THE RIGGED GAME

THE RIGGED GAME

Corporate America And A People Betrayed

John Hively

Montreal/New York/London

Black Rose Books No. II343

National Library of Canada Cataloguing in Publication Data

Hively, John
The rigged game : corporate America and a people betrayed / John Hively

Includes bibliographical references and index.

ISBN: 1-55164-281-6 (bound)   ISBN: 1-55164-280-8 (pbk.)
(alternative ISBNs 9781551642819 [bound]   9781551642802 [pbk.])

1. United States--Economic conditions--2001- 2. Big business--United States.
3. Corporate power--United States. I. Title.

HC110.15H58 2005   330.973   C2005-902393-7

Cover photo entitled "Lunch Atop A Skyscraper" Charles C. Ebbets, 1932

BLACK ROSE BOOKS

C.P. 1258	2250 Military Road	99 Wallis Road
Succ. Place du Parc	Tonawanda, NY	London, E9 5LN
Montréal, H2X 4A7	14150	England
Canada	USA	UK

To order books:
In Canada: (phone) 1-800-565-9523 (fax) 1-800-221-9985
email: utpbooks@utpress.utoronto.ca

In United States: (phone) 1-800-283-3572 (fax) 1-651-917-6406

In the UK & Europe: (phone) 44 (0)20 8986-4854 (fax) 44 (0)20 8533-5821
email: order@centralbooks.com

Our Web Site address: http://www.blackrosebooks.net

Printed in Canada

TABLE OF CONTENTS

ACKNOWLEDGEMENTS

The beginnings of this book can be traced to the many writings of the late economist, Thorstein Veblen (1857-1929). In his book, *Theory of Business Enterprise* (1904), he argued that all recessions begin in the financial markets. He did not actually provide any theoretical premise from which to proceed. The economic points he argued, however, made sense to me, and my curiosity running wild, I proceeded, slowly at first, to conduct research into this area. I continued to read everything I could that had been written by him. His ideas were absolutely fascinating, at least to me. For example, in 1919, he boldly forecast the coming of the Great Depression. It was at least ten years away he proclaimed. He was the only person of note to see the coming of the economic disaster. Veblen's prediction made me realize more than ever before that he knew exactly how the economy actually functioned, more so than anyone else, and by a wide margin.

I entered the Ph.D. program in economics at the University of Tennessee, Knoxville in 1994. I wanted to study other theories about how the economy actually functions. It took less than a semester for me to recognize that I didn't believe what I was being taught. It was a waste of my time. Veblen's theory had me hooked. I left the program to pursue other interests, and now and then I continued to research this issue. By 2001, I felt the time had come to write the book.

Critical input and feedback into the writing of this manuscript was provided by Rick Anderson, Shirley Andrade, Peter Forsyth, Ron Green, Anita Hively, Michael Hively, Lois Poole and Michael Sloan.

There were times when I thought about giving up this project, but one of the above would say something, now and then, that would keep me going. There were other times when I took a break from researching and writing it, and then someone else, like a friend named Greg Margolis, said something to inspire me. I was also stirred to continue by stories of people who succeeded against great odds, including Fanny Lou Hamer, Ella Baker, U.S. Grant, Woody Guthrie, Myles Horton and so many others. So I persevered by relying heavily on all of these other people, some dead and some alive. Many thanks to my publisher Black Rose Books, and especially to Linda Barton, for just knowing they were interested in publishing it helped to keep me going.

dedicated to
Michael and Opal Hively

to
Lorraine Cavener
Anita Hively

and to the memory of
Thorstein Veblen

Chapter One

INTRODUCTION

Are you working more and earning less than five, ten or twenty years ago? Does it seem that what you earn every year doesn't quite keep up with the yearly rate of inflation? Even if you are doing better today than ten or twenty years ago, do you sometimes worry that economically something is not quite right for the citizens of the United States? Do you fret about your children's future? Are you suspicious that what the experts have told you all of your life about how the economy functions does not seem quite right? Is the financial return from your college education getting to be worth less and less today than ten years or more ago? Does it appear as if our political and business leaders lie to us quite often, but sometimes you just can't figure out exactly how or why? Has your engineering or computer programming job been shipped overseas? What about your customer service job? Has it been shipped overseas, as well? Have your health benefits, wages, salaries and retirement packages been reduced or eliminated during the last ten to twenty years? Do you wonder how and why the wealthy folks throughout the world have gotten richer while the poor and middle classes have seen their real income and wealth drop during the last thirty years? Do you wonder how all of these issues have arisen during arguably the greatest twenty-five years of prosperity in U.S. history? It probably won't surprise too many people to discover that the U.S. economic system, heavily dominated by publicly traded, limited liability corporations, has been built to achieve all of the above. And this is precisely why the general trend is for more and more people around the globe to work more and earn less.

The autumn of 2003 found Bill, a forty-two year high school graduate, taking another two-dollar an hour pay cut to add to the cutback he had been forced to swallow the year before. His health care premium jumped by double digits again that year, and this time the corporation he works for isn't picking up the increase, although its profits are on the rise. Bill paid for the growth of his health care insurance right out of his own wallet. He is a highly skilled mechanic in a steel fabrication shop. Bill has been a journeyman mechanic and welder for twenty years. He complained to me that things aren't what they used to be. His years of work experience count for nothing as they are generating less personal income than ever before, especially when measured against the forces of ruthlessly growing inflation. His property taxes have gone up, as well as his monthly electricity bill. He pays the highest electricity rates in the state of Oregon to Portland General Electric (PGE), a subsidiary of the bankrupt and disgraced Enron Corporation. "My standard of living is definitely in decline," he lamented, "I don't know why." But Bill is hardly alone. In fact, this appears to be the trend for the bottom 98 percent or so of income earners throughout the world.

Over the past thirty years, the super-rich have improved their percentages of income and wealth, while the vast majority of people throughout the world have seen their percentages reduced.[1] During these years, a transfer of income and wealth has been occurring from one group to the other. Ultimately, you just have to follow the money in order to discover how this has been achieved. It should come as no surprise that affluent people have created an economy in which they can acquire more and more income and wealth as easily as is possible than ever before. Along with the interrelated political markets, corporations and the financial markets were created to accomplish this goal.

Because of how they are structured, especially relative to the financial markets, the major corporation's of the world possess insatiable appetites for income and wealth similar to a never-ending and famished swarm of locust that just happen to come across a wheat field ready for harvest. The insects eat most of the crop ensuring the farmer receives a diminished reward for his or her efforts. The following year the swarm of locust returns just a little bit larger than before and consumes just a little bit more, reducing the living standard of the farmer even more so than the previous year. This process continues year after year and leaves the farmer in increasing poverty. Like the swarm of locust relative to the helpless farmer, the corporate economic system–something completely different from a competitive capitalist economy—is rigged to ensure a continuous unequal distribution of income and wealth in favor of the most affluent consumers, and at the expense of the vast majority of the world's citizens, and there is no end in sight.[2] Because of this, just like the farmer above, people will increasingly continue to work more and earn less as long as the current system is in place.

The proof of the pudding is in the eating, and likewise the evidence is constantly mounting as working people continue to experience declines in their standards of living from the middle class suburbs of North Carolina to the rain soaked streets of Portland, Oregon, from the central highlands of China to the far away tropical forests of Central and South America, across the Atlantic to mineral rich yet impoverished Africa, to the deserts of central and northern Mexico, to the suburbs of New York City, and all the way to France and Germany. Citizens all around the world are paying the price for having a world-wide economy dominated by large scale corporations and their allies in political offices.

In the spring of 2003, *Time Magazine* reported that "Shrinking paychecks are the new reality for many Americans." The magazine provided plenty of examples.

> Over the past year, steel worker Eugene (Lou) Costello has endured pay cuts of 15%, 10% and 12.8%, plunging his annual income base pay from about $50,000 down to about $33,000. "I feel like a marathon runner who sees the finish line but when he gets close, his coach holds up a sign that says he has 25 more miles to go," says Costello, 61, who works for Wheeling Pittsburg Steel in Mingo Junction, Ohio. "I'm going to have to work until I die." Costello chose to work in steel mills rather than the coal mines where his father toiled because he believe steel jobs were more secure. Now he is scrapping plans to build a long-planned retirement house and says he will not be replacing his 13-year-old pickup truck anytime soon. "You have to make choices," he says, "between a house payment, a car payment or medicine."

Costello was not alone in his predicament. In the autumn of 2003, Saul was a worried pest exterminator. He was at the top of his company's pay scale, but he heard his job might be eliminated because the corporation he works for can hire someone for half of his pay. In the year 2002, unionized custodians for the Portland School District of Oregon lost their jobs and were replaced by a company paying its employees considerably less. The same school district saw its teachers work ten days for free as part of their new contract, effectively reducing their pay in the spring of 2003. A Microsoft mid-level executive earning $100,000+ experienced the elimination of his job. An office manager of an investment firm saw her working hours dramatically increased when several disgruntled employees quit and were not replaced for many months. Despite the extra hours she worked, her salary was not increased, effectively cutting her pay. She worked more and earned less. This is becoming commonplace in the United States, as well as throughout the world, and increasingly so when compared with past decades.

It is normally assumed by the alleged experts that Costello and others are victims of an economic system going through an evolutionary transformation from a manufacturing to an information based economy. *Time Magazine* revealed that nothing could be further from the truth. High paying jobs in engineering and computer programming are going overseas, and they are not coming back. According to the article in *Time*,

> Michael Tucker, 49, fumes when he thinks about computer programmers overseas working for $20,000 a year—"and to them, that's good money." He was making $80,000 a year at a programming job in Chapel Hill, N.C., before Temtec USA laid him off last October in a broad cost-cutting move. He has been unable to land a regular paycheck, despite sending resumes to 300 U.S. tech firms. Now with unemployment benefits running their course, he's trying his hand at commissioned sales for a human-resources company in his hometown. He says he is finished with tech and moans that "computer programmers are the textile workers of the future."

Highly paid computer programmer jobs are the heart of the information age, since computers and the Internet represent the foundation, if not the entire package, of any information based economy. Intel and hundreds of other corporations are moving highly skilled information based jobs overseas, including engineering positions. With the exception of the position of CEO, no corporate job is safe anymore from becoming an export. A business manager located in the United States can easily access information about a corporate plant in Russia, Pakistan, China, Mexico or Vietnam. The ability to obtain such information makes it convenient for corporations to shift any and all jobs overseas where the price of labor, environmental standards, health and safety laws, and the standard's of living are considerably less than what is generally allowed by law, social awareness and social pressure to exist in the United States. *Time* noted that a "call-center employee" for a U.S. corporation receives $20,000 a year in the U.S., hardly a great sum, but in India the person doing the same job earns only $2,500 each year. Michael Tucker lost his job because somebody else was willing and capable of doing the same thing for one-fourth the pay, and most likely with little or no benefits, as well. Among other white collar industries, *Time* reported that between the years 2003 and 2008, "financial-services firms" planned to transfer 500,000 jobs from the USA to foreign countries.

This long-term race to the economic bottom is not just a phenomenon of the United States. Even as *Time* reported that millions of Americans were discovering "shrinking wages," other people throughout the world were also experiencing declines in their standards of living. The Oregonian newspaper reported on May 8th, 2003 that the already bleak economic situation in Venezuela had worsened. Since 1998 poverty had grown roughly 10 percent there, meaning 68 percent of the population lived in unimaginable poverty. People there reside in houses made of cardboard and corrugated tin, but it would be a mistake to assume this depth of poverty is a product solely of Venezuela. Hundreds of thousands of people work for U.S. corporations in the North of Mexico, and they and their families live in exactly the same dire poverty on the U.S. side of the border, principally in Texas.

When U.S. corporations export jobs, they reduce the standards of living provided by these positions, and often compel people to live in horrible poverty, as well. The management of Hershey's of Pennsylvania decided to export poverty when they closed a packaging plant in the United States, and then moved it to Guadalajara, Mexico, placing it firmly within the Maquiladora free trade zone established by the Mexican and U.S. governments in 1965. One of Hershey's lay-off victims, Denise Brightbill, had earned $25,000 a year working on a packaging line. This was hardly an astronomical sum. It was not even possible to purchase a house in many places in the United States with such low pay, nor even rent a decent apartment. Ms. Brightbill visited Mexico to see just what had become of her former $25,000 a year job. She met Margarita Curiel, who was performing the same work for Hershey, but earning only $2,871 per year. According to the Reverend Philip Wheaton,

> Margarita lives with her mother, father, two sisters and three children
> in an extremely crowded house with only three rooms plus an outdoor
> kitchen. To make it, the Curiels must combine Margarita's income with
> those of her father and sister. Yet Hershey's continues to sell its candy
> products for the same price; by firing Denise and paying Margarita only
> survival wages, Hershey's has vastly increased its profit margin.[3]

Margarita and her family live in extreme poverty by any measurable standards. The job in which Denise once earned a lower class living in the U.S. now pays a wage that is 87 percent less.

In the Maquiladora zone, there were roughly 1.2 million jobs provided by mostly U.S. based corporations in the year 1999. Depending on whose estimates are used, 25 to 40 percent of those jobs were lost from 1999 to 2003. Many of them were shipped to Vietnam and China where the new holders of these positions will earn about one-tenth of the pay as the former employees in Mexico, who recollect, received only about one-tenth of what Americans formerly earned while toiling at these jobs. Why were jobs exported to Mexico, and then exported to Asia where the workers toil in even greater poverty? What are the forces continuously compelling these jobs to pay less and less? Aren't living standards supposed to improve for the vast majority of people working in a free market economy?

The justification for the establishment of capitalism was its theoretical promise of a rising standard of living for all of those who participated in the production of goods and services. The mounting evidence suggests theories justifying this economic order were all incorrect in their assessments of its promise. The system is failing. Why does Margarita do the same job Brightbill once performed, but only earn about 13 percent of her former wages? Why are Bill, Michael Tucker and Denise Brightbill, along with hundreds of millions of other people throughout the world, working more and earning less? Conversely, why does a tiny minority of affluent and politically powerful people experience a rising tide of prosperity?

The answer to these trends ultimately, as well as the solution, can be found in the financial markets and the structure of publicly traded, limited liability corporations. Although economists are often unwilling to admit the obvious, major corporations are managed differently than competitive businesses such as local coffee shops, local manufacturers, auto repair shops, barbers and hairdressers, local contractors and retail stores. It is not rationale to assume a similarity exists between a competitive owner-operated business and a major corporation whose owners take no part in its day-to-day operations. Therein hides a dirty little secret that helps account for the rising tide of the mal-distribution of income and wealth in favor of the most affluent of citizens.

Notes

1. See appendix one for details.
3. Income is money that is acquired. A limited list includes wages, salaries, interest and dividend income. Wealth is comprised of what you own. Your total assets are your wealth. This includes houses, cars, savings, stocks and bonds.
2. Wheaton, Philip E., *Unmasking the Powers in Mexico: The Zapatista Prophetic Alternative to the New World Order*, EPICA: Washington D.C., 1998, p. 10.

Chapter Two

THE BAKERS OF FINANCIAL DEBAUCHERY

The trade of a joint stock company (Business Corporation) is always managed by a court of directors (board of directors). This court, indeed, is frequently subject, in many respects, to the controul (sic) of a general court of proprietors (shareholders). *But the greater part of those proprietors (shareholders) seldom pretend to understand any thing of the business of the company*; and when the spirit of faction happens not to prevail among them, give themselves no trouble about it, but receive contentedly such half yearly or yearly dividend, as the directors think proper to make them. —Adam Smith, *The Wealth of Nations*, 1776 (Parenthesis and italics mine.)

Mike Sloan is the only paid employee of House Magic, an S-corporation based in Portland, Oregon. Mike and Laurie, his wife of twenty-five years, manage the day-to-day affairs of the company. Sometimes Sloan builds houses, and sometimes he buys existing homes and remodels them. Laurie is responsible for paying the bills, bookkeeping, filling the dishwasher now and then, and along with her husband, raising their children—Sara, Amanda and Molly. Mike hires subcontractors for a few services such as carpet installation, plumbing, electrical, and every now and then foundation work. Although he possesses significant skills in all of these fields, he hires people who specialize in these vocations because they are more efficient than him. Otherwise, he performs all of the labor on each house because he possesses all of the necessary skills. Mike knows what every tool is used for, and he knows the price he paid for every one of them. He can look at a house and recognize within a few minutes if it can pass an inspection to be eligible for a mortgage loan. Now and then, he has filled out the paperwork and sold houses directly to customers without the help of real estate agents. In all my years of knowing Mike, never once has he worried that financial market analysts might anticipate lower profits for his business than the previous quarter, an event that usually depresses the price of a corporation's stock. That's because House Magic does not issue stock. Mike and Laurie are the investors, shareholders and the stakeholders. Their investment is counted in time, significant amounts of labor, skills and their own money.

Like Mike Sloan, Lois Poole never worried about what the members of a board of director's thought of her management of Java Man. When she owned the coffee shop in Portland, Oregon, she had no need for such a board. She was responsible only to herself and to her customers. Lois needed many skills in order to be successful. She ordered products directly from venders, hired employees, trained and supervised them, and determined what marketing strategies to adopt. She was also the accounts receivable and the accounts payable clerk, and she did her own bookkeeping. Lois was at the café most days serving coffee and pastries and talking with people who wandered in to her shop, such as the goofy bus driver who came in almost every day and always lamented that he didn't have a girlfriend, and that he really wanted to be a teacher.

Back in 1997, a fellow by the name of Rick Anderson started Eyedesign, a graphic design company located in Portland, Oregon. He invested his own money to get the business off and running, and he possessed all of the necessary skills to be successful. Anderson had been an employee with several graphic design companies after graduating from Washington State University with a degree in you guessed it, graphic design. Rick had experience and knowledge of the things he intended to produce. This is typically a prerequisite for starting a successful profit seeking enterprise, unless the business is a fair size publicly traded, limited liability corporation. Don't worry about that issue now. We'll get to it a little later. Needless to suggest, Rick has all of the graphic design skills necessary to fill the needs of his clients, but he also possesses many other talents that are necessary to be a successful business person. He seeks potential customers so he is also a salesperson, and Rick does his own books, and stays up-to-date on all of the newest technologies in his field. Since he is in a competitive line of business, Anderson manages his company very efficiently, if only to save a few dollars here and there. Along with the contributions of his wife Nancy, Rick's endeavors have given the couple the abilities to provide a nice middle class upbringing for their two daughters, Sierra and Cilesse.

I used to work at Yesterday Records almost thirty years ago. A gentleman named Bob Gallucci started the enterprise with a friend, whom he later bought out. Bob seemed to know everything about the history of rock and roll, rhythm and blues, and just about anything you could buy on vinyl. To my eye, Galluccui's small shop was crammed with records and somewhat untidy, but he always seemed to know just were everything was. He knew the value of original vinyl disks. When somebody brought old records to sell to him, Bob knew what he could pay for them, as well as what he could sell them for. Gallucci did his own bookkeeping. And he was a wonderful salesman simply because he knew his product well, and he enjoyed sharing his knowledge with his customers. Among many others, he made Elvis Presley, Chuck Berry, Buddy Holly and Fats Domino come alive in that cramped little shop. Luckily, for both Gallucci and his customers, Bob didn't have to worry about pleasing his shareholders, because he didn't have any. He called his own shots, so he didn't have such people telling him what to do. Besides, what would they have known about his business anyway?

Sloan, Poole, Gallucci and Anderson provide examples of people taking chances in life by owning and managing their own businesses. Such people stick their necks out and risk their own money and labor. The successes of their businesses are dependent on their knowledge of how to efficiently manage their operations, and also their abilities to develop relationships with their customers. Bankruptcy and the end of their businesses and their livelihoods would be the results if they were unable to provide goods and services efficiently and knowledgably. These things are what make their companies radically different from the major corporations that currently dominate the economy and the politics of the nations of the world.

The owners of corporations typically have nothing to do with managing their businesses. These people may not even know what goods and services their corporation produces. Often, the owners don't even know where the headquarters are located, nor do they know where its goods and services are manufactured. They don't know who their customers are, and often they can't even name the person in charge of managing the affairs of their businesses. In short, most owners more often than not don't know anything about their own business corporations, although some may have vague generalizations on this matter. For example, an owner of General Motors Corporation (GMC) probably knows the company manufactures cars and its headquarters are located in Detroit, Michigan or thereabouts, but their knowledge does not extend much beyond these thoughts. On the other hand, GMC is one of the most recognizable business firms in the world. With respect to lesser known corporations, some owners may not even possess this miniscule amount of knowledge.

The people who are the owners of corporations are called shareholders, investors, or stockholders. They possess pieces of paper called "certificates of stock," or sometimes called "shares," and these indicate ownership of one or more corporations. For example, the owner of a certificate of stock issued by the Ford Motor Company is an owner of that business entity.

Most corporations that issue stock pay dividends. Dividends are payments from corporations to their stockholders. These disbursements most often come directly from profits. Corporations can also dip into retained earnings in order to provide some portion of dividend payments to shareholders. Retained earnings are that part of profits that are held in reserve by corporations for future use, rather than given immediately to shareholders. They serve as rainy day funds for the times when earnings are limited or nonexistent, and they are often used to enhance dividend payments at some point in the future.

More or less, the price of a corporation's stock is determined by the abilities of its managers to generate earnings. If profits drop from the previous quarter, some owners will sell their stock. The value of the shares will typically sink if large enough numbers of owners decide to sell because of the depressed return on investment. Conversely, if the earnings of a corporation rise, more often than not investors will be enticed to purchase its stock due to the greater return on investment, and this buying frenzy will drive its share values upward. This is especially the case if earnings improve consistently from one quarter to the next over long periods of time. Investors are attracted to stocks that are constantly rising in price.

Investors purchase and sell the shares of corporation's in the financial markets. These markets exist in many cities throughout the world: Tokyo, Berlin, Chicago, London, and Buenos Aires are only a few of the cities that are home to financial markets. New York City has the most celebrated financial market—Wall Street.

Business firms on Wall Street and in other financial markets bring buyers and sellers of stocks together. They are called brokerages and investment banks. These firms employ analysts to determine how well corporations are being managed. Among other things, these people examine the accounting books and perform other research in efforts to ascertain which corporations are going to be profitable and which are not. The purpose of the analysts is to lessen the risks to investors by giving them an idea of what to expect regarding the near-future earnings performances of corporations. These people help investors make decisions to buy or sell the stocks of the enormous number of corporations whose shares are publicly traded.

Analyst's expectations of corporate profitability often determine whether or not the values of stocks rise or fall. If these experts decide certain corporations will not meet their earnings expectations, large numbers of investors will often sell their stock holdings in these firms, which usually sends their values tumbling down. Conversely, if the analysts foresee higher earnings than expected for certain corporations, investors will purchase these stocks, typically sending their values up, up and away. Examples of this relationship between financial market analysts and their expectations can be read almost daily in local and national newspapers. Generally, phrases such as "Wall Street expectations," "analyst's expectations," "expectations," and other such expressions are used to demonstrate the corporate earnings prospects analysts provide investors. Some examples are provided below.

- J.C. Penney fell $1.16, to $18.89. An analyst at *UBS Warburg, Linda Kristiansen, reduced her expectations* for 2003 earnings to $1.45 a share from $1.55 a share. She said the company's Eckerd drugstore unit would have lower profits. (*New York Times*, April 10, 2003, p. C8. Italics mine.)

- Amazon.com fell $1.46, to $25.06. Daryl Smith, *an analyst at J.P. Morgan Securities, recommended that investors sell shares of the company because of slowing consumer spending and concern that the war will hurt profits.* (*New York Times*, Friday, April 11, 2003, p. C8. Italics mine.)

- Diversified manufacturer Englehard didn't do much better, dropping 1.15, or 4.9%, to 22.15 after *Credit Suisse First Boston downgraded the stock to underperform* (sic) from neutral and proffered a 12-month price target of $23, just 85 cents above the shares' closing price. (*Wall Street Journal*, April 10, 2003, p. C3. Italics mine.)

- Microsoft's earnings increased nearly 82 percent in its fiscal fourth quarter, helped slightly by a tax benefit. *But the latest quarter's results fell short of analyst's expectations and the stock fell Thursday.* (*Oregonian*, July 23, 2004. Italics mine.)

As you can see from the evidence above, when the profits of corporations fail to meet analyst's expectations, even if there is an 82 percent increase in earnings, the payment of dividends will often be lower than anticipated, and this provides investors with strong incentives to sell their stocks. The results are usually drops in the share prices of the slacker corporations, and such events indicate the corporate management team is not doing its job very well.

Publicly traded, limited liability corporations are managed from the top down by chief executive officers (CEOs). As you might expect, these captains of industry and finance are guided with a view as to how their abilities to generate profits will be greeted by analysts and investors of the various financial markets. These corporate heroes will rarely appear as if they are doing a really bang up job if their leadership decisions result in persistently dropping profits, from say $200 million one quarter to $150 million the next, and then to $125 million the following quarter. Sure those are pretty good earnings, but CEOs whose business strategies lead to fairly consistent downward or even stable income will look like incompetent clowns next to the alleged geniuses that are able to ensure earnings rise consistently one quarterly period after another. Many investors are quite happy to sell their shares of corporations with declining or stable profits, and then demonstrate their keen business intellect by purchasing stocks undergoing long term upsurges in earnings.

The abilities to enhance profits, dividends and stock prices from one quarter to the next on a fairly continuous basis is the only method by which our corporate heroes are able to demonstrate their managerial wizardry to shareholders, analysts and investors. The reason for this is straightforward. Most if not all publicly traded limited liability corporations are simply too large for anybody to manage their day-to-day operations very well, if at all. And this is why meeting those analyst expectations fairly consistently, especially with rising earnings from one quarter to the next, is used exclusively as a gauge of CEO competence.

You would think these captains of industry who are paid millions of dollars every year should know exactly how the corporations they are in charge of managing develop, produce and market their goods and services on a day-to-day basis. But how can any one person, or any small group of people, know everything that goes on in a corporation spread across large geographic areas ranging in size from cities and counties to all away around the Earth, with tens or hundreds or thousands of employees, as well as numerous contractors and subcontractors in different countries whose employees and owners speak different languages? Add to that those businesses that produce multiple products, and the need to know how each one is developed, produced and marketed, and it isn't difficult to come to the conclusion that our corporate heroes really can not acquire enough skills and knowledge in a life time to understand how to efficiently manage the day-to-day operations of corporations. Depending on how each product is produced, they would have to possess considerable skills as lathe operators, engineers, product designers, graphic designers, truck drivers, computer programmers, inventory specialists, accountants, bookkeepers, customer service providers, merchandisers, machine operators, sales persons, assembly line workers and managers, quality control inspectors, and hundreds of other job classifications.[1] Furthermore, in addition to the above, if CEOs were truly efficient, they would need to possess exact knowledge of what all employees are doing during all minutes of all working hours, and that is simply not possible when there might be more than three people working under their direction.[2]

Former Secretary of the Treasury Paul O'Neill provided a lucid example of how it is impossible for one person to efficiently manage major corporations. When O'Neil was chief executive of Alcoa, and one of the best executives in the U.S., he proved to be adept at raising earnings, and one day he bragged about the company's increasing profits at a meeting of shareholders in Pennsylvania. A worker from one of Alcoa's Mexican factories, Juan Tovar Santos, appeared before a microphone at this same meeting. He told of how more than 100 employees had been made so sick by vapors from a gas leak that they had to be taken to a hospital.[3] In response to this accusation, O'Neil insisted that conditions were pristine in the factory. He argued that Alcoa's manufacturing plants in Mexico were so clean people could eat off the floors. In reply, Mr. Santos declared that O'Neil's assertions were lies. He then showed shareholders news clippings of the disaster proving O'Neil did not have too many clues as to what was happening in the corporation that he was in charge of overseeing. Alerted by Santos revelations, he eventually fired the manager of the plant for keeping this information from him.[4] How efficiently managed was a corporation so large that its chief executive didn't know that a hundred employees were injured on the job and sent to the hospital, especially when these actions were reported in the local newspapers? If he didn't know what was going on in the factories, it's more than likely that he did not possess an abundance of detailed knowledge of how his workers produced Alcoa's goods and services.

When O'Neil was the U.S. Secretary of Treasury (2001–2002), he was a strong advocate for enhancing CEO accountability. In a conference with "financial executives" in Florida early in 2002, he argued that our captains of industry and finance should know what is occurring within their corporations, and they should be held "responsible for it." As might be expected, the CEOs objected to this idea. One of them protested, "'I would resign rather than be expected to know everything that's going on in my company. It's just not tenable. That's what I have a board for, that's what I have a chief financial officer for. I simply can't be held responsible for what all of those people do.'"5 Apparently, many CEOs recognize their own impotence to be able to control the affairs of their own companies, and at least one of them thinks it is wise not to know much of what the people under his authority are actually doing while on the job. You can't create a situation to manage operations much worse than that, but that's precisely how publicly traded companies are structured. On the other hand, there are many ways our corporate heroes can enhance their companies earnings while being completely ignorant of how to manage the day to day affairs of their corporations.

Another of our mighty captains of industry worked for five years with one publicly traded, limited liability corporation. He received a generous retirement package and stocks valued at $48 million when he departed. Under his leadership, despite a U.S. trade embargo, his U.S. corporation betrayed every citizen in the United States when it acquired $75 million in business with our enemy Iraq using its European subsidiaries. Our hero also increased the amount of his company's corporate welfare payments from the U.S. federal government by 91 percent during his short tenure. He also enhanced the number and value of public assistance programs his corporation received through foreign governments by using his political connections. On the other hand, our hero's record at managing the operations of this corporation was not overly impressive. One "accounting irregularity" during his reign of error was $100 million.6 When this executive merged his corporation with another, it was "hit with several hundred million dollars of unexpected losses, including an estimated $100 million on a single pipeline project in South America." His company failed to meet deadlines on road projects in North Carolina and Texas, and ran into trouble. The company had bid "$20 million or less" for each of these projects yet lost as much as $4 to $5 million on several of them. The losses may have ranged from 20 percent of their bids or more. His corporation's stock price "lagged its competitors in the final year and a half of his tenure." Prior to being hired, this person had worked for the federal government for decades, as an elected representative as well as one of those seemingly life long and inefficient government bureaucrats, and he barely had any experience in private industry. What qualifications did this person possess that a corporation decided upon him to be CEO when he knew almost nothing of the business, and had almost no experience outside of government? His predecessor said the decision to hire him was based on his abilities "to make the proper strategic decisions, and to establish relationships," and was not based on his skills to manage operations.[7] How efficient is it when your CEO does not need to know anything of what your corporation produces? Dick Cheney, ex-congressman, former secretary of defense, and vice president of the United States from 2001 to 2009, was appointed to be the CEO because of his connections in government, and he did not fail in this regard. He was the ultimate corporate welfare queen with all kinds of political relationships that enabled his company to receive generous welfare handouts of one sort or another from many governments. His political connections offset his inabilities to manage operations very well. After leaving the post of defense secretary, but before becoming vice president, he was the CEO of Halliburton Corporation for five years.

Cheney was hardly the only captain of industry who didn't know how to manage operations very well at all. It is likely the vast majority of CEOs have only vague notions as to how their businesses function. It's not a particular requirement for the job. And that's why many corporations seek those inefficient government bureaucrats to be their CEOs. Since profits must always rise, corporate management teams usually feel the need for sales and markets to grow in order to help consistently boost dividends. Public assistance programs provide such nifty boosts to earnings growth. The story of Cheney at Halliburton also demonstrates why corporations are often more inefficient than government agencies, something that will be demonstrated later in this book. Inefficiency throughout corporations, the need to constantly grow, CEO ineptitude, the desire on the part of our corporate captains to remain un-responsible and often clueless as to what their subordinates are doing, coupled with the need for constantly rising earnings are the reasons why corporations are more and more heavily reliant on public welfare handouts, not to mention accounting gimmicks, such as those that occurred at Enron and other corporations. But no matter how it is achieved, so long as our heroes can keep those profits on the rise, everybody demanding success of corporations are regularly kept quite happy.

In order to ensure the captains of industry and finance are managing the affairs of their companies properly on behalf of stockholders, every corporation has a board of director's serving as guardian angels. However, the ability of any board to do this successfully is dubious at best, and very likely impossible. The experience of George W. Bush provides a revealing example of this self evident truth.

Bush served on the eight member board of directors of Harken Energy Corporation for several years. He owned hundreds of thousands of shares of the business. While on the board, Bush was also a member of a subcommittee studying the potential effects of a corporate restructuring. He had "'detailed knowledge of the financial pressure Harken was under and of the demands being placed on (it) by its creditors.'"[8] Like all board members, he could only examine data and listen to managerial testimony to ascertain how well the company was being managed. The future president sold the majority of his Harken stock on June 22, 1990, eight days before the company announced huge losses. Analysts were shocked at the earnings report, and the price of Harken stock dropped 25 percent from four to three dollars per share. As a person with inside information not yet available to the stock buying public, when Bush sold his shares he committed a felony. But Bush denied having any knowledge of the impending losses when he sold his stock, despite being both a member of the board and an owner of Harken. Although his claim may appear to be an act of fantasy, or even a dubious rationale for legal salvation, at least to some degree, his knowledge of Harken's situation was normal for most people on any board of directors.

Most board members of publicly traded, limited liability corporations are relatively clueless when it comes to the matters of determining the effectiveness of the decisions made by CEOs. First of all, members typically do not make any of the decisions having to do with any of the day-to-day operations of their corporations, so their ignorance in this area is usually even greater than the captains of industry. Of course, since our corporate heroes have little or no knowledge of what actually occurs in their far flung commercial empires, then what knowledge would board members possess, especially since many of them attend to the business of their corporations for only a few hours a month, if that much? The best answer to this question is obvious; although often handsomely rewarded, other than possessing some generalized knowledge, they're a largely clueless bunch. This is especially true since it is not uncommon for people to be members of several different corporate boards, diluting what little time and what little expertise they have or might be able to acquire with respect to each business over which they supposedly serve as guardians. Many board members, and perhaps most, may be ignorant to one degree or another of some of the goods and services their corporations provide, as well as where they are produced, and who makes them. Consequently, their lack of knowledge makes it very difficult for them to effectively oversee the job performances of the various captains of finance and industry. However, with the apparent exception of George W. Bush at Harken Energy, board members are intelligent enough to be able to read the bottom line, and this consists of growing earnings, dividends and share prices. If a stock price is sinking, the board members know this is bad, whereupon they will exert pressure on their corporate hero to boost profits, or risk being booted from his or her position. If their captain is then successful at increasing earnings, the board members know such a turnaround is a good thing because it will allow the corporation to raise dividend payments, which typically enhances share prices, and subsequently provides the illusion that they are somehow knowledgeable about the business entity over which they serve as guardian angels. So long as the earnings and share prices of the vast majority (if not all) publicly traded corporations typically rise one quarter after the next, board members will generally not interfere with or take offense with any management decisions.

Back in 1776, as quoted at the beginning of this chapter, the economist Adam Smith noted, with few exceptions, that shareholders seldom exert any pressure of any kind on either management or board members since they are usually completely ignorant as to how to effectively produce the goods and services of any such business.[9] Once in a while, shareholders put pressure on their directors, but it is a fairly unusual occurrence. This just goes to show that things haven't changed at all in 229 years.

Because of the all around ignorance of shareholders and board members, our corporate heroes can be cunning as a fox when it comes to accumulating earnings. Their primary goal is to ensure profits rise to meet or surpass financial market expectations from one quarter to the next—but not by too much. Increasing profits 150 percent over the previous quarter might prove to be truly foolish, because such an outcome means investors will expect even higher earnings the following period, something any CEO might be hard pressed to accomplish. The prudent thing to do then is to enhance profits significantly, but generally not by 150 percent, or by any amount they cannot likely surpass in the near future. To help regulate earnings and avoid such a dreaded calamity,

CEOs use the device called retained earnings, which are profits corporations keep for a rainy day fund, rather than disburse to shareholders. Unfortunately, accumulating too large of a rainy day fund might anger investors, who then might self-righteously demand that some or all of this money be allowed to flow into their bank accounts and wallets, and they might even bring pressure to bear on board members to do just such a thing. To keep retained earnings at levels that will avoid the wrath of shareholders and board members, our corporate heroes also regulate profits by making unnecessary purchases in order to soak up whatever earnings are significantly above the expectations of the financial analysts. Among other things, superfluous factories will be built and new equipment and technology will be ordered that is uncalled for. Marketing budgets will be raised and charitable donations will be increased to help the cause. Other corporations will be purchased, or merged with, in order to retain a greater degree of control over prices, but also to help soak up excessive earnings. Accounting tricks can be used to hide excessive profits, just as these actions concealed a paucity of earnings at Enron, WorldCom and others. Below is an example of this kind of corporate corruption.

Freddie Mac Discloses Its Understated Profits

Freddie Mac, the second-largest financier of mortgages, understated its pretax profits for the past three years by as much as $6.9 billion, in part because it wanted to report those gains in future years...For the first time, Freddie Mac also acknowledged that in some cases it had deliberately manipulated accounting rules so that its profits would be near *Wall Street's forecasts*. (*Oregonian*, June 26, 2003. Italics mine.)

Once profits are hidden, the wizards of corporate finance can make them reappear out of nowhere—just like magic! Just when it looks as if earnings will fall below Wall Street expectations, victory is whisked away from impending defeat by the wonderful managerial wizardry of the captains of industry and finance, or so it appears to all of those whose hopes and dreams have been saved by our heroes. Unlike people who own and operate their own businesses, corporate head honchos find profit concealing very practical as a tool to help foster an illusion of managerial competency.

During a period of brisk business, our corporate captains will also regulate the expansion and contraction of profits by hiring unnecessary staff. Then, when there is a downturn in earnings, they will lay off these profit-soaking employees in order to help align income with the expectations of the financial market analysts. This tactic allows income to be transferred from the former employees to investors via higher dividends. Below is an example of a corporation that magically discovered enhanced earnings when the CEO decided to lay-off profit-soaking employees in order to better align costs with projected revenue.

Worldcom Eliminates 3,700 Jobs At Its Worldcom Group In The U.S.

JACKSON, Miss: WorldCom is eliminating 3,700 U.S. jobs *to better align costs with projected revenue.* (Italics mine.)

The cuts announced Wednesday were limited to the company's WorldCom Group, which includes the high-growth data, Internet and international businesses. They amount to 6 percent of WorldCom Group's employment and 4 percent of the company's 75,000 member global work force.

WorldCom also is the nation's No. 2 long-distance provider, which it operates through its MCI Group. (*Oregonian*, April 4, 2002, pg. D1.)

The difference between total costs and total revenue is profit. When a corporation can arbitrarily cut jobs in order "to better align costs with projected revenue," it is effectively regulating its profit margin. Why did the corporate heroes of WorldCom hire these people in the first place? At one time it was prudent to hire superfluous employees to soak up excessive profits so as to not exceed Wall Street expectations by too much. And then as if by the wave of a magic wand, the wonderfully talented CEO of WorldCom produced higher earnings during a downturn of income when he laid off profit-soaking people. All publicly traded corporations can soak up excessive profits. These self-regulating actions bring longer-term stability in the growth of earnings than would otherwise be the case, and this makes it easier to meet or exceed the expectations of financial market analysts from one quarter to the next. This in turn ensures that stockholders, financial market analysts, prospective investors, and the various boards of directors are overly impressed with the managerial expertise of our corporate heroes.

When letting superfluous employees go doesn't turn the earnings picture around sufficiently, the jobs of necessary staff are shipped overseas, or employees suffer cutbacks in hours worked, wages, salaries and benefits. The savings from laying off people and substituting lower-cost labor in their place, and or reducing employee compensation, is passed on as enhanced dividends to stockholders. The *New York Times* provided an example below.

Black And Decker Will Move Some Operations Overseas

The Power tool maker Black and Decker said yesterday that it plans to move some power tool and hardware operations to Mexico, China and Central Europe from the United States and England, reducing its workforce by about 2 percent. Black and Decker announced the plan as it reported a fourth quarter net loss, including a charge of nearly $100 million for the restructuring. But the company, based in Towson, Md., forecast earnings growth for 2002. Black and Decker said that it would cut 2,400 jobs in the United States and England and replace about 1,900 of those at lower cost facilities in Mexico, China and the Czech Republic. (*New York Times*, January 30, 2002, pg. C5.)

Note that Black and Decker expected "earnings growth" during the year 2002. This was the year it laid off 2,400 employees in the United States and England, and transferred 1900 jobs to "lower cost facilities" in other countries. The difference of 500 jobs was evidence the company had arranged for the 1900 new employees to work more hours at less pay than its former American and British workers, especially since the new guys were "low cost" employees. The difference between what was paid to the U.S. and British workers, and what was later paid to the low-wage workers, was an enormous savings for the corporation. This was likely a significant part of its anticipated profits and dividend payments during the year 2002.

Exporting work to lower wage countries is one of the principal methods by which our corporate heroes are able to increase earnings. CEOs will look like complete qeniuses when they raise profits and dividends by taking thousands of jobs that pay twenty dollars or so an hour in the U.S., and exporting them to Guatemala, Mexico or the Czech Republic where the wages might be only two dollars an hour. When things get tough and the profits drop a little, these two dollar an hour jobs can then be transferred to Vietnam or China where wages are maybe a hundred dollars a month. When you figure some people in these countries work ten to sixteen hours per day, six days a week or more, the hourly wage translates into roughly ten to twenty-five cents per hour. The difference in worker pay multiplied by thousands, or even hundreds of thousands of jobs, is considerable enough to boost corporate profits and dividends even further. It doesn't take a brilliant mind to lead his or her company on a race to the economic bottom by transferring the wages, salaries and benefits of employees to dividends via this method. In fact, this is among the least imaginative techniques by which corporations can keep those dividends, earnings and share prices constantly rising.

Currently, as measured in terms of income and wealth, the lowest 80 percent of the population of the United States hold only about 4 percent of all corporate stock. The top 1 percent of U.S. citizens own about 48 percent, while the next lowest 19 percent possess the remainder. The reason for exporting relatively high paying jobs from high wage nations to low wage countries is to transfer the difference in compensation from the lowest 80 percent to the upper 20 percent, although this transferred income principally goes to the top 1 to 2 percent wealthiest of consumers. These actions allow dividends and earnings to rise, but simultaneously reduce the demand for goods and services since working people have less income. Since affluent shareholders quite often provide no labor for the corporations they own, these consumers receive "free," or what some might call "unearned," income. But this money is not so free because the price is always paid by working people, and not just via these particular income transfer mechanisms. Along with other negative impacts on the demand for goods and services, even when these conspicuous transfers do not occur, in order to keep earnings rising, CEOs hold worker compensation in check, especially when inflation is factored into wages and salaries, and this also inhibits the expansion of the demand sector of the economy. One conspicuous reality with regard to their negative impact on the demand sector is that people who receive free income via dividends act as a drag on the success of their own business firms, on their employees, and on the national economy, much in the same manner as a "parasite unto its host."[10] Worst yet, rich folks usually reinvest their unearned income, which, as will be shown later, quite often depresses the demand for goods and services even more. The roles played by investors, especially those who own large numbers of shares, is the direct opposite of the roles played by working citizens and the highly skilled owner/operators of businesses who, in direct contrast to mostly rich shareholders, add to the total stock of income and wealth of the United States.

The legal structures of publicly traded limited liability corporations ensure that investors and their guardian angels react to a completely different set of incentives than owner managed businesses. With few exceptions, shareholders and their angels can only examine the bottom lines in order to ascertain how well their captains of industry are managing their corporations, and it doesn't take much skill to do that. So long as their CEOs make the proper decisions that ensure constantly rising earnings from one quarter to the next, investors and their guardians are usually quite satisfied. Owner operators, in contrast, typically need to possess high levels of intelligence, business shrewdness, skills and knowledge to ensure the success of their business entities. Their know-how allows them to manage their own business operations. They are under pressure to produce quality goods and services efficiently. Their livelihoods are jeopardized if they don't achieve this result, which is a dilemma shareholders and their guardians don't need to worry about at all.

In contrast to owner-operated businesses, CEOs are provided with incentives that are often at cross purposes with the owners. For example, not too many owner operators desire to successfully hide profits from themselves, which would be stupid for them to do. And many if not most CEOs possess little or no knowledge of the day-to-day operations of their firms because of the sheer size of their companies. They just need to be able to raise earnings from one quarter to the next fairly consistently, and there are many ways this can be achieved without knowing how to produce goods and services efficiently at all. More and more, for example, our heroes just need to possess political connections, or obtain more free trade policies that make it easier to export jobs to lower wage countries.

You can rest assured Corporate Welfare Queen Dick Cheney, former CEO of Halliburton Corporation, does not have the skills to step in for Mike Sloan and manage the day-to-day operations of his business firm, House Magic. It is difficult to believe that Cheney is capable of laying the foundation of a garage faster and more efficiently than Sloan, or building a house, or remodeling a kitchen. Skills are necessary to do these things, but Cheney can only offer businesses the use of his political connections for obtaining corporate welfare at taxpayer expense. Since Mike Sloan is not in need of government handouts because he actually works for a living, it is highly unlikely he would hire Cheney anyway— unlike Halliburton Corporation.

Sloan is in a competitive business. He needs to build and repair houses faster, cheaper and with higher quality than his competition. His livelihood is at stake if he can't. Cheney received a $48 million dollar retirement package from Halliburton for just five years of mediocre management. Mike Sloan can only dream of earning such a retirement parcel despite his wonderful skills and efficiencies. How competitive can publicly traded corporations be when their captains need to know very little of their day-to-day operations? In addition to what was discussed above, there is another devious method corporations use to help generate gigantic profits that allows them to pay mediocre CEOs millions of dollars every year. That's the next dirty little secret.

Notes

1. In a general sort of way, CEOs can also decide to enhance the productivity of employees through the purchase and application of new technologies, among other actions open to them. However, our heroes have little experience and knowledge in actually operating such new equipment. Often, the purchase of new equipment is used to absorb and regulate profits.
2. There are some corporations in which all of the shares, or a majority of them, are held by just a few people or family members, and they are not publicly traded. However, those corporations that are just limited liability companies that reach a certain point in size beyond some small level are managed just as inefficiently as those that are publicly traded.
3. Santos also depicted Alcoa managers so miserly that janitors were stationed at bathroom doors in order to limit employees to just three sheets of toilet paper. You have to wonder how cost effective it was to pay janitors to ensure employees use only three sheets of toilet paper every time each one of them sat down on a toilet. How efficient in the production of goods was this corporate decision?
4. Dillon, Sam, "Profits Raise Pressures On U.S.-Owned Factories In Mexican Border Zone: The Dividing Line," *New York Times*, Feb. 15, 2001, p. A 16.
5. Suskind, Ron, *The Price of Loyalty: George W. Bush, the White House, and the Education of Paul O'Neil*, Simon & Schuster: New York, 2004, p. 232-233.
6. *Yes!* "The page that counts." Fall 2002, p. 11.
7. Henriques, Diana, "Cheney Has Mixed Record In Business Executive Role," *New York Times*, Aug. 24, 2000, p. A. 1.
8. From *Times* Staff and Wire Reports, *Los Angeles Times*, "Questions Raised on Bush Son's Dealings," March 8, 1992, p. A-21.
9. Unlike owner operated businesses, absentee owners are blessed with the knowledge that they will never be held legally responsible if their captains make decisions on their behalf that damage the environment or their product or service injures or kills people. Generally, the CEOs of each corporation are also not held responsible for their decisions that negatively impact the lives of other people. This provides a disincentive to make decisions that harm non-corporate citizens while the drive for ever-increasing profits gives them motivation to ignore making decisions that can and do harm people. Such a legal situation, along with the ignorance of absentee owners and members of the Boards of Directors, also provides a fertile environment whereby our corporate heroes are able to make decisions that benefit themselves, often to the detriment of share owners.
10. There are, of course, exceptions to this rule. Bill Gates and Paul Allen of MicroSoft are examples of people who are wealthy, and deservedly so. Oprah Winfrey became wealthy because of her considerable talents. There are plenty of people who fit into this category. However, these people are also probably wealthier than they might otherwise be because of the speculative construction of publicly traded, limited liability corporations.

Chapter Three

INFLATION: THE ILLEGAL DRUG OF CHOICE
OF THE CORPORATE ECONOMIC SYSTEM

> Federal Reserve Chairman Alan Greenspan said Tuesday the economy
> has picked up so much momentum that deflation, a widespread fall in
> prices, is no longer a threat and *companies are regaining pricing powers*.
> —*USA Today*, April 21, 2004, p. B1. (Italics mine.)

On October 7th 2003, *USA Today* reported that Americans were flocking in
rising numbers to Canada to purchase pharmaceutical drugs that were significantly less expensive than in the United States. According to the newspaper,

> Mary Music of Strongsville, Ohio, says her 11 medications for choles-
> terol, high blood pressure and heart problems cost her $900 for a three-
> month supply from Canada. Buying them at home, she says, would
> cost more than $3,000. Since her first bus trip to Canada, the 80-year-
> old has been ordering her drugs by phone from the same pharmacy. "I
> just think it's a shame that we have to cross the border to get them."

Prior to the autumn of 2003, Music had been very fortunate indeed at being able
to purchase the medications she needed in Canada, because she saved herself
$2100 every three months. If she had been compelled to purchase her drugs in
the United States, the $2100 overcharge would have gone directly to pharma-
ceutical corporations. At least a major portion of the $2100, if not the whole
amount, would have gone towards ensuring constantly rising profits and dividends, primarily for wealthy shareholders.

In order to stop these elderly citizens from seeking affordable pain relief
medicine in Canada, on behalf of the pharmaceutical corporations, President
George W. Bush signed the Medicare prescription drug law late in 2003. The
new law made it illegal for U.S. citizens to travel to Canada to purchase less ex-

pensive drugs there. Since then, Music would have committed a criminal act every time she purchased drugs in Canada. In one stroke of the president's pen, she and millions of other citizens were deprived of the benefits of free trade under the NAFTA treaty because their actions undercut the rising profits of the U.S. corporate pharmaceutical cartel.

Senator Orrin Hatch supported the anti-free trade approach of the industry. He argued,

> Many of my constituents have written, asking why they cannot use the lower-cost medications from Canada. The answer is easy: it is just irresponsible for Congress to jeopardize public safety by allowing the unchecked reimportation (sic) of drugs...If we truly care about our seniors and other patients who depend upon prescription drugs, we should not expose them to what amounts to pharmaceutical Russian roulette.[1]

The good senator failed to mention that pharmaceutical and health corporations had provided him with more campaign funds than any other industry between 1999 and January 2004. Without these legalized bribes, had he acted on behalf of citizens, he could just as easily have said, 'It is just irresponsible for Congress to jeopardize public safety by allowing the unchecked upward spiral in the price of drugs. If we truly care about our seniors and other patients who depend upon prescription drugs, we would not allow fellow citizens to go without their medicines due to the continuous growth of the inflationary prices set by the industry.' Unfortunately, the industry pays him to say things justifying their anti-market price structure, and this ensures citizens such as Mary Music are not represented at all by the good senator in their battle against the drug cartel that is taking place in the supermarkets of politics.

When President Bush signed the legislation into law, he certainly had his priorities straight. The drug cartel had paid him a handsome sum of nearly $500,000 during the 2000 presidential campaign to support their price structure and keep their dividends rolling upward. Supposedly, with this bill, the government agreed to subsidize citizens a portion of their prescription drugs provided they meet certain requirements. The cost of the program was somewhere in the vicinity of 1.2 trillion dollars. Less than a year after the president signed the bill into law, newspapers reported that the prices of many drugs had risen beyond the subsidies the federal government was willing to provide seniors, leaving the few of them who qualified for the program as badly off as before. Only the pharmaceutical corporations, and their mostly wealthy shareholders, benefited from the president's public assistance program, which was never intended to help senior citizens. It gave the pharmaceutical industry a completely captive market, and provided them with an estimated $1.2 trillion in government welfare handouts over ten years, and all at taxpayer expense.

The new legislation also prohibited officials of the Medicare program, which represents about 40 million citizens, from negotiating the price of prescription drugs with pharmaceutical corporations.[2] The Veteran's Administration has successfully negotiated prices with the drug cartel for years. Nonetheless, Senate majority leader Bill Frist said he supported the bill because the government should not be allowed to fix prices.[3] The good senator had received over $120,000 from the industry in just a few years prior to the new drug law, which is probably why he supported this corporate welfare bill, and why he concluded negotiating lower prices with price-fixers was somehow an act of fixing prices.[4] Unfortunately, Mary Music, like more than two hundred million other citizens, did not have the income to purchase the legislative assistance and sound logic of such powerful politicians at such fancy price tags.

The actions of the Federal Drug Administration (FDA) also help the pharmaceutical drug industry drive prices for prescription medicines skyward. Although drugs sold in Canada are certified as safe by that government, and although many of these drugs come from manufacturers in the United States, the FDA ensures that the industry is protected from competition by not approving of the less expensive Canadian drugs U.S. citizens need. This is why the United States has the highest pharmaceutical drug prices in the developed world. It also explains why this drug cartel is the "most profitable of all businesses in the United States."[5] If drugs made in the United States and exported to Canada are allowed back into the USA via Canadian pharmacies, the entire price structure set by the captains of Drug Cartel USA and the U.S. government would be undermined, along with their abilities to constantly expand earnings and dividends.

Because politicians of the U.S. government are well paid partners, Drug Cartel USA is able to use the legislative favors it purchases to help fix the prices of prescription drugs at increasingly higher levels. In turn, the government endorsed fixed prices help to fuel the habitual yearly rise in the inflation rate. However, the pharmaceutical cartel is not the only industry that relies on the help of the government to pass on increasingly higher fixed prices to citizens.

Shortly after he took office in 2001, President George W. Bush refused to place caps on the rapidly rising prices of energy in California. The president was (and perhaps still is) a good friend of Kenneth Lay, corporate hero of Enron, an energy company. Both Captain Lay and his corporation had given hundreds of thousands of dollars to Bush as a candidate for governor of Texas, and later as a presidential aspirant. During those first few months of the Bush administration, Vice President Dick Cheney headed a task force to determine national energy policies. With their campaign contributions, Enron officials had purchased six top secret meetings with Cheney and his team. What was discussed during those encounters has been kept secret. The Bush administration has even gone to court in order to keep the records of these meetings from the public. What we do know is that President Bush refused to interfere with the manipulation and fixing of increasingly higher energy prices in California during those months. We do not know if determining a federal policy of "inaction" on these matters was among the national policies discussed during the meetings of the energy task force, but "inaction" was the evident path chosen. This policy was extremely harmful to the public good, yet it was very helpful to Enron and Kenneth Lay.

In California, the price of electricity had surged upward hundreds of percent starting in the summer of 2000, and continued to rise unabated until the summer of 2001. Rolling blackouts, where large areas went without electricity, were common. At the time, although unknown to the public, Enron was facing an imminent financial meltdown, which was successfully hidden from stockholders and the public by the use of fraudulent accounting practices. Although proof did not exist until later, at the time, some skeptics strongly suspected the power crisis in California was completely contrived. The conservative news media did their duty and chose to ignore the obvious and instead insisted that population growth had brought about the rise in prices, as if the number of people living in California had jumped 1000 percent during the previous year. It did not take a mental wizard to understand that the price of energy usually will not jump hundreds of percent in a matter of months unless the supply has been rigged to ensure such an outcome. Combined with the accounting fraud committed at Enron, the energy crunch and its artificially rising prices was probably a last ditch effort to save the company and keep its stock value high with a flood of illegally obtained cash. Thanks to the president's policy of "inaction," since citizens paid criminally higher utility bills during the crisis, Enron's wealthy shareholders got something for nothing when they reaped the benefits of this inflation driven income transfer scheme with higher dividends and stock prices. In addition, the president's "inaction" policy delayed the collapse of Enron for many more months later than would otherwise have been the case, which was very convenient for the president's benefactor and close friend, Kenneth Lay. At the very least, big money given to a politician had ensured that Enron officials were included in national energy policy meetings, what was discussed would be kept secret from the public, and prices in California were allowed to explode upward.

Although it may appear to be a ridiculous idea that the president and vice president of the United States aided and encouraged Enron's income transfer scheme against the citizens of California, such a scenario would be unerringly consistent with the president's economic policies of using the powers of the federal government to transfer income and wealth from working people to his self-proclaimed base of "the haves and the have mores." His pharmaceutical drug and energy policies discussed above are just two of many examples. Others will be exposed in the following pages.

The purchase of presidential, legislative and regulatory favors in the supermarkets of politics is among several methods used by corporations to ensure themselves the power to manipulate the prices of their products, if not completely control them, and this helps to fuel the yearly rise of inflation. The inability to wield a powerful influence over the prices of their products would have grave consequences for the entire corporate economic structure.

Consumer demand plays a role when the captains of "corporate price gouging" set prices, but it is insignificant compared to the insatiable demands for constantly higher dividends and stock values required by the super-rich investors of the financial markets. These demands exercise a powerful influence on the cost of goods and services, as well as the price of labor the citizens of the United States receive.[6] Controlling prices allow our corporate heroes to raise or lower the costs of their goods and services based on how much they need to expand their quarterly earnings in order to attract more buyers than sellers to their stocks. This is particularly true in the long-run.[7] Price manipulation is why inflation continues to rise even during recessions, which are periods of time when demand for goods and services are slack. Prices should experience deflationary pressures during these times, but reaching such a point would be harmful to the financial health of the corporate economic system.

Generally, in a largely controlled market, there are only a few major firms numbering roughly one to twelve. When it comes to being serious rivals, the resemblance is closer to co-conspirators who possess slight competitive streaks vis-à-vis each other, a defective emotional condition similar to slightly jealous siblings. The corporate family of each industry, although largely dysfunctional, pulls together during times of crisis to protect their common well being. When such a business firm needs to increase the price of its goods or services, other corporations in the industry must also raise their prices. Below is an example provided by corporate manufacturers.

Sign Of The Times? Prices Rise For Paper, Eating Out

Georgia-Pacific said this month it would boost the price of its toilet paper, tissue and paper towels 6% to 9%, and the price of Dixie Cups, plates and plastic utensils 4% to 6%. In March, Kimberly-Clark said the price of Kleenex, as well as Cottenelle and Scott toilet paper and Viva paper towels, would jump 6%. In February, P&G said it would raise the price of Bounty towels and Charmin toilet paper 5% to 6%. All moves are effective midsummer. The three companies make the lion's share of the toilet paper, paper towels and tissue in the U.S., and their decision to raise prices could mark a significant turning point for the *pricing power of consumer-product makers*. (*Wall Street Journal*, April 13, 2004, p. B1. Italics mine.)

In the example above, the major corporations in the paper products industry raised their prices by approximately the same amounts. Further, P&G jacked-up its prices in February, followed by Kimberly-Clark in March, and finally Georgia-Pacific in April 2004. Notice, "All moves are effective midsummer." In other words, these corporations simultaneously pushed their prices up.

For corporate America, such cooperation is considered to be competitive. Strangely, some people think of it as being cutthroat competition, but the reality for many industries is remarkably one of collaboration, as shown below.

FedEx Increases Rates

FedEx raised rates an average 3.5 percent Nov. 20, with the increased effective Jan. 7. United Parcel Service raised its rates on express shipments as much as 4 percent Nov. 2. The increases were imposed a month earlier than last year to give customers more time for budget planning, the companies said. (*Oregonian*, Nov. 30, 2001)

Shortly after reporting the FedEx price rise, the *Oregonian* newspaper reported the following, "Airborne, the third-largest U.S. air freight carrier, will raise rates as much as 4 percent as of Jan. 2 for express and ground shipments *to counter increases by larger rivals* such as FedEx" (Italics mine). You might wonder how competitive an industry is when all the major players are increasing the prices of their services to "counter increases" by their rivals. Under competitive conditions, rivals would "counter" their opponents with price decreases and enhancements in the quality of their goods and services. Alas, as the examples above and below confirm, competitive conditions among major publicly traded corporations are largely an illusion hyped by the corporate news media.

On December 3, 2002, the *Seattle Times* reported, "Airborne said it will raise rates for its Airborne Express overnight-delivery unit by as much as 4 percent *following similar increases by rivals FedEx and United Parcel Service*" (Italics mine). This story is remarkable given that the economy was still feeling the effects of the recession of 2001, unemployment was still swelling, corporate profits were down, and the rise in prices came barely after the twin towers had been wiped out. Demand was slack, and yet the three largest private delivery corporations in the USA all raised their prices in solidarity. In doing so, the cartel members gave themselves better opportunities to raise earnings, dividends and share prices during a period of slackening demand than would otherwise have been the case. That inflation rises during recessions should raise caution among the members of the media that competition among producers of goods and services is not as pronounced as they claim.[8] For the most part, the system of publicly traded corporations disallows long-term price competition. An example is provided below.

Paper-Makers To Lift Paper Prices, A Sign That Demand Is Rebounding

STAMFORD: International Paper and Weyerhaeuser, the world's biggest paper makers, plan to increase the price of paper used in copy machines and books by about 5 percent, the first sign of increasing demand, analysts said. Domtar Inc. and Boise Corp. also plan to increase the price of so-called uncoated paper by $40 a ton at the beginning of next month, analysts said. The paper sells for about $740 a ton now. The increase would be the first in 17 months and likely will boost profits for paper-makers that have struggled with declining earnings and losses *because of lagging demand*, according to Pulp & Paper Week, a newsletter that tracks prices. (*Oregonian*, March 21, 2002, page D1. Italics mine.)

Just who are the analysts that are proclaiming the price increase of 5 percent by "the world's biggest paper makers" is an indication of increasing demand for paper products? The same article contradicts the analysts because it is "lagging demand" that has brought about an increase in prices, and it is expected the amplification of paper costs will "boost profits." The reporters and editors of the corporate news media do not question the make believe fairy tale that the analysts created out of thin air.[9] Six days after the article was published in the *Oregonian* newspaper, it printed a different story.

Boise Corporation Lowers Earnings Expectations For The First Quarter

---

BOISE: A weak paper market prompted the Boise Corp. to alert the financial industry on Tuesday that is expects a first quarter loss substantially larger than Wall Street has been anticipating. The Idaho-based company, which just changed its name from Boise Cascade, said red ink for the January-March quarter 2002 could hit 20 cents a share. "Security analysts estimates of our first quarter 2002 results have been generally rising in recent weeks due to improving conditions in our building products business," Boise Chairman George Harad said in a statement. "However, we expect that improvement to be more than offset by *weak conditions in our paper business*," Harad said. (*Oregonian*, March 27, 2002, page C2. Italics mine.)

According to the Chairman of Boise Corporation, six days after the view of the analysts was uncritically published in the news media, demand in the "paper business" was so "weak" that it was going to "offset" the "improving conditions" in the building products business for Boise Corporation. How was it that this corporation, along with the other leaders in the paper products industry, was able to increase the price of paper products during a time of "weak conditions" in the industry? The answer was that major producers were working together to set prices at what the market would bear. Along with its alleged rivals, Boise Cascade announced its price increase six days before, one might conjecture, so as to alert the "security analysts" that something was being done to increase earnings, and to provide them with an idea of what to expect so far as future earnings were concerned.[10]

John Kenneth Galbraith in his seminal work on corporate behavior, *Economics and the Public Purpose*, accurately noted that a corporate cartel member that unilaterally ratchet's up its price but discovers that its partners fail to do so must retract the increase.[11] There are times when it may not be prudent to raise prices, and cartel members will resist the price increases of their fellow conspirators.

Three Largest Airlines Tack $20 To Price Of Certain Fares

NEW YORK: The nation's three largest airlines raised the price of certain round-trip fares by $20 for leisure travelers ahead of the July Fourth holiday. The ticket price increases introduced by American and matched by United and Delta on Wednesday apply to 14-day advance-purchase companion fares that require a Saturday night stay. A spokesman for American, which initiated the move late Tuesday, said the change applies to the lowest fares in the carrier's pricing structure. Nevertheless, the fare increase is the industry's fourth such effort since mid-April and comes at a time when the biggest airlines continue to lose millions of dollars a day. *Major carriers' three previous attempts to raise ticket prices were short-lived as competitors, most notably Northwest Airlines, refused to go along.* (*Oregonian*, July 4, 2002, page C2. Italics mine.)

Galbraith's analysis of price setting by corporations is confirmed in the example above. Three times the airline cartel refused to go along with the unilateral price increase of a wayward member. In this respect one could argue that competition compelled a corporation to terminate a price increase. However, a more realistic explanation is that a rebellious cartel member wanted to increase prices unilaterally, but the other members decided the time was not good to do so. However, when American Airlines made the decision to raise prices, the cartel decided to go along with the price enhancement.

Although cooperation in setting prices is practiced in the long-term by most any industry dominated by publicly traded corporations, there are other methods used to ensure that any short and long term rivalries are aborted or limited in one way or another. Large corporations, for example, have many advantages over smaller rivals and newcomers to their industries, and they will use any trick in the book to try to keep potential foes from springing up. One method of dealing with a budding upstart is simply to purchase them, and then put them out of business, but there are other ways to limit competition as well. For example, in 2004 a jury found the Weyerhaeuser Corporation guilty of illegal monopolizing behavior in the alder saw-log market. The company hoarded alder logs "to the point of letting logs rot—to force shortages. The shortages made it difficult for competitors to obtain logs and *drove up prices*" (Italics mine).

Weyerhaeuser also made pacts with large timberland owners to guarantee its own supply, leaving its smaller competitors at a huge disadvantage in obtaining logs.[12] Citizens and small businesses paid higher prices for this conspiracy while Weyerhaeuser shareholders and corporate officers reaped all the benefits.

Purchasing competitors, even long-time and large scale rivals, is a major method our corporate heroes use to help raise prices to perpetual new highs. This is so common a practice as to be tedious to recite all of the times it has occurred. However, to give an idea of how common it is, a person only needs to look at a single issue of the *New York Times*. On April 18, 2003, on a single page, the *Times* reported "National Steel Accepts Bid From U.S. Steel"; "Citizens (The Citizens Financial Group) Agrees to Pay $285 Million for Port Financial," and "Russell (a maker of sportswear) Buying Most of Spalding Sporting Goods Unit."[13] On March 11, 2003, the *Times* reported that U.S. Steel anticipated a first quarter 2003 loss of earnings. Despite the loss, on April 22, 2003 the *Times* reported "The National Steel Corporation won bankruptcy court approval yesterday to sell its assets to the U.S. Steel Corporation for $850 million." The same newspaper reported the following day that "The Bethlehem Steel Corporation won a judge's permission yesterday to sell its assets for about $1.6 billion to the International Steel Group." With these mergers, according to the Times, U.S. Steel remains the biggest producer in its industry followed by International Steel. The incentive for purchasing their competitors is to control prices by eliminating opponents, abolishing potentially devastating price wars, thereby ensuring constantly rising profits, dividends, stock values and prices—and always at the expense of citizens who earn their income by working.

Although technically not a purchase, when two corporations merge into one, the effect is the same as if one rival purchased another. Quite often, the spokespeople of merging partners maintain that the integration of two corporations of the same industry is done so as to ensure better efficiency, along with higher quality goods and services, and lower prices. But the central reason for merging is the same as when purchasing foes, to exercise better market control for pushing prices upward in the long run by reducing the number of competitors.

It is absolutely imperative for publicly traded corporations to maintain control over the prices of their goods and services over the long haul. Our captains of industry would be rightfully accused of sailing their corporate ships onto the rocks of insanity if they engaged in long-term fights to the death with their foes because such contests would ignite the deflation of prices, and this would bring about stable or declining earnings, the exact opposite of outcomes that give CEOs the appearance of being competent at their jobs, and which makes board members and shareholders happy. Consequently, the incentives guiding our heroes in the management of the affairs of their businesses gently nudge them toward less quarrelsome and more cooperative means of dealing with semi-rival CEOs, who also want to see their profits go up one quarter after the next. In the short-term, our captains may decide to engage in brutal dog fights with their adversaries, but typically, unless such combat brings their foes to their knees relatively quickly, the corporations of any industry are not able to withstand the downward pressures on earnings such belligerent action fetches. In the United States, a prime example of long-term unfettered competition occurred in the middle to late nineteenth century when the prices of farm products plummeted for several decades. Nowadays, that kind of foolish struggle is reserved only for small, localized businesses—the real capitalist economy. If such long-term and cutthroat competition existed today among publicly traded corporations, such insane behavior would bring about the self-liquidation of the system, as well as put an end to the built-in scheme that allows for income and wealth to freely flow from working citizens directly into the already bulging wallets of wealthy shareholders, board members and CEOs.

In the publicly traded corporate economic system of the United States, some long-term competition does exist, but it is in the financial markets, rather than the markets for goods and services. Corporations seek investors to purchase their shares, which if successful will inflate their stock prices upward. Likewise, our corporate heroes do not want investors to sell their stocks, which could drive values downward and make any corporate captain appear ineffectual. Therefore, there exists a continuous need to push stock values upward to attract prospective shareholders. The little investors are insignificant in achieving the aims of CEOs because their purchases are way too small to impact share prices. Therefore, the various captains of industry want to appeal to investors with millions and billions of dollars to purchase their stocks. The financial clout of the super-rich gives them the power to demand constantly rising dividends and stock prices from the captains. If our heroes fail to achieve this target fairly consistently, these big time investors might sell off their shares and turn around and purchase the stocks of more successful companies. Therefore, one on-going rivalry in the financial markets exists between wealthy investors on the one side, and the captains of price gouging on the other.

The competition between these two groups significantly influences what goods and services are produced, and also the quantities necessary and their prices. These factors have some significant bearing on how much labor is necessary to produce goods and services, and what wages and salaries will be paid. All of which suggests that another primary competition being waged today is occurring in the interrelated financial and labor markets. Cash is increasingly redirected from worker compensation, and instead is more and more directed to enhance profits to help push dividends up. That's why people are working more and earning less despite the long-term growth in worker productivity. This long-term competition is taking place all over the world, and is being fought between citizens with jobs and small business owners on one side, in struggle against corporations, CEOs, board members, extremely rich shareholders, and their political allies on the other side. Unfortunately, only the latter group appears to know the war has been continuously waging for over thirty years, and it appears it will continue for many decades into the future.

To a relatively minor degree, corporations compete against each other in the political markets. Solar power companies, for example, might try to purchase legislation favorable to their industry. Electric, gas and oil companies may oppose some of the laws supported by the solar companies simply because they may pose a threat to their profits.

However, the most sinister competition in the political markets pits major corporations and their super rich allies against 80-year-old ladies on fixed incomes, as well as other working citizens. The ability of the corporate drug lords to purchase legislation in the political markets helps to explain why the prices of pharmaceutical drugs are so excessive in the United States. These battles in the supermarkets of politics are typically one-sided affairs in favor of corporations and the rich, and that's because the members of these two groups can afford to pay the expensive prices charged for legislative goodies. Along with corporate cooperation in setting prices and other tactics, these purchases in the political markets ensure the continuous upward spiral of prices.

Decades ago, the conservative economist Milton Friedman falsely assumed that the long-term rise of inflation was brought about by the growth in the money supply. Increase the money supply and the cost of goods will rise. In other words, goods will always follow money. A sizable number of academics, businesspeople, politicians and average people came to subscribe to this error of thought. Their beliefs were based on the assumption that the economic system in which they lived was a close approximation to the free market economy laid out by the economist Adam Smith more than 200 years ago in his book, *The*

Wealth of Nations. According to Friedman and his supporters, governmental institutions such as the Federal Reserve Bank, have always created inflation by increasing the money supply. Adam Smith is widely considered to be Friedman's intellectual father, but he was no fool. In 1776, he wrote, "Money...necessarily runs after goods, but goods do not always or necessarily run after money." Obviously, Smith knew his subject matter very well.

Perhaps mislead by some ghostly prankster, such as a demented "invisible hand," Friedman assumed Smith's free market economic theories supernaturally removed themselves from the pages of *The Wealth of Nations* and conjured up some magical spell that has shaped and controlled economic reality, beginning somewhere between 150 and 200 years ago. If Smith were alive today, never being ideologically rigid in the manner of Friedman and others, and having been far more intellectually gifted as well, it is doubtful he would have concurred with this assumption. For starters, Smith largely excluded corporations from his theoretical models of a utopian and competitive business world because, as he observed, they were extremely inefficient and not very competitive at all, especially those in manufacturing. In his day, as in contemporary times, corporations relied heavily on purchases in the political markets in order to gain profits at the expense of laboring people. Smith observed that political power provided merchants and industrialists with the leverage to raise the prices of their goods above what normally would have been obtainable under real competitive conditions. If inflation were anything more than a short term phenomenon, Smith knew a real market economy as he had devised it could not have evolved. His comprehensive theories was essentially a plan to put an end to the economic and political system that granted rich people the powers to transfer income and wealth from laboring people. He wanted to replace that system with a more egalitarian economy in which the acquisition of income and wealth would be based on everybody's productive abilities. Therefore, in all likelihood, Smith would have observed too many similarities between the parasitic economy of his day and the contemporary corporate economic structure. Consequently, he would have disagreed with Friedman's assertion that a market economy came into existence roughly 150 years ago, dominates today, and is a close approximation to Smiths' theories. Smith would have been shocked and saddened that affluent people and corporations dominate the political and economic institutions of today. He would have been dismayed that the corporate economic system had been legislatively pieced together during the past 300 years in such a way so as to ensure a continuous stream of income and wealth transfers from working citizens to rich persons, and that's the next secret many politicians and rich folks don't want you to know.

Notes

1. Barlett, Donald L., and Steele, James B., "Why Your Drugs Cost So Much," *Time Magazine*, Feb. 2, 2004.

2. With the passage of this new corporate welfare program, some, but not all, elderly citizens could receive a discount on drugs. However, *USA Today* reported in May 2004 that the rapid rise of pharmaceutical drug prices had wiped out whatever savings these citizens might have received through the discounts offered through this program.

3. Barlett and Steele.

4. Opensecrets.com.

5. Barlett and Steele.

6. The Federal Reserve also has had a hand in increasing inflation most notably in the early nineteen twenties, and then later in the early nineteen eighties.

7. There are, of course, times when CEOs will not raise prices, and there are times when prices in certain markets will fall in the short term. Also, prices, generally, are not allowed to increase too much. Usually when corporations raise prices, such as the California energy crisis of 2000-01, the public will become outraged unless the conservative news media diverts their attention with lies and distortions.

8. It is true that there exists some competition among members of the same industry. To be more competitive, for example, sellers of clothes, shoes and other things will export jobs to low wage countries in order to acquire a competitive advantage against their rivals. Eventually, however, after all of the alleged competitive corporations have moved jobs overseas, prices tend to become stable throughout an industry, and then begin a long-term process of rising.

9. Thorstein Veblen pointed out a century ago in *Theory of Business Enterprise* that, "The first duty of an editor is to edit and omit all news articles with a view to what the news ought to be." Most major newspapers and television stations are corporations, or they are owned by corporations, and they operate with the same incentives as any other publicly traded corporations. A major duty of any editor is to ensure that dividends and share prices rise one quarter after the next, and this influences the shape of "what the news ought to be." Of course, in the long haul, the conservative news media tries to manipulate public opinion as to what is right and good: the corporate economic system is always "good," and the same is true for whatever is good for it.

10. Price increases have a wake effect that is felt throughout the economy as first one corporation, and then others in industries different from the price raising firms, but economically interlocked with them, must raise prices as well. For example, if the steel industry raises the prices of its products, users of steel, such as automobile manufacturers, may be compelled to raise their prices. If they do not follow the lead, the price they pay for goods and services from other corporations will have to be absorbed, and this will have a negative impact by reducing profits. Generally, this will make the laggard corporation's stock drop in value since dividend payments will have to decline. The only logical thing to do in order to avert such a potential disaster is for all of the effected corporations to expand prices. On the other hand, absorbing the price increases can be used to soak up excessive profits for those who are doing very well.

11. Galbraith, John Kenneth, *Economics and the Public Purpose*, Houghton Mifflin Company, Boston: 1973, chapter 12.

12. *Oregonian*, "Weyerhaeuser guilty of illegal monopoly," May 21, 2004, p. B1.

13. *New York Times*, April 18, 2003, p. C4.

Chapter Four

ANATOMY OF A PARASITE

Implicitly or explicitly, most economic theorists consider the modern economic system of the United States to be roughly equivalent to a natural ecosystem. Various species of business institutions compete against each other in this environment. This is the man-made equivalent of a finely balanced bionetwork, in which all of the laws of nature apply. During a period of business expansion, it is an economic system that is considered to be in a finely tuned equilibrium. The law of Nature applies to each industry just as surely as it pertains to the natural world, or so the experts suppose, because the belief in the existence of this natural state of economic affairs serves as the foundation of most business cycle theories.[1] Since God and Nature are one and the same in these theories, this dog-eat-dog world must be perfect, or a close approximation.[2] This is the reason why economists are most likely to blame something other than the economy for those troublesome times known as "recessions," which are sometimes called "bust cycles" or "economic downturns."

It should come as no surprise that economists and business experts typically blame government interference with the free markets of the United States as causing recessions. If markets are allowed to function properly without government interference, so the reasoning goes, recessions would not occur. However, some economists also blame the actions of people for bringing about economic downturns. Economists and business people fail to understand that recessions are built right into the system.

Some experts have insisted that the Federal Reserve Bank of the United States pushed the economy into economic slumps when it drove interest rates higher, making goods and services less affordable, and thereby putting a damper on consumer and business spending. Liberal economist Paul Krugman, for example, claimed these actions on the part of the Fed ignited the last six recessions. However, during the boom cycle, the recessionary forces built within the economy were already compelling the captains of industry and finance to redistribute income from working citizens to shareholders typically before any actions on the part of the Federal Reserve occurred. This process is what weakened the demand sector and sparked every recession for as long as statistics have been available.

Rather than governments, some economists blame the collective stupidity of people for causing economic downturns. For example, some experts theorize that inflation eats away at the earnings of citizens during business expansions. Supposedly the entire citizenry are not bright enough to realize this has occurred until relatively late in the boom periods. Upon discovering that their spending power is not as great as they once thought, citizens collectively express shock and dismay and cut their spending immediately, and this allegedly reduces the demand for goods and services, and leads the country into recession. This hypothesis is backwards and not realistic at all. Okay, it sounds just plain dumb, but it serves the purpose of blaming the victims of recessions while leaving the system guilt free. Rather than a "theory," this explanation should be more properly labeled as a "guess," and not a very educated one at that. Perhaps it could be called a "fairy tale" in defense of the system.

Since these explanations for the birth of recessions are bogus at best, the only conclusion we can come to is that we do not live in an economic system that is "perfect," or even a remote approximation. As we have seen in a previous chapter, we do not live in a competitive economy, except for that part in which small owner-operated businesses exist. We know corporations need to exercise great amounts of control over the prices of their goods and services in the long-term. Price competition between these organizations is minimal at best, and usually only a short-term phenomenon. If a truly competitive environment among businesses represents economic perfection, then such a condition does not exist in the United States among the economically dominant publicly traded corporations.

How A Recession Occurs

A recession is really nothing more than an adjustment to the terms of the distribution of income and wealth between working people and wealthy shareholders. We know from chapter two that the earnings of publicly traded corporations must always move upward every quarter in order for our corporate heroes to demonstrate their wonderful managerial abilities.[3] Although corporations manufacture goods and services in order to generate earnings, we saw in chapters two and three that they also depend upon expropriating income and wealth from working people in order to generate profits (and in ways that are not covered until the later chapters of this book). As any business expansion unfolds, wealth and income need to be increasingly shifted from working people to wealthy shareholders because at some point dividends rise at faster rates than earnings. Such a situation cannot continue indefinitely. A corporation can dip into retained earnings to make up the difference but eventually they're all used up. And so profits must be elevated in order to keep dividend payments escalating upward. At this point, more or less, our corporate heroes often raise the prices of their goods and services faster than normal, and usually in harmony with the price increases of their overly cooperative rivals. When boosting prices doesn't do the trick, and as more and more corporations experience dividends racing upward more rapidly than their incomes, they all need to reduce expenditures. Jobs are cut, wages and salaries are frozen, and business-to-business transactions are cancelled or curtailed. This is why job creation typically begins to gradually slow as more and more businesses enter that phase of the business cycle in which dividend growth exceeds the rate of profit growth. Many of those profit soaking employees are shown the door, but many necessary workers find themselves unemployed, or with reduced hours and pay. It's not uncommon for staff to be laid off, while others are forced to pick up the slack with little or no additional compensation. Work more and earn less. Sounds familiar, doesn't it? These CEO actions slash business costs, and cause profits to rise faster than before, dividends then continue to surge, stock prices roll upward, and the good times continue, or so it appears. Unfortunately, there is a negative side to transferring the income of employees to rich shareholders via rising dividends. As should be expected when large numbers of working folks experience unemployment, declining or stagnant pay, and reduced working hours, their demands for goods and services slowly begin to erode, although perhaps not statistically noticeable at first.

Imagine you just had your hours at work reduced from forty-two to thirty-nine per week. You're earning $30 an hour forty hours a week, plus time and a half for those extra two hours, so your pay just dropped $5240 a year. You might now decide not to purchase that new car you wanted since you can't afford the payments anymore. It would be cheaper just to repair the old car. And that washer you own; it's not the best, you could use a new one, but you're just a little timid about making such a big expenditure. Your kid wanted that boom box, but it costs $150, and sure you can still afford it, but maybe he'd be just as happy with something a little bit less expensive. What are you going to do about those credit cards you have? Instead of spending money, perhaps you might feel a little safer paying them off just as fast as possible. That pay cut means you're not going to be buying as much stuff as before.

On the other hand, thanks to your sacrifice, the company you work for now has $5240 extra in profits, and this has occurred in order to pay ever higher dividends to some rich guy who doesn't even need the money. He's not going to go out and buy a couple of washing machines or some hot new car or stereo. The guy probably already made those purchases long ago with the dollars he already had. A person can only eat so much, so he's not likely to go to the nearest supermarket and buy more steak and eggs with that money. Most likely this man is going to purchase things to earn money; he's going to make speculative investments by buying such things as stocks, bonds, land and foreign currency, and none of these purchases fuel the demand for goods and services much at all. Since you are spending less this year on things that actually stimulate the economy, and this rich guy is not taking up the slack with money that formerly went to you, this transfer of income actually weakened the demand sector.

Now imagine the same thing that happened to your paycheck is occurring increasingly throughout the economy. Tens of thousands, and then hundreds of thousands of people are put in the same situation as you, or perhaps their situations are worse than yours because they become unemployed, and all just to make sure those profits, dividends and share prices are always rising one quarter after the next. At some point during each business expansion, however tiny and faint, the stagnant and declining financial abilities of growing numbers of citizens to purchase goods and services at prices necessary to support constantly rising profits and dividends begins to diminish. At this point, corporate profits are typically soaring, thanks in part to the sacrifices made by you and your fellow working citizens.[4]

When the demand for goods and services begins to drop, it becomes more difficult for the captains of industry and finance to keep those profits rolling upward at the same pace as dividends. Gradually, more and more corporate rulers come to the conclusion that costs must be reduced even more, and that means more reduced hours for employees, pay freezes, and of course those dreaded lay-off notices. However, much of this is hidden by other factors.

Interest rates will sometimes drop for many people as the boom cycle enters its twilight period, and credit will be approved for citizens not previously deemed credit worthy. Among other things, this expands the demand for goods and services, helping to off-set the rising lay-offs and other cost reductions on the part of businesses that are occurring. These trends help to slow and camouflage the deterioration of the business expansion.

As progressively larger numbers of corporations struggle to provide ever rising dividends in the face of deteriorating demand for their products, the declining economic situation first gets noticed in the durable goods industries, where the hours of workers begin to slowly fall, beginning many months before a recession appears. A durable good is anything that is expected to last more than three years. Examples include stereos, cars, car parts, computers and clothes dryers. Long-term payments and relatively high prices probably act as a deterrent for those citizens experiencing layoffs, reduced hours, wage and salary decreases, or stagnant pay. Of course, durable goods corporations are also undergoing their struggles to keep dividends rising in the face of slackening demand for their products, so the industry gets hit twice as hard as other sectors of the economy, more or less. This probably explains why the entire manufacturing sector, including both durable and non-durable goods producers, always shed jobs prior to the coming of recessions, with but one easily explainable exception.

Before an actual recession strikes, the unemployment rate slowly begins to shoot upward as other industries accelerate their lay-offs, reduce employee hours and trim business-to-business expenditures. This is why, prior to the beginning of official recessions, the ranks of people in poverty swells, and this is also why the number of people applying for welfare, food stamps and unemployment benefits surges upward during the latter stages of business expansions.

The slackening demand for goods and service eventually forces corporate profits downward, but average dividend payments typically rise to historic levels, thanks to the sacrifices of you and your fellow citizens. Although the labor liquidation process fuels the surge of dividends, it erodes the abilities of working people to purchase the goods and services necessary to sustain the boom cycle, and in time the economy enters into an official recession.

The economic bust cycle is pretty much an extension of what occurs during the months leading up to a recession. A rising tide of unemployment sweeps through the nation for many months after a downturn officially commences as jobs and employee hours continued to be transferred into dividends, reducing the demand for goods and services even further. In turn, corporate profits continue to drop so much that even average dividend payments typically droop, at least a little bit now and then, although not all that much. During this time, more shareholders will sell their stocks than buy, driving the values of the stock markets downward. Rather desperately, our corporate heroes then accelerate the lay-offs even more in order to transform more salaries, wages and benefits into dividend payments as a means to drive share values upward. This is why, with slight interruption, dividend payments and the unemployment rate rise simultaneously during the latter stages of business downturns.

As can be seen, an economic contraction occurs because the livelihoods of working citizens are transferred to mostly wealthy consumers in order to keep those free income payments known as dividends constantly rising during the business expansion, yet the boom periods also typically begin because of this same transfer of jobs into these laborless income payments.

The Boom Cycles

I suppose by now it won't surprise you to learn that, with few exceptions, the unemployment rate continues to rise for a few to several months after the official end of recessions, and this fuels the rise in dividend payments, usually to historic highs.[5] Throughout business downturns and the early part of expansions, unemployment insurance, declining interest rates, an extension of credit via lesser standards, and lower rates of inflation, among other things, help to offset layoffs and reductions of hours and keep a fair degree of demand for goods and services at relatively high levels, although lower than prior to the end of the preceding boom period. Corporate earnings begin to rise because of the cutbacks that take place during the economic bust cycle, as well as the lay-offs that occur during the beginning months of the boom period, and because of the stabilization of demand at lower levels. As earnings rise, our corporate heroes then hire new employees, increase marketing budgets, and purchase new plant and equipment, either because these actions are necessary to meet rising demand, or to hide excessive profits.[6] Regardless, such actions stimulate the demand for goods and services on the part of both citizens and businesses. Corporations then hire even more employees, the unemployment rate begins to drop, and the economy expands and begins the cycle again.

During all phases of the business cycle, the rich must always receive rising returns on investment at the expense of all others. Sometimes income and wealth transfers are more conspicuous at one or more points during the business cycle than at others, but they are always there throughout each cycle to one degree or another. For the most part, the income-to-dividend transfers are least visible during the middle portions of the business expansions, but they still occur, only at lower levels than during the beginnings and ends of boom periods, or so it appears. During recessions, the total quantity of wealth the rich possess is generally greater than what it was at the end of the last boom period. Sometimes it may appear by the end of recessions that the wealth of the affluent has actually declined vis-à-vis the rest of the world's citizens. Whenever and if this happens, they are illusions created by declines in the values of corporate shares, which are assets held mainly by the wealthiest citizens. This temporary drop in values provides the false impression of a narrowing of the income and wealth gap between affluent and working citizens.

Slowly, over the decades, as the demand for goods and services degenerates more and more due to the mal-distribution of income and wealth inherent within the construction of the corporate economic system, working people will be less able to afford the goods and services of these business entities at prices necessary to sustain continuously rising earnings and dividends. Consequently, with the passing of each new business cycle, a rising percentage of wealth and income will need to be expropriated from working people, who will possess less and less real income and wealth for the rich to steal.

Unmitigated disaster will likely occur before the system is outlawed via legislative or revolutionary action. A parasite that grows faster than its host will die when it has sucked its victim's life dry. We have probably already passed the halfway mark in the life of this freeloading corporate economic system. In the calculable future, perhaps in as little as ten years, but definitely in fifty years or less, it must self-liquidate.

Evolution Of The Corporate Economic System

A competitive world of small businesses existed in the United States from roughly 1620 to 1840. Corporate forms of business institutions then existed, but they were few and far between. After the year 1783, state legislatures provided corporate charters for public spirited purposes, such as the building of bridges, canals and railroads. Corporate economic and political power rose significantly during the American Civil War, from 1861 to 1865. Prior to 1864, recessions likely occurred due to drought, war, or the end of wars, or other such calamities. For example, most U.S. citizens then were members of farm families. Drought damaged crops dampened demand for industrial products, leading the economy down the road to recession. Typically, the end of wars decreased government demand for goods and services, which also sent the economy into recessions.

Somewhere between 1861 and roughly 1890 to 1900, corporations began to dominate the economy. It is likely that several of the recessions within this period began in the financial markets, if not all of them. For example, a recession began in April 1865, the month that Robert E. Lee surrendered the Army of Northern Virginia to U.S. Grant. Although beyond the scope of this study, it might be reasonable to suggest that our corporate heroes recognized that the war was effectively over, government demand for goods and services was going to drop, and the lay-offs began in order to provide higher dividends in the face of imminent declining earnings.

In 1904, Thorstein Veblen, in *Theory of Business Enterprise*, wrote that corporations had come to rule the economy by 1900. He correctly reasoned that the economic and political power of small businesses had taken a subservient role to publicly traded, limited liability corporations. Arguably the most brilliant economist of the twentieth century, he claimed that all recessions began in the financial markets. However, due to the paucity of statistics, it is difficult to establish proof of this assertion for the period from roughly 1890 to 1919, but the data that does exist for this time frame indicates potential truth to his theory. Although limited, the evidence indicates the recessions within the years 1919 to 1928 likely began in the financial markets. On the other hand, the evidence clearly demonstrates that from 1929 onward all recessions began in the financial markets.

Notes

1. When analyzing the economy, this is why economists employ such intellectual tools as "natural growth" and the "natural unemployment rate."
2. The belief that God is Nature and visa-versa serves as the foundation, if not the whole package, of most economic theories, from John Locke and Adam Smith to Karl Marx, and to all of their modern economic disciples, whether they know it or not, such as Milton Friedman and Richard Lucas.
3. See chapter two.
4. Unknown to Krugman and his more conservative contemporaries, during the months prior to the onset of official recessions, more and more publicly traded corporations raise prices to offset the slow drop in the demand for goods and services brought about by the cutbacks in employee hours and lay-offs, a process set in motion in order to ensure dividends and stock prices roll higher. Upon detecting these inflationary pressures, and under the false assumption that the demand for goods

and services is higher than the supply, the Federal Reserve pushes interest rates upward to keep inflation in check. Therefore, the actions of the Fed are reactions to what is occurring in the financial markets, and not, as many people believe, reactions to the theoretical inflationary pressures caused when the demand for goods and services falls short of supply. However, the unintended actions of the Fed adds its weight to an economy already in the process of sinking into recession by further reducing the demand for goods and services, and resulting in more lay-offs and cutbacks. On the other hand, interest rates have often risen and the economy has expanded despite this. Consequently, it should be obvious that relatively mild increases in interest rates have little or no impact on whether or not an economy goes into recession, making Krugman's hypothesis untenable.

5. Seven of the ten post-World War II business expansions began with rising unemployment rates for various numbers of months. The recession of 1948-49 is the most obvious example of a recession in which the unemployment rate declined with the beginning of the following boom period. The recessions of 1980 and 1981-82 also experienced declining unemployment rates beginning with the following business expansions. However, two things occurred immediately after the recessions of the early 1980s. After a few months of enhanced real hourly earnings at the beginning of the following boom cycles, declines in real wage rates occurred for many months afterward, which made it less necessary to continue to lay off employees in order to transfer the income of working people to the affluent via dividends. People simply received lower real wage rates, rather than the complete loss of their jobs, in order to provide rising dividend payments to the freeloading class.

6. Retained earnings, remember, are that part of profits not paid out in dividends. This money is saved by corporations, and provides a financial cushion between rising profits and rising dividends, helping to ensure that the expectations of financial market analysts are met. Also, recollect from chapter two, our corporate heroes will hide profits. These two actions ensure that earnings are higher than dividend payments, at least for a while during a boom period, and they help our corporate heroes to regulate profits.

Chapter Five

HARD TRAVELING DURING THE GREAT DEPRESSION
(1929–1940)

Opal Brown turned nine years old in 1929, the year the Great Depression struck. Born in 1920, her mother had died in the process of giving birth. Opal was forced to live with the family of her Uncle Jim after her father abandoned her for good in 1925. Jim had his own kids to worry about, and he wasn't particularly happy with having another child to feed. Nonetheless, from a material point-of-view, life with her relatives was not the best, but it wasn't all that bad either, that is until the financial gale force winds of the Great Depression swept her life, as well as the lives of tens of millions of others, spiraling out of control.

Jim's job at the local factory vanished long before the unemployment rate officially crested at 25.3 percent of the population in March 1933. Unemployment insurance did not exist at the time and the family had to scrape by using whatever means possible. Because Jim and his wife were always looking for jobs, Opal found her days working around the house rising while her hours at school diminished.[1] Finding food to eat was far more important than education for struggling families. During the immediate months after Jim lost his job, family members were compelled by the force of circumstances to skimp on such basic necessities as food, heat, water and soap. As the days and months rolled along, the family succumbed to poverty and its offspring—hunger and despair. Jim and his wife took out their frustrations on Opal with frequent beatings and verbal abuse, but sadly, she had yet to experience the complete torment offered by these difficult times.

Before the decade was over, Opal was forced to do quite a bit of hard traveling as she was passed around from one home to the next like a baseball during warm-ups. At some point during this period, Jim could not feed his own family much less Opal, and she was sent to live with another relative who was also tee-tering on the edge of financial insolvency, a situation quite common for tens of millions of other people during the decade. Barely able to feed themselves, the adult members of the new family looked upon the young girl as a burden. When they fell over the edge money-wise a few months later, Opal was again pushed out the door and forced to live with others who also felt she was a heavy load to handle. She found herself unwanted and shoveled from one home to the next throughout the decade.

These events left deep psychological scars on Opal, and with the exception of her last few years, they wielded a powerful influence on her life. Fifty years later, even if someone else offered to pay for her meal, she would still order the cheapest item on the menu of any restaurant. Opal would typically order one appetizer, and she always considered that to be her dinner, lunch or breakfast. If her friends or relatives objected, sometimes they could coax her to order the cheapest entrée by stressing that they were purchasing the meal for her. Opal al-ways used bars of soap until they eventually became microscopic in size. She hoarded everything. Deprived of a meaningful education, Opal was always em-ployed in jobs that paid at or near minimum wages, usually as a seamstress or a maid. During her life, she married three different men. However, life's circum-stances had conditioned her to remain emotionally aloof to them, as well as to her eight children. She never learned how to bond with other people until the day her grandson Michael was born. Opal realized at the age of seventy-three that his birth represented a second chance at a life that had been stolen from her by the emergence of the economic tidal wave of sixty-two years earlier.

The economic tempest exerted a permanent influence on nearly all aspects of Opal's life, but it also wielded a powerful impact on tens of millions of other peo-ple. Echoes of The Great Depression reverberate throughout our national and per-sonal psyches, political and economic institutions, and other aspects of our culture. John Steinbeck wrote about dust bowl refugees in his classic novel "The Grapes of Wrath," which was also made into a popular movie. Although a work of fiction, the book mirrored much of what was occurring throughout the coun-try to millions of sharecroppers and other farm families during the Depression. Many of these people and their families had been forced off of their lands by drought and depressed prices for agricultural products, and they were made to compete against an ocean of unemployed people for a few lousy beacons of salva-tion known as jobs. Some of their fellow citizens derisively called them Okies, be-cause many were from Oklahoma, yet hundreds of thousands came from other states ranging from Texas to Mississippi and from the Gulf of Mexico all the way north to Nebraska. Along with millions of former industrial workers, the Okies rambled and roamed throughout the country looking for work during the 1930s.

Woodrow Wilson Guthrie, otherwise known as Woody, may have been the most famous of these wayfaring people. He left a dust plagued Oklahoma and road the rails and thumbed and walked his way across America only to discover that the land of milk and honey was a myth. He witnessed firsthand the horrors experienced by millions of people made homeless by the unfolding economic tragedy, including people who died from starvation even while farms were producing an over-abundance of crops. Among other subjects, Guthrie wrote songs about the struggles of these tens of thousands of nomadic people, cut loose from their roots, drifting aimlessly from city to town in search of work, whole families living in card board shacks alongside the highways, all desperately clinging to the hope that they might be able to feed their families something as simple as flour soup on any given day. Just about everybody has heard at least one of Woody's musical compositions, such as "This Land is Your Land." However, his musical influence drifted significantly beyond this one tune. Among many others, his songs have been recorded by Bob Dylan, Bruce Springsteen, Pete Seeger, U-2, Emmy Lou Harris and Willie Nelson. Furthermore, his music indirectly influenced others such as the Beatles, who had been inspired by Dylan, whose musical genius had been ignited by Guthrie, who had been deeply moved by the sufferings endured by his fellow citizens, during the Depression.

Besides having an effect on culture, the economic hard times also served as the major reason the role of government expanded in economic affairs. Many programs were enacted during the decade in order to reverse the economic misery. The Social Security Administration was established, and it still successfully provides retirement benefits to those whose working days are over. The Fair Labor and Standards Act established the minimum wage and the forty hour work week. It also restricted the use of child labor. Most citizens still appreciate these laws more than sixty years later. The Tennessee Valley Authority was a project started in order to provide electricity throughout much of the southeastern United States, and it is still doing its job today. The Federal Deposit Insurance Corporation was legislated into existence in order to insure bank deposits, and it still does its job quite well. The Securities and Exchange Commission was created in order to ensure that corporations were accurately reporting their earnings. During the last twenty years or so, it hasn't done its job very well simply because it has been overly politicized and under funded. The Food, Drug and Cosmetic Act came into being during 1938. This legislation required manufacturers to list the ingredients in food, drugs and cosmetics, and this law seems to be functioning just fine today, more or less. These are just a few examples of how government became more involved in the lives of just about everyone who has lived during the last seventy-seven years. The echoes of the financial catastrophe of the 1930s still ring clear.

The impact of the Great Depression on the United States is obvious. What is less certain is why did it occur? What were the seeds out of which it sprouted? Once it began, why did the economy continue to implode until the arrival of President Franklin Roosevelt and his New Deal policies? And why did the president's programs successfully stop and reverse the economic disaster?

The seeds of the economic holocaust lay in the prior decade. This was the ten year period known as the Roaring Twenties. By some erroneous accounts, it was a period of prosperity unprecedented in the history of the United States. As the years of the decade passed by, well known politicians and economists, such as Irving Fisher, predicted the good times would last forever. There were a few pessimistic voices of dissent, such as the economist Thorstein Veblen, the only person of note to predict the coming of the Great Depression, but nobody listened to him. In a state of the union address to Congress on December 4, 1928, President Calvin Coolidge boasted, "'No Congress of the United States ever assembled, on surveying the state of the Union, has met with a more pleasing prospect than that which appears at the present time. In the domestic field there is tranquility and contentment...and the highest record of years of prosperity.[2] In reality, the prosperity of the Roaring Twenties was not quite what the president suggested it was. On close inspection, the decade roared for wealthy people mostly while the efforts of tens of millions of working and small business people failed to deliver to them the promise of increasing living standards. Rising prosperity for most people was simply a myth.

Farmers, for example, did not fair well during the decade. They represented nearly 50 percent of the population by the latter half of the 1920s. These people were stuck in an agricultural depression throughout those years, and they were worse off in 1929 than they had been in 1920.[3] In addition, large areas of the United States did not experience economic progress, such as the Southeast and the Southwest; and a large section of the middle class, especially small businessmen, did not prosper. A number of industries were in the doldrums during the ten year period, including coal, textiles, shoe and boot manufacturers, and the railroads.[4]

The richest 1 percent of the population held 31.6 percent of the total wealth of the United States in 1922, but their share climbed to 36.3 percent by 1929.[5] The mal-distribution of wealth in favor of the freeloading class accounted for a significant degree of the uneven economic advancement of the mislabeled Roaring Twenties.[6] In order to attract increasing investor dollars as the decade unfolded, the captains of industry diverted more and more income from working people to dividend payments, and with their rising flow of free income, the wealthy purchased increasing numbers of shares, creating a stock market bubble. However, this income transfer process also weakened the demand for goods and services as tens of millions of people suffered stagnant and declining incomes and affluence as the decade rolled by.

During the 1920s, average yearly dividend payments rose almost 5 percent from 1923 to 1924, and then they increased 5.5 percent from 1924 to 1925. That wasn't such a big deal. But then they popped up more than 9 percent from 1925 to 1926, and that was kind of a big thing. And then, beginning with a tremendous leap in December 1926, dividend payments skyrocketed over 200 percent by 1930. And that was surely a big deal. This flood of free income was a financial adrenalin rush that pushed the values of the stock markets higher, adding to the total portfolios of wealth and income of the most affluent of consumers. These rapidly expanding dividends fueled the growth of the Dow Jones Industrial average from 95.11 on November 15th 1922 to a high of 386.1 on September 3rd 1929, an increase of over 300 percent. This rise in value occurred because corporate profits, dividend payments and share prices increased every year, but especially after 1926.

Throughout the 1920s, there were few corporate shareholders compared to the population as a whole, and they were mostly extremely rich consumers. Therefore, most if not all of the corporate income that pushed dividends and stock prices higher were directed toward the wealthy, and much of their free income was transferred from the working people who needed to buy the goods and services necessary to keep the economy moving forward.

Experts considered rapidly growing stock prices and dividends as signs that the economy was quite healthy. In this case, they were completely wrong. Too much income had been expropriated from working people in order to fuel the stock market bubble and the economic expansion.

The mal-distribution of wealth began to noticeably impact the demand sector especially after 1926. Veblen had pointed out that in order for the corporate economic system to survive, "...prices have to be maintained or advanced." As early as 1927, deflation struck as prices dropped -1.7 percent, indicating that demand throughout the economy was less than the supply of goods and services. It was not a coincidence that prices began to dive shortly after dividend payments began their spectacular rise in December 1926. The consumer price index dropped another -1.7 percent during 1928 even though the number of employed citizens rose. Deflation in the face of rising employment demonstrated that the one sided distribution of income and wealth had undermined the demand for goods, services and money at prices necessary to sustain the system.

Average monthly dividend payments in 1927 rose almost 80 percent from their levels of 1926. This was in large part sparked by a tax cut for the wealthy that year. In order to attract this newly available cash, our corporate heroes had to offer higher dividend payments. This was achieved by laying-off employees, and or reducing their wages and salaries, and the difference between the old rates and the new was transferred to wealthy shareholders in the form of free income.[7] These actions weakened the demand sector, and by 1927 the economy already teetered on the edge of the Great Depression. All that was needed was something to push it over the brink and into the abyss.

Calvin Coolidge was a great supporter of Big Business, which was made up of corporations controlled by wealthy people. He especially liked these rich people, and so as might be guessed, the president signed legislation into law in 1928 granting them their fourth big tax cut of the decade. You probably have already deduced that this was the final spark that ignited the Depression. On account of his action, dividends exploded upward nearly 50 percent beginning late in 1928. CEOs knew that significantly higher dividends typically persuaded the affluent to invest the newly available cash in the financial markets, which helped to bid up the price of stocks, and made our corporate heroes look awesome at doing their jobs. Unfortunately, this time the corporate economic system could not withstand such illusions of managerial wizardry so soon after the enormous 1926-27 increases. The massive boosts of dividends that began in late 1928 were the final blows that crippled the demand sector, and forced the system to begin the inevitable process of self-liquidation, a development brought about solely by the transfusion of jobs, wages and salaries into dividends.[8]

Inflation equaled 0 percent during 1929. Prices had been maintained, and net corporate profits had risen 28 percent from the fourth quarter of 1928 to the third quarter of 1929. Things looked to be picking up. Unfortunately, much of these earnings were gained by lowering employee pay rates and laying people off, and these actions weakened the demand for goods and services. The economy statistically reached its peak in August 1929, and then stumbled into the Great Depression.[9]

As the economic hurricane commenced, as corporate earnings dropped like rocks beginning in the fourth quarter of 1929, our corporate heroes remained committed to their traditional methods of raising profits and dividends; they cut costs by liquidating jobs and reducing wages, and this weakened demand for their products even more. CEOs could have lowered the dividend payments of share-holders, rather than sending them upward. This would have allowed them to avoid reducing employee hours and slashing jobs, which would have stabilized the demand sector, kept profits stable, and prevented the Great Depression. Unfortunately, earnings must always rise in order to drive dividends and stock prices higher. Our heroes recognized that failure to do this would have dropped the values of their stocks and made them look ineffective, if not completely incompetent.

Corporate earnings fell constantly from late 1929 through 1933. With each quarter, as profits dropped, the captains of industry simply laid-off more people, and reduced more wages and hours of employees. And when earnings were lower the following quarter, and the next and the next and the next, the vicious job liquidation cycle was continued as more and more people received their lay-off notices, or discovered their hourly wages had been reduced for the umpteenth time, or their working hours had been further reduced. These interrelated processes continuously weakened demand, which undermined profits, and forced more lay-offs in a seemingly never ending downward cycle.

Dividends continued their relentless upward surge for fifteen months after the Depression was set in motion, in spite of dramatically declining profits. Then in the sixteenth month, December of 1930, these payments finally dropped a little, from $294.7 million to $290.5 million, a decline of slightly less than -1.5 percent. This ended the string of increases. However, deflation was –2.3 percent during 1930 and this indicates how much the demand for goods, services and money to buy things had dropped. When the decline in prices is taken into account, the actual spending power of $290.5 million in 1930 was $297.46 million in 1929 dollars, a boost over the same month of the previous year. Even if the impact of deflation is not taken into account, CEOs still pushed dividend payments upward an average of 18 percent in every month of 1930 over the corresponding months of 1929. As you by now realize, this was achieved by magically transforming the wages and salaries of millions of working people into free income for rich shareholders via constantly rising dividends. As you should also by now expect, the unemployment rate rose all during 1930, breaching 7 percent by the end of the year, up from 2.7 percent in 1929. Personal income dramatically dropped in every region of the country.

During the year 1931, many of the captains of industry must have been in a panic. The previous year had been awful for business, but during the following twelve months conditions just got worse and worse. The unemployment rate skyrocketed to 16.3 percent while wages and salaries continued to spiral downward. Prices dropped another -9.0 percent, corporate profits plummeted even more, and the gross domestic product (GDP) slid downward another -6.4 percent. In what ways did our heroes respond to the bleak and worsening situation? They continued to lay off employees and reduce wages so that dividends could be kept at high levels. During the first seven months of 1931, dividends continued to swell, averaging over $346 million a month, an increase over the same period of 1929 by 13.3 percent. When comparing all twelve months, these total free income payments in 1931 were 5.2 percent higher than in 1929. For the rich to achieve such soaring sums of unearned income, working citizens had been forced to pay the price through unemployment, starvation, homelessness, and myriad other maladies that came with such large transfers of income and wealth.

The following year, 1932, the liquidation of jobs raged unabated as the unemployment rate surged over 20 percent and continued to rise. GNP plummeted further, prices collapsed another -9.9 percent, and total corporate profits were negative.[10] Even dividend payments diminished a bit, but not all that much. With deflation factored in once again, the free income payments in 1932 were only slightly less than those of 1929. Even without deflation factored in, dividends were still higher in February, August and November of 1932 than they had been during the corresponding months of 1929. Average monthly dividends in 1932 were still over 11 percent higher than in 1928, the last non-recession year. With deflation factored in, this amounted to 37.4 percent more in unearned income corporations paid shareholders during 1932. How could our captains have accomplished this when total corporate profits were in the red? The explanation is simple. Some companies earned money during those months, and this enabled them to pay dividends directly from earnings. Corporations also obtained money by issuing rapidly depreciating bonds and issuing new shares, as well as getting loans from commercial banks. But all of these methods likely only added up to a small fraction of the dividends paid during the year for most companies. The majority of corporations had little choice but to continue slashing jobs, and magically transformed them into dividends. CEOs also continued to reduce the wages and benefits of tens of millions of those who still had jobs. These courses of action continued to cause the corporate economic system to self-liquidate.

Early in 1933, the official unemployment rate shot upward beyond 25 percent, and the army of the unemployed was still growing by legions. Prices, wages and salaries had plummeted further. GDP had dropped -45.6 percent since 1929, and was still in the process of withering away even more. The Dow Jones Industrials had toppled from its towering high of 386.10 on that exuberant day of September 3, 1929, back when prosperity appeared as if it were going to continue its unabated advance into infinity. But by March 1, 1933 the once cocky investors had been laid low by the less lofty value of only 52.97, a tumble of -86.2 percent in less than four years. All of the income transfers used by our corporate heroes to provide shareholders higher dividends had ultimately proven to be economically devastating.

For historians and economists the important questions have always been, "Why did the Great Depression continue to worsen?" and "Why did it last so long?" The reply to these questions can be found in the answer to another question, "Why were dividend payments able to rise during every month of the Great Depression for the first fifteen months over the corresponding months of 1929, a time when earnings were sinking faster than the Titanic? Just as importantly, how was it that for twenty-three months after the recession began, real dividend payments rose while the unemployment rate simultaneously jumped to 16.3 percent, and wages, salaries, GDP and corporate earnings plummeted?" The answers were simple. The corporate economic system had been created to ensure that there flowed continuous income and wealth from those who work for a living to the rich, who received all that free money, even during lean times. The system had reached a point in its freeloading life where it simply had to self-liquidate itself in order to feed the wealthiest of consumers the livelihoods of millions of people to achieve the desired goal of always increasing profits and dividends.

Over the decades, there have been many suggestions offered as to why it was possible for this economic debacle to occur, none of which are tenable. All of these assumptions were developed around the notion that publicly traded corporations operated with the same incentives, and in the same ways, more or less, as other business forms and all interacted together in competitive environments. We have seen in chapters two and three that this assumption is false. These excuses, especially those from the conservative point of view, tend to place the responsibility for the coming of the Depression on anything other than the corporate system itself, thereby acquitting the system and its leaders of any guilt in the development of the debacle.

The least likely of these explanations was developed by the economist Milton Friedman. He claimed the Federal Reserve Bank lowered the money supply from 1929 to 1933, and this action exacerbated what should have been a mild recession, and transformed it into the monster known as the Great Depression. Apparently, his reasoning was that the decline of the supply of money made it exceedingly difficult for sufficient numbers of consumers and businesses to acquire enough cash to make adequate quantities of purchases to keep the economy rolling forward. However, Friedman's guess was always bogus because interest rates fell during these years, and this fact revealed the demand for money dropped at faster rates than the supply. For example, short-term interest rates for business loans declined from a high of 5.8 percent in 1929 to 4.9 percent in 1930, and down the rates went to 4.3 percent in 1931, a -26 percent plunge. Meanwhile, the money supply dropped -5.7 percent in 1930, and then -12 percent in 1931. During the recessions that began in January 1920 and July 1981, the Federal Reserve Bank had cut the money supply and interest rates rose, a normal consequence of its actions. Reduce the supply of anything and the price usually rises. Why did interest rates do the opposite and drop during the years 1929 to 1933, a time when the money supply also contracted severely? The answer is that the demand for money was shrinking before, and faster than, the supply during this period, because the system was self-liquidating.

Recollect that during the business expansion of the 1920s, consumer prices had dropped in 1927 and 1928, and this showed that goods and services were being produced at rates higher than the demand for them. These were also the years when rapidly rising dividend payments, which were in large part achieved via wage reductions, first applied the brakes on the abilities of working citizens to purchase goods and services in quantities and at prices necessary to keep the economy moving forward. Prices stabilized in 1929. However, throughout that year jobs and wages were again transferred into fast rising dividends, and once again these payments severely crippled the demand sector to such a degree that prices were forced downward again beginning in 1930.[11] Large drops in interest rates were unable to offset the weakening of the demand sector caused by the massive rise in dividends from 1926 to 1933. Normally, declining interest rates would have boosted the demand for goods and services since the cost of borrowing money would have been cheaper. Such a scenario would normally have also applied upward pressure on prices. Instead, the constant transfer of jobs and wages into dividends had weakened, and then shut off, the demand for money to pay for the goods and services necessary to keep the economy from collapsing. Friedman was completely wrong; the system had simply self-liquidated.

By early 1933, the corporate economic system had obviously failed miserably, and the process of self-liquidation was moving rapidly towards its obvious conclusion. Millions of hungry people roamed the streets of the cities in search of food and jobs. Grumblings of discontent could be heard throughout the nation. Historian Arthur M. Schlesinger Jr. described the bleak situation in early 1933.

> The fog of despair hung over the land. One out of every four American workers lacked a job. Factories that had once darkened the skies with smoke stood ghostly and silent, like extinct volcanoes. Families slept in tarpaper shacks and tin-lined caves and scavenged like dogs for food in the city dump. In October the New York City Health Department had reported that over one-fifth of the pupils in public schools were suffering from malnutrition. Thousands of vagabond children were roaming the land, wild boys of the road. Hunger marchers, pinched and bitter, were parading cold streets in New York and Chicago. On the countryside unrest had already flared into violence. Farmers stopped milk trucks along Iowa roads and poured the milk into the ditch. Mobs halted mortgage sales, ran the men from the banks and insurance companies out of town, intimidated courts and judges, demanded a moratorium on debts. When a sales company in Nebraska invaded a farm and seized two trucks, the farmers in the Newman Grove district organized a posse, called it the 'Red Army,' and took the trucks back. In West Virginia, mining families, turned out of their homes, lived in tents along the road on pinto beans and black coffee.[12]

People who would never have given a thought of committing violence or theft found the circumstances unbearable and did what they had to do in order to survive. Many parents were unable to feed their children and forced them to leave home, although they had no where else to go. These wayward youngsters found themselves riding the rails with other children and often with tragic results. In his autobiography, *Bound for Glory*, Woody Guthrie recalled that a twelve or thirteen year old boy had died of starvation after accidentally being locked in a rail car.[13] In 2004, seventy-eight year old Florence Bain recalled that her former mother-in-law, in violation of the prohibition on the manufacture of liquor, made gin in her bathtub in an attempt to avoid starvation. Some of her best customers were local law enforcement officials. For rapidly rising numbers of Americans, the situation was the same.

Like an exhausted and dazed boxer only one or two blows away from a knockout loss, in early 1933 the corporate economic system teetered on unsteady legs, badly battered and dazed, ready to collapse and die. Sensible people recognized it either needed to be abolished or reformed before the epidemic of poverty and anarchy encompassed every citizen in the United States. Playing the role of a compassionate referee willing to step in and save a boxer from receiving blows he no longer could defend against, in 1933, the new president, Franklin Delano Roosevelt, decided to use the powers of the federal government to step in and save the system.

Even as FDR was inaugurated into office on March 4 1933, tens of thousands of citizens had already lined up to withdraw their money from banks all around the nation. This was called a "run on the banks." Depositors lost their money if they were not among the first to withdraw their cash.[14] And this caused people to panic and run as rapidly as possible to their banks to withdraw their money before the funds were all gone.

Banks only held a small percentage of total deposits in reserve since the rest had been lent to people to buy houses, appliances, cars and to start businesses. If too many citizens wanted to withdraw their money at the same time, lending institutions were forced to go out of business when they ran out of funds.

Since the beginning of the Great Corporate Self-liquidation in 1929, over 9000 banks had gone out of business. If allowed to follow through, the consequences of the masses of people making their runs on their banks in 1933 would have been to force more lending institutions out of business, which would have driven the unemployment rate up, and further weakened the banking system. For the rest of the tottering economy, this "run on the banks" might very well have been the knockout blow.

Two days after President Roosevelt was sworn into office, he declared a national bank holiday in order to stop the massive run on the nation's banks that was by then already in progress. All banks and the stock markets were closed for ten days in order to determine which were too weak to stay solvent, and which should plan to reopen. It also provided time for the administration to sooth the panic felt by depositors. On March 12th, the president announced that only the financially soundest banks would reopen for business. One-tenth of the nation's lending institutions were not allowed to do so. When their banks reopened for business at the end of the holiday, people knew they were financially sound, leaving depositors with few reasons to engage in "runs on the banks."

The series of reforms enacted by FDR were called the New Deal, and they collectively had two intentions: raise prices by pushing the demand for goods and services upward, and restore citizen confidence in the system. Brief descriptions of some of the New Deal legislation are given below, while some were outlined earlier in this chapter.

Legislation passed to raise public confidence in the system included the establishment of the Securities and Exchange Commission and the Federal Deposit Insurance Corporation (outlined earlier).

FDR's programs to stimulate demand and raise prices included the National Recovery Administration (NRA). The NRA attempted to fix the prices of goods and services in about 500 industries. It also provided such things as minimum wages, maximum hours of work, and the right for workers to bargain collectively. These reforms also made sure that many workers were paid overtime rates when they worked over forty hours per week.

The minimum wage law eliminated the problem of constantly dropping wages during the Depression, which had put downward pressure on the demand for goods and services, and which in turn had pushed prices lower. This law ensured that some degree of demand would remain in place during future recessions since wages would no longer be allowed to drop below the minimum level.

The Civilian Conservation Corps (CCC) provided employment to young, unmarried men. They planted trees, maintained forest roads and trails and built flood barriers, among other things. The CCC paid its workers $30 a month. It employed about three million men.

The Public Works Administration (PWA) spent six billion dollars during the Great Depression putting people to work building schools, libraries, roads, dams, levees, courthouses, and other things. These programs provided cash for the unemployed, and helped increase the demand for goods and services.

The Federal Housing Administration provided loans for the construction and repair of homes, which stimulated the growth of more jobs. The United States Housing Authority gave federal loans for home improvements throughout the nation, and this also created jobs. The Rural Electrification Administration furnished inexpensive electricity to isolated rural areas, which provided jobs and helped to encourage the economic development of these areas.

There were plenty of other programs intended to stimulate demand and prices. Some of them provided work or job training and included the Civil Works Administration, the Works Progress Administration, the National Youth Administration, and the Federal Emergency Relief Act.

Legislation to increase prices without necessarily resurrecting demand included the Agricultural Adjustment Administration, which paid farmers to limit their production, thereby applying upward pressure on the prices of farm goods. Before it could take effect, farmers were paid to slaughter excessive livestock and plough under overabundant crops in order to rapidly raise prices.

The New Deal quickly stopped the Great Depression cold in its tracks, and then began to reverse its tidal wave of misery. The economy recovered during the years 1933–37, but it was a slow process. The unemployment rate dropped to 21.7 percent in 1934, slid to 20.1 percent in 1935, shrank to 16.9 percent in 1936, and tumbled down to 14.3 percent in 1937. During each of these years, GNP gradually rose and average yearly dividend payments improved (They acted as a drag on economic recovery). There was also a resurgence of inflation: 3.1 percent in 1934; 2.2 percent in 1935; 1.5 percent in 1936 and 3.6 percent in 1937.

For all of his pragmatism when faced with an economic meltdown, Roosevelt was fiscally conservative. The economy would have recovered much more rapidly had the government spent tens of billions of additional dollars above what had actually been spent on New Deal programs. And higher rates of pay for everyone would have swiftly boosted the economy to new heights. Instead, although the New Deal represented a vast increase in federal responsibilities, Roosevelt's programs were significantly under funded, and they were unable to reverse the huge crisis as rapidly as might have otherwise been the case.

The 1937-38 Recession

Roosevelt's fiscal conservatism uncovered a gigantic problem during the 1937–38 fiscal year. With the economy apparently on the road to recovery, the president and his top advisors decided the time was ripe to reduce federal deficit spending. They had incorrectly reasoned that the corporate economic system had mended enough to stand on its own two feet. In spite of the massive number of New Deal programs that had resuscitated the moribund economy, the system once again began the process of self-liquidation when the life-support of deficit spending was sufficiently scaled back. The still queasy economy tepidly peaked in May 1937 and then quickly began to expire. Corporate earnings staggered to their apex in the second quarter, stumbled downward more than -17 percent the following period, and collapsed unconscious, more or less dead to the world, in the fourth quarter having suffered another -34.5 percent plunge of earnings.[15] By the third quarter of 1938, total profits had toppled by -80 percent from the second quarter of the previous year.

Faced with a federal government intent on balancing its budget and thereby reducing its stimulus to the economy, our corporate captains resorted to the tried and true methods by which they had always demonstrated their managerial magic. They enhanced dividend payments for as long as possible by liquidating jobs, wages and employee hours.[16]

Despite the steep plunge in corporate income from one quarter to the next, cumulative dividend payments increased every month of 1937 through October compared to the corresponding months of 1936. The unemployment rate surged to 19 percent in 1938 as millions of jobs were simply transferred into dividends. The manufacturing sector, for example, shed over two million employees by July 1938, and those who still had jobs suffered from reduced hours and wages. Meanwhile, the service industries lost 282,000 jobs from 1937 to 1938.[17] Working people in other sectors of the economy also similarly suffered from these transfers of income.

This corporate self-liquidation within the Great Depression also saw the re-emergence of deflation. Prices fell –2.1 percent in 1938. This demonstrated that the demand for goods and services, and the money to pay for them, deteriorated far more rapidly than the drop in production. In 1939, overall prices tumbled another –1.4 percent despite a rise in the federal budget deficit, an 11.9 percent surge in the money supply, a fall of the unemployment rate to 17.2 percent, and the growth of GNP. The growth of the money supply did not, nor could it, have any impact on an economic tragedy brought about by the weakening of the demand sector via the transfusion of jobs and wages into dividends.

The demand for goods and services has always been the vital organ on which the life of the U.S. economy flows, as well as the livelihoods of all citizens. Who would produce anything for sale or trade if there was no demand for it? Only a "fool" is the answer. Very little is produced if the demand sector is on its death bed. After the federal deficit was scaled back, the economy staggered around for a while, providing higher dividends, but at the expense of working people. With demand badly weakened by the income transfers occurring throughout the nation, in November 1937, the system dropped to its knees, completely exhausted, without the strength to be able to support constantly rising free income payment to the rich without additional government relief.

The recession of 1937-38 proved for all time that the corporate economic system could no longer sustain itself. As a private welfare program created for the rich, it had sucked the great body of citizens financially dry for far too long, and just like any parasite that continuously grows faster than its host, it slowly weakened and then killed all parts of the economy in the process. The New Deal had acted as a life-support system for a terminally ill patient. Once it was disconnected even to a slight degree, the economy staggered and fell flat on its face, just like any life form experiencing its final moments.

Roosevelt, upon seeing the damage caused by reducing federal spending on his programs, reversed course and more than doubled the deficit in 1939, increased it slightly in 1940, and nearly doubled it again during 1941. During those three years, GNP surged nearly 40 percent, the unemployment rate dropped to less than 10 percent, corporate earnings rose, the stock markets flew higher, and inflation reared its head again during 1940 and 1941.

The United States entered World War II in December 1941 and federal deficit spending exploded. Unemployment was virtually wiped out by 1943, GNP nearly doubled its 1941 level by 1945, and corporate profits shot up.

The principal economic lesson of the war as it applied to the New Deal was that Roosevelt's fiscal conservatism had hindered its effectiveness. Had the president doubled or tripled federal spending for New Deal programs above what had actually occurred during his first two terms, it is very likely the corporate self-liquidation would have been completely reversed by 1935 or 1936. Sweden and Germany had both risen from the misery of their Great Depressions by 1935 because their governments had not hesitated nearly so much as Roosevelt's to put people to work and reinvigorate the demand sectors.

The New Deal provided built-in stabilizers for the economy, much like the shock absorbers of cars smooth out the rough patches of roads and bestow much greater comfort to passengers. And Veblen had been proven correct; the corporate economic system could not possibly survive without stable or rising prices. Perhaps because many of Roosevelt's advisors had been influenced by Veblen and his unique and highly realistic economic points of view, these stabilizers (unemployment insurance, Social Security, minimum wages, etc...) were introduced to strengthen the demand sector and raise prices during times of economic hardship. In doing so, gradually over a period of more than thirty years, they were able to offset the economic and political inequality constantly manufactured by the corporate system, and this ensured a rising tide of prosperity for an ever growing number of U.S. citizens.

Notes

1. Opal somehow managed to graduate from high school.
2. Galbraith, John Kenneth, *The Great Crash*, Houghlin Mifflin: Boston, 1961, p.6.
3. Chase, Stuart, *Prosperity: Fact or Myth*, Charles Boni, Jr.: New York, 1929, p. 179.
4. Chase, pp. 173-174.
5. Batra, Ravi, *The Great Depression of 1990*, Simon and Schuster: New York, 1987, p. 118.
6. With three notable exceptions, all lengthy economic expansions have brought about a conspicuous mal-distribution of wealth in favor of the most affluent consumers. These exceptions occurred during major wars.
7. There number of people employed in manufacturing declined from 1927 to 1928. In 1927, there were, on average, 10,001,000 people employed in this industry compared with 9,947,000 in 1928. A large increase in employment did occur in manufacturing during 1929. There were 10,702,000 people employed in manufacturing, on average, during that year, but at lower weekly rates of pay than the year previous. Average weekly earnings by production workers in manufacturing peaked during 1928. Average hourly earnings for this class of workers from 1924 to 1927 were $.54. The average number of hours worked per week for these people dipped from forty-five to forty-four and four-tenths in 1928, and then dropped another two-tenths during 1929. Average yearly wages for full time employee's rose in several other industries from 1928 to 1929; transportation 2 percent; wholesale and retail trade 1 percent; finance, insurance and real estate 1 percent; and services 1 percent. However, these professions represented a minority of workers. Besides production workers, people in other industries saw stagnation, or a decline, in wages from 1928 to 1929. Construction workers saw a drop of –3 percent, while workers in gas and electric utilities, telephone and telegraph companies, and government workers experienced stagnate pay. Thus, the decade of the twenties represented a period of financial stagnation or decline for most people.
8. U.S. Department of Labor, Bureau of Labor Statistics, Employment, Hours, Earnings, 1994, p. 70.
9. http://www.nber.org/cycles.html.
10. U.S. Commerce Department, Survey of Current Business, Annual Supplement, 1936, p.54.
11. Deflation was: -2.3 in 1930, -9 percent in 1931, -9.9 percent in 1932, and –5.1 percent in 1933.
12. Schlesinger, Arthur, Jr., *The Crisis of the Old Order*, Houghton Mifflin Company: Boston, 1957, p. 3.
13. Guthrie, Woody, *Bound for Glory*, Plume: New York, 1983.
14. This helped to decrease the money supply. When someone deposits money into a bank, the bank is required to keep a reserve, or part of it, on hand, say 10 percent. The rest of the money is lent. The result is the increase in the money supply. The money supply declines when depositors withdraw money from their banking accounts.
15. U.S. Commerce Department, Survey of Current Business, Annual Supplement 1940, p. 60.
16. The average weekly hours in this sector of the economy peaked in March 1937 at 41.1, two months before the business boom reached its apex. By January 1938, employees in this industry worked only 33.5 hours a week, a -18.5 percent decline.
17. U.S. Department of Labor, Bureau of Labor Statistics, Employment, Hours, Earnings, 1994, p. 787.

Chapter Six

THE AGE OF FINANCIAL EQUALITY (1946–1972)

After World War II, the New Deal offset and slowly reversed the mal-distribution of income and wealth rigged into the corporate economic system. Along with other government policies that came along later, Roosevelt's programs ensured that growing numbers of Americans shared in the rising tide of prosperity for the next thirty to forty years. The top 1 percent of the population did not hold more than 32 percent of the total wealth of the United States from 1940 to 1973. Sometimes this figure dipped to as low as 21 percent.[1] This range was adequate to sustain the economy and prevent another corporate self-liquidation for a while. Thanks in large measure to the New Deal; the period 1940 to 1973 is an exception to the historical mal-distribution of wealth inherent within the legislatively constructed corporate economy.

Some post-World War II government legislative acts are covered in this book, interspersed among the recessions. Many of these programs were enacted purely as corporate welfare programs. Others appear to have been created for the benefit of people, but gradually many of these evolved to one degree or another into public assistance for corporations. Many programs and policies were used to ensure a continuous stream of income that flowed upward from those at the bottom to those at the top, regardless of the consequences to working people.

The Military Industrial Complex

Containing the spread of communism after World War II is usually the reason cited for having established the permanent war economy in the United States. The communist system was a terrible threat to rising corporate profits. This is because U.S. businesses were unable to expand earnings by spreading into older or newly established communist nations, and this also made them incapable of stealing the natural resources, as well as the land and labor of the citizens of any nations that adopted a communist system. On the other hand, when the federal government began building the permanent war economy, it was unlikely to have been lost on policy makers and their business allies that government spending on World War II had virtually wiped out unemployment and dramatically boosted GNP. Spending on the war had stimulated the demand for wartime items, raised corporate earnings, and created higher demand for workers in these industries than the peacetime economy. This had quickly reduced unemployment and put upward pressure on wages, salaries and benefits, and in turn, raised the demand for consumer items. This kept the demand sector stronger than would otherwise have been the case and was also good for corporate profits.

Nonetheless, looking at it from the perspective of more than sixty years of history, it appears that the primary reason for establishing and maintaining a permanent war economy has been to keep corporate income rising at tax payer expense. It was established, or evolved into, an income transfer program. The martial economy does serve as an economic stabilizer because it keeps people employed permanently, more or less, and helps to diminish the effects of economic downturns. However, one could reasonably suspect that this was a happy coincidence to the real reason for the massive rise of military spending during peacetime. Containment of the spread of communism was a primary rationale only because communism represented a threat to corporate earnings. Conservatives accurately point out that communism was dictatorial, and therefore a human rights violator, yet it's also true that the U.S. government has used covert and overt means to install right-wing military dictatorships all around the world. Therefore, the fight against communism was never waged on behalf of democratic freedoms. That was always a lie. And the proof is in the outcome. Despite the collapse of the Soviet Union over a decade ago, which completely discredited communism as a challenger to the capitalist system and eliminated its strongest warlike threat, U.S. military spending has continued to expand, and the search for potential enemies appears to be a game that will never end. Nor can this game ever stop so long as corporations exist. The need for constantly expanding profits will ensure that the illusive peace dividend will never be allowed to come into existence.

The New Corporate World Order

It was during the war, after the tide had turned in favor of the United States and its allies against Germany, Italy and Japan, that the idea of constructing a new world order began to bear fruit. At Bretton Woods, New Hampshire, during July 1944, representatives of forty-four nations gathered to decide the fate of the world's people. The purpose of these meetings was to unite the world economically, bringing about interdependence, and theoretically reducing the likelihood of war among the participants.

Some critics suggest U.S. corporate representatives entered into these negotiations with the primary goal of obtaining access to the world's markets, raw materials and cheap labor. There may be some truth to this claim since it is highly unlikely these discussions were held for the benefit of the local auto mechanic, nurse, doctor, butcher or baker living in Omaha, London, Atlanta, Paris or Brooklyn. Instead, they were most likely held with an eye toward enhancing corporate financial performance by opening up the markets of war devastated Europe and Asia to U.S. corporate penetration, as well as to continue U.S. economic and political domination of Latin America. For seventy or more years prior to these meetings, corporations had increasingly dominated the U.S. economy, and except for an occasional recession, life had not been so terrible for the majority of citizens. So it may have appeared to the non-corporate influenced negotiators that what was good for publicly traded companies was fine for the rest of the world's economies.

The memories of the Great Depression wielded a powerful influence over the meetings at Bretton Woods. The delegates there wanted to avoid another such calamity. Although some corporate representatives may have been seeking ways to enhance their bottom lines through these discussions, most of them likely were trying to fix the system of international trade for the betterment of mankind. In June 1930, near the very beginning of the Great Corporate Self-Liquidation, the United States government had enacted the Smoot-Hawley Act. It raised tariffs on foreign goods entering the U.S. to historically high levels. Other countries retaliated by raising their tariffs against U.S. products. World trade slowed because of these actions. Some people thought these events contributed to the severity of the Depression, and perhaps were even the primary cause. Nowadays we know that international trade represented only a tiny fraction of the world's production of goods and services when Smoot-Hawley was enacted into law, and its influence on the unfolding economic calamity was non-existent or minor; but the representatives at Bretton Woods may not have known this in 1944. They wanted to make sure nothing like The Great Depression would ever happen again. Therefore, these people developed two organizations to regulate international trade: The World Bank and the International Monetary Fund.

The World Bank was established to provide loans in various foreign currencies so as to make it easier for lesser developed and war devastated nations to buy goods and services from economically advanced countries. These actions served to enhance corporate profits by stimulating the demand for goods and services. The bank itself has always operated much as a corporation does. Its leaders have always sought to convince countries to borrow money, even if they could not afford to pay it back. Bankruptcy is often the outcome when individuals borrow money for which they cannot make the payments. The results are similar when governments borrow money they can not hope to pay back, only they default on their loans, and hurt their international credit ratings.[2] When nations have been compelled by force of circumstances to borrow, the outcome for citizens of these countries has been devastating.

The International Monetary Fund (IMF) was originally created to promote stability in international monetary exchanges, to enhance and expand the growth of free trade throughout the world, and to ensure financial resources were made temporarily available to members experiencing balance of payment problems. The IMF transformed itself into a lending institution, as well as a loan broker for private banking interests, due to the Arab oil embargo of 1973-74. The Oil Producing Export Countries (OPEC) suddenly found themselves awash with cash from the high priced oil, and so they deposited much of their money in U.S. banks. Bankers couldn't just let the cash sit in their safes though. They needed to find borrowers, so private banks and officials of the IMF and the World Bank convinced the governments of lesser developed countries to borrow money for economic development. Industrial countries experienced strong inflation during this time, and the interest rates charged borrowing nations were correspondingly high. Since government officials of lesser developed countries were not stupid people, they must have had some overriding motivation to secure these loans on such terrible terms. There is no telling how much bribery was involved in getting them to agree to borrow the cash at such high interest rates. In time, many debtor nations found themselves unable to make even their monthly interest payments, which was rolled over and added to the principle. They dug themselves deeper into debt when this occurred, and of course their worsening financial conditions sometimes led them to default on their loans, wreaking their international credit rating in the process. To avoid such a calamity, these nations borrowed even more money so they could make their minimum monthly payments, which were often just the interest due that month, and this just piled on more debt. The high interest rates paid by these nations ensured a constant flow of income to the lender banks, and helped ensure continuously rising banking profits. Developing countries have been at a disadvantage vis-à-vis their lenders ever since—and with dire results (See chapter eight).

Foreign Aid

U.S. foreign aid programs sprang up after World War II. Taxpayer money has been given to foreign governments, and they are supposed to use the money to help their citizen's rise out of poverty. But the benefits of these loans have rarely gone to the majority of the people of these countries, even though it is they who have almost always been burdened with increased poverty, misery and famine, a point noted by economist Peter Bauer. He wrote, "…it should always be remembered that most of official aid goes to governments not to the destitute people shown in aid propaganda."[3] Typically, the only people who benefit from U.S. foreign aid have been the wealthy elite of these countries, along with U.S. corporations and their shareholders. This is one of the reasons why poverty has been on the rise in Africa and Latin America for decades despite billions of dollars of U.S. grants and loans during the last sixty years.

In order to obtain U.S. foreign aid, the governments of poor countries must agree to use the funds to purchase goods and services from U.S. corporations. Instead of using the aid to create an industrial base that might help poor people rise out of poverty, or using these funds to create locally and ecologically sustainable interlocking economies servicing the needs of local citizens, U.S. corporations supply the requirements of these people—for a handsome profit. If something, such as a dam, needs to be constructed using foreign aid funds provided by the United States, aid recipients must use the services of U.S. corporations to do the job. That doesn't do much to develop anybody's economy. If weapons need to be purchased using the aid, to say, suppress a revolt of people tired of being immersed in poverty, U.S. corporations will get the call to supply the weapons, leaving the local people who remain after the carnage still destitute, and perhaps even more deeply so than before. Foreign aid, therefore, is not an economic development plan. Instead, the way in which the funds are disbursed makes it is an anti-development, poverty expanding, corporate welfare scheme.

The Central Intelligence Agency

The Central Intelligence Agency (CIA) was established in 1947 to gather information about foreign countries. In 1948, the CIA was given the power to carry out covert operations to overthrow other governments. This authority has typically been used against nations that have enacted, or were thinking about carrying out, legislation that threatened corporate earnings.[4] The two earliest examples of this occurred in Iran and Guatemala, but they were followed by many more.

In 1953, after the democratically elected parliament of Iran voted to nationalize its oil industry, in partnership with British intelligence, the CIA arranged for the overthrow of Iranian Prime Minister Mohammad Mosaddeg. Shah Reza Palavi, a U.S. puppet dictator, was installed in his place. The shah tortured and killed thousands of his fellow citizens during the next twenty-five years to make his country safe for corporate profits. Needless to say, the very cold relationship that exists between Iran and the United States today is due to this covert action.

In 1954, the CIA arranged the overthrow of the democratically elected government of Guatemala because it had threatened to nationalize the assets of the United Fruit Company, a U.S. corporation. The U.S. government installed a right-wing dictatorship in its place. For the next four decades, to make Guatemala safe for ensuring ever-rising U.S. corporate profits, tens of thousands were killed and tortured.

Since its inception, the CIA has been one of the principal organizations in the world engaged in terrorist activities, and its actions have been responsible for the overthrow of many governments, as well as the deaths and torture of hundreds of thousands of people. Because its primary purpose appears to be to ensure U.S. corporate earnings rise, it suggests the agency was founded as a corporate welfare program, at least in part.

The official rationale for its founding was that communism was an alleged threat to capitalism and democracy, and we needed to keep an eye on those nations. However, since our government has preferred to overthrow democratically elected governments on behalf of U.S. corporate interests, it can be suggested with a high degree of confidence that solely ensuring a world-wide business climate so that corporate earnings can continuously surge upward was the primary purpose for establishing the CIA.

The Recessions Up Until The Near-Corporate Self-Liquidation

It can be boring to read how each economic contraction unfolded since they all began the same way, more or less. You only need to read maybe one or two of the recessions in order to get the idea of how they all followed the same pattern. The final stage of the boom periods leading up to the beginning of each recession are highlighted in the following pages. Read the notes at the end of each chapter if you want more details. Although the notes contain many of the less important yet still significant details of each recession, I suspect they will not very entertaining reading for many people. On the other hand, some readers might find the footnotes fascinating. Please read as much as you want if you are one of these hard core economic history buffs.

As a review, recollect from chapter four that during business expansions total corporate dividends at some point grow faster than total profits. That's not really good for publicly traded corporations, and something needs to be done to bring income more in line with ever-growing dividends.

Now imagine we are in charge of just one corporation. Its dividends grew more rapidly than earnings during the last few quarters. Dividend payments always need to rise, but they cannot continue upward much longer unless profits grow at similar rates. Although we can't sell many more goods and services than what we do now, we can raise our prices just a little more than normal because our competitors are willing to do the same. However, that still won't be sufficient to keep those profits soaring high enough to keep up with those speeding dividends, so we must cut costs. Maybe we don't really need the services of some employees all that much, so we lay them off. For example, we can cut our marketing budget by hiring less expensive contractors. Some other workers are necessary, but their jobs can be done more cheaply if they are outsourced, either overseas or to some local contractor with less costly employees. A business in India is willing to provide customer service cheaper than our corporation because it is able to pay its employees considerably less than the U.S. hourly minimum wage. So we make the decision to cut our customer service agents and hire the foreign firm. Why don't we send the jobs of our computer programmers and some engineers to India? That would save a bundle of money. Let's do it! That office Christmas party can be cut out of the budget completely, but that means' not hiring the local catering service which then has to reduce the hours of its employees. We can also merge departments. That's a good idea. This way, some more people can be laid off, including a manager or two or three, and their high priced salaries and benefits will no longer be our burden. Sure that means some employees are going to have more responsibilities and be forced to work longer hours, but we can reduce or freeze their current wages and salaries, and decide to slice their benefits, as well. Forcing them to work more and earn less saves the company money. Meanwhile, we can trim or eliminate some or all charitable donations, although that means some low paid people working with children or persons with disabilities will be laid off by their organizations. We can cancel that contract for the 100 computers. The supplier will probably need to lay off an employee because of this, but oh well, that's life. Instead of having a Mexican contractor manufacture our products, we can ship those jobs to China, a nation where wages are far lower than in Mexico. We'll save a bundle with that action.

Due to our brilliant decisions, we reduced costs and enhanced profits. Now we have produced surging profits, we can declare higher dividends, and hopefully this will lead to higher share prices, and guarantee that our bonuses will reach to the sky.

Our actions raised profits all right, but they also weakened the demand sector since so many people lost their jobs. We reduced the hours of some employees, and they don't have as much money to spend as before. We froze the wages and salaries of others, and this decision also served to trim their demands for goods and services because inflation is eating away at their immobile earnings. Along with our very cooperative competitors, we raised the prices of our goods and services, and this further reduced the spending power of consumers. We can't forget that we cut medical, dental and vision benefits for our employees, forcing companies that provide these services to reduce their payrolls. We reduced our business-to-business transactions, and our own actions lowered the demands for computers and a catering service. These businesses were forced to lay off employees because of the scaled back demand for the things they produce.

We achieved our goal of keeping dividends and our share prices rolling upward. Maybe our wealthy investors purchased a few more trinkets than they might normally have, but for the most part, their new found wealth was reinvested. By and large, dividend payments are not used to purchase new goods and services; and so because we transformed wages, salaries and benefits into dividends, the impact of these unearned income payments was to actually reduce the demand for goods and services.

Now imagine the above scenario unfolding throughout the economy as corporations are riding a wave of prosperity known as a business expansion. Over time, a swelling number of them discover their dividends are growing more rapidly than their earnings, and they begin to reduce jobs, employee hours and other costs, including business-to-business transactions. More or less, profits are able to rise more rapidly at first, but the cost cutting actions reduce the demand for goods and services. Not so long afterwards, more and more businesses cannot keep earnings rolling upward in the face of falling demand. They find themselves struggling to give shareholders higher dividends one quarter after the next, especially since these expenditures are racing far ahead of corporate income.

As this process unfolds, it first becomes noticeable in the manufacture of durable goods. Employees in these industries gradually begin to experience reduced hours long before any recessions occur. Durable goods are often relatively expensive items, such as automobiles, stereos, refrigerators; basically anything expected to last three years or more. These often require monthly payments, and people who have lost their jobs, or experienced reduced hours at work, or frozen pay, might be thinking that it is not a good time to add monthly payments to their budgets. Maybe these people can still afford to purchase a $100 boom box, but it's a luxury many decide they can afford to do without until their financial fortunes brighten.

Typically, jobs losses throughout the manufacturing industries rise many months before the recession occurs, and the unemployment rate jumps. The number of people thrust into poverty also surges upward prior to all recessions for which there are statistics. All of this is due to the massive rise in the numbers of people whose pay checks were diverted into dividends.

As all of these cost reductions occur throughout the economy, there comes a point in time where demand becomes extremely slack, and more and more corporations find themselves with falling profits; but dividends must always rise. And so the transfer of jobs and employee hours into dividend payments accelerates until the economy actually enters a recession due to the drop in demand.

During the economic downturn, the transfer of wages into dividends continues unabated. This is why, as mentioned in chapter four, dividend payments almost always drift upward with the unemployment rate. Lost jobs are always the primary fuel providing dividend growth, even as the economy plunges into some of its worst recessions.

The Recession Of 1948-1949

The first recession following the Great Depression officially began in November 1948. That's the month when the boom period peaked, and then we began sliding into the bust cycle. However, the economy had entered the last phase of the previous business expansion more than a year earlier. For the first several months of 1947, dividends grew more rapidly than earnings. To offset this im-

balance and keep dividends rolling up, our corporate heroes were forced to trim expenditures and divert that money to enhance profits and dividends. Among the methods used to do this were curtailing business-to-business transactions (resulting in layoffs and cutbacks in hours at other firms), slowing the growth of employee wages and salaries, cutting employee hours, and of course lay-offs. This is why job growth slowed significantly that year compared to 1946. While earnings rose because of these and other cutbacks, throughout the economy the demand for goods and services slowly dropped. Those who experienced lay-offs and reduced hours at work were not in very good positions to pay for things they no longer could afford. CEOs were faced with stagnant or declining demand due to their own decisions, as well as weakening profits, and so collectively they laid off more employees, cut more pay rates and more worker hours. This reduced the spending power of citizens even further, and started a snowball effect. Workers in the durable goods industries began to experience a statistically noticeable slide in their hours at work beginning in December 1947. The manufacturing sector shed 150 thousand jobs from August through November 1948. And the unemployment rate rose steadily from a low of 3.5 percent in May 1948 until hitting 4.0 percent in December of that year. Once again, our corporate heroes had brought about a recession with their decisions to transform wages into profits and dividends. This weakened the demand for goods and services and resulted in the recession that began in November 1948.

At least in part, because of the reductions of hours and the elimination of jobs, total corporate profits continuously rose throughout the first three quarters of 1948.[5] Total corporate earnings sank -6.2 percent in the fourth quarter of that year even as total dividend payments accelerated upward over 5 percent, unrelentingly fueled by the sacrificial lay-off victims. In the fourth quarter of 1949, although average corporate earnings had dropped -21.8 percent from just five quarters earlier, dividend payments still surged 8.5 percent higher.[6] The unemployment rate meanwhile skyrocketed to 7.9 percent by October that year, fueling the rise of dividends. The livelihoods of working citizens had been sacrificed once again on the golden cross of corporate finance so the rich could receive higher unearned income payments.

New Deal programs, such as unemployment insurance, helped the economy shift from a bust to a boom cycle. Such policies also allowed for a more rapid increase in dividend payments to the wealthy because they spurred demand for corporate goods and services in spite of the slack demand that typically

comes with rising unemployment. Social Security recipients also stimulated demand since they had guaranteed incomes, and this allowed them to continue to purchase items without fear of losing their jobs. The minimum wage law stopped any potential precipitous drops in personal income. The New Deal's pivotal role had been to strengthen the demand sector during hard times, and it was working just fine.

There are critics who argue that Roosevelt's programs were designed to save the corporate system. They might be correct to one degree or another since the outcomes produced by the New Deal suggest that policies designed to help the unemployed may have been constructed with a view toward sustaining corporate profits and dividends. This also may suggest that any aid provided to the victims of the corporate economic system is coincidental, and necessary, to its maintenance, and therefore, just another corporate welfare program to prop up a system that would otherwise collapse upon itself.

The Recession Of 1953-1954

The next bust cycle officially ignited in July 1953, but the economy had entered the last phase of the business expansion many months earlier. As is the usual story, dividend payments had grown at faster rates than earnings all through 1951. For the first three quarters of 1952, profits continued to head downward, and this time they dragged dividends with them, although the former dropped at much faster rates than the latter. The growing chasm between them needed to be made up somehow. The captains of industry proceeded to do what they always do under these circumstances; they cut jobs and hours at work forcing job growth to slow dramatically when compared to 1950. Because of these actions, profits rose in the fourth quarter of 1952, and in the following two quarters, as well. Unfortunately for our corporate heroes, their actions also resulted in gradual drops in the demand for goods and services. Citizens employed in durable goods factories eventually experienced a gradual decline in the hours they worked beginning as early as December 1952. The manufacturing sector began a mild hemorrhage of jobs as 8,000 of them were eliminated from May through July 1953. And the unemployment rate rose steadily from 2.5 percent in May to 2.6 percent in July 1953. Once again, during the months prior to a recession, the actions of our corporate heroes led to weakening demand throughout the economy. The result of this labor liquidation process was another recession.[7]

Average corporate earnings dropped by a massive –27.0 percent in the fourth quarter of 1953. Despite this, dividends dropped only slightly during the period, and they were still awfully close to historically high levels.[8] By December 1953, the unemployment rate had jumped to 4.5 percent. Corporate profits dipped again in the first quarter of 1954 and remained weak throughout the year while total dividends expanded at historic rates. When the recession ended in May 1954, the unemployment rate had grown to 5.9 percent, but it continued to grow until reaching 6.1 percent in September, indicating jobs were still being transformed into dividends after the end of the economic bust.

The Recession Of 1957-58

The next recession officially began in August 1957. As you know by now, the economy had entered the last phase of the business expansion more than nine months earlier. This time average corporate earnings dropped during the first three quarters of 1956 while dividends continued skyward like a rocket to the moon. Job growth slowed to a virtual standstill as CEOs began to slash and burn jobs and cut pay rates and employee hours to make up the difference between the growth of dividends and income.

Earnings skyrocketed during the final quarter of 1956, but the demand sector had been damaged. Worst yet, the job liquidation process still continued. Citizens employed in durable goods saw their hours reduced from forty-one and three-tenths a week in December 1956 to forty and two-tenths in August 1957. Then CEOs began slashing over 200 thousand manufacturing jobs from February to August 1957. And as should be expected, as the layoffs expanded to include other industries, the unemployment rate rose steadily from a low of 3.7 percent in March to 4.1 percent at the peak of the expansion in August 1957. And once again, people were castoff and made orphans of the financial storm so their incomes could be diverted as "free income" to the affluent. The result was another recession.

As the economic tidal wave picked up steam, dividends rose to historic levels even though profits plummeted. Our corporate heroes continued to slash jobs in order for the rich freeloaders to receive their always rising dividend payments. And that's why the unemployment rate and dividends continued to rise together during the recession—as usual. The process of transferring jobs into dividends continued even after the end of the recession in April 1958.[9]

The Recession of 1960-61

The next recession officially began in April 1960. You know the events that transpired by now. The economy had entered the final stage of the business expansion at least nine months before the recession erupted. The economy had added 6 percent more jobs from June 1958 to July 1959. The growth of dividend payments outpaced the rise of earnings from the second to the third quarter of 1959, and then these two variables diverged even more in the fourth. Job growth then slumped as CEOs began to terminate jobs and cut pay rates and employee working hours in growing numbers in order for profits to catch up with the growth of dividends. Because of these actions, total corporate earnings surged upward in the first quarter of 1960, but the drop in demand caused by these income transfers ensured that employees in the durable goods industries experienced a gradual decay in the hours they worked from forty-one and two-tenths in January 1960 to forty and one-tenth in April. CEOs in manufacturing eliminated over 100 thousand jobs of their fellow citizens from February to April 1960. As usual, the unemployment rate shot upward from a low of 4.8 percent in February to 5.2 percent in April—the peak of the business expansion.

Average dividend payments stayed the same in the first and second quarters of 1960 before jumping to an historic high in the third quarter, and another in the fourth, and once more in the first quarter of 1961.[10] This was achieved despite corporate profits that tumbled during each of the last three quarters of 1960, and again in the first quarter of the following year. The unemployment rate reached 6.9 percent at the bottom of the recession in February 1961, but it continued to shoot upward until May when it struck 7.1 percent.[11]

The Nineteen Sixties Economic Boom

Two things brought about a massive economic expansion in the United States during the 1960s. Government spending for the Vietnam War pushed the economy to great heights, and served as a corporate welfare program. In addition, the Great Society programs of President Lyndon Johnson provided a similar yet smaller momentum to the economy. The number of people living in poverty during the decade dramatically dropped. The poverty rate plunged from over 20 percent of the population in 1959 to less than 13 percent in 1969.[12]

The distribution of income and wealth in favor of the most affluent also declined during the boom. The top 1 percent of the population held 31.6 percent of the total wealth in 1963, but this regressed to slightly less than 25 percent by

1969.[13] This is a normal trend during major wars.[14] Government expenditures raise the demand for goods and services during such times and this creates more jobs. A shortage of workers usually pushes wages up, which slices into corporate profits and dividends. Also, the federal government will generally put pressure on corporations to keep profits at certain levels since citizens are sacrificing their lives for the good of the alleged mutual cause. In the old days, not so long ago, patriotic captains of politics sometimes marched arm-in-arm with many captains of finance and industry on this issue, and generally they brought public pressure to bear on overly enthusiastic profiteers of patriotism.[15] Along with labor shortages, which typically compelled corporations to raise wages and salaries in order to attract more employees, political and social pressure served to put a lid on overly excessive corporate profits that were being expropriated at taxpayer expense and the lost lives of American soldiers. Along with the programs of the New Deal, the war and the expenditures on it helped to create a greater degree of financial equality than what normally occurs during periods of peace, with the exception of the Iraq war of 2003.

The Recession Of 1969-1970

The next recession officially began in December 1969. As usual, the economy had entered the last phase of the business expansion many months earlier. Dividends grew more rapidly than profits in the first quarter of 1968 and this continued through the third quarter of that year. In order to expand earnings enough to continue paying ever rising dividends, the captains of industry and finance cut jobs and employee hours. This caused job growth to sag in the middle of 1968, and then drop steadily all through 1969 as more and more business firms found dividends racing past income. Profits rose sharply in the fourth quarter of 1968, but to get there CEOs had collectively had clipped the wings of the demand sector. Drooping demand led to flopping corporate income all through 1969, but average dividends still surged to historic highs every quarter. CEOs now had little choice but to begin slashing additional jobs and cutting pay rates and more employee working hours. They did so in great enough numbers to bring about a drop in the demand for durable goods and other manufactured items. As a result, the durable goods captains steadily sliced average employee hours from forty-one and six-tenths per week in November 1968 to forty-one and two-tenths in December 1969. Manufacturing CEOs terminated the jobs of over 200 thousand American citizens from August through December 1969, while the unemployment rate slowly crept upward from 3.4 percent in May

1969 to 3.7 percent in October of that year, but then it declined to 3.5 percent in November and December.[16] As usual, these lay-offs and lost hours were transformed into dividend payments and brought about another recession.

The loss of jobs and hours could have been worse. CEOs paid higher dividends in part by using retained earnings, which declined through every quarter of 1969 and through the second quarter of 1970.[17] This was normal because, as explained earlier, sometimes an economy does not necessarily go into recession when total corporate profits fall, especially if there are other ways to increase dividends than by reducing the hours of employees or by eliminating their jobs. This may explain why the unemployment rate gradually moved upward to 3.7 percent by October, before dropping down to 3.5 the following two months. Rather than transfer jobs into dividends, our corporate heroes used money from retained earnings to enhance those free income payments to the wealthy. The recession ended in November of 1970. It had been a mild bust cycle, yet this was just the calm before the approaching economic storm.

Notes

1. Batra, Ravi, *The Great Depression of 1990*, Venus Books: Texas, 1987, p. 118.
2. Korten, David C., *When Corporations Rule the World*, Kummarian Press, Inc. and Berrett-Koehler Publishers: West Hartford and San Francisco, 1995, p. 162.
3. Bauer, Peter, *From Subsistence to Exchange and other Essays*, Princeton University Press: New Jersey, 2000, p. 42.
4. U.S. government military interventions on behalf of corporate interests were common long before the CIA was formed.
5. (More information about the recession of 1948–49) In the first and second quarters of 1949, corporate profits decreased compared with each previous quarter. Average dividend payments were the same in the first quarter of 1949 as the last quarter of 1948, before declining slightly in the second and third quarters.
6. Federal Reserve Bulletin, July 1950, p. 866.
7. Average corporate profits declined from the second to the third quarter of 1953.
8. Federal Reserve Bulletin, June 1954, p. 652.
9. Dividend payments rose almost 8 percent and established another historic record during the first quarter of 1958 although total corporate profits had plummeted again. The transfer of incomes into dividends drove the unemployment rate from 5.2 percent in December 1957 to 6.7 percent in March 1958. Starting in the second quarter, corporate profits rose throughout 1958. This was achieved by more cutbacks in jobs and hours worked. The unemployment rate shot up to 7.5 percent in July, and thereafter began to decrease. Dividend payments during the second and third quarters of 1958 remained tied for the second highest in history up to that time before declining in the fourth quarter, and then heading up again in the next quarter.
10. "The Federal Reserve Bulletin" of July 1961 shows corporate dividends increased in the third and fourth quarters of 1960, before declining slightly in the beginning quarter of 1961. However, the "National Income and Product Accounts of the United States, 1929–97" have dividends reaching a

peak in the third quarter of 1960, and then moving downward a bit in the fourth quarter and the first three months of 1961, before moving rapidly upward. The fourth quarter of 1961 was another historic high for average corporate profits.

11. (More information on the recession of 1960) The unemployment rate stayed at 6.5 percent or higher until October 1961. However, dividend payments continued to increase from the first quarter of 1961 to the last quarter by over 5 percent—another historic high. Yet corporate profits did not surpass the level of the first quarter of 1960 until the last quarter of 1961, a period of almost two years. For many months after the recession ended, unemployment rose and or remained high in order for corporations to be able to increase dividend payments to the wealthy.

12. DeNavas-Walt, Carmen, Proctor, D. Bernadette, Mills, J. Robert, "Income, Poverty, and Health Insurance Coverage in the United States," U.S. Census Bureau, August 2004.

13. Batra, Ravi, p. 118.

14. Statistics provided by Wesley Clair Mitchell, founder of the National Bureau of Economic Research and former student of Thorstein Veblen, show that the 5 percent highest income earners received 34 percent of all income in 1916. The United States entered World War I in April 1917. The top 5 percent received only 29 percent of the total national income in 1917, 26 percent in 1918, and 24 percent in 1919. "Income in the United States, National Bureau of Economic Research," 1920, p. 116.

15. The apparent exception to this was during the administration of President George W. Bush (2001-2009).

16. (Additional notes for the 1969-70 recession) Corporate profits continued to decline from one quarter to the next during 1970, excluding the third quarter when they rose. Dividend payments were more than 5 percent higher in the last quarter of 1970 than they had been during the first quarter of 1969, even though average corporate earnings were –20 percent less. The unemployment rate raced from 3.4 to 6.1 percent during the same period in order to ensure the higher dividends. In November 1970, at the end of the recession, the unemployment rate reached a historically mild 5.9 percent. However, it climbed to 6.1 percent in December 1970, and continued to float around 6.0 percent throughout 1971. All through that year, aggregate corporate profits remained below their peak of the first quarter of 1969. Nonetheless, total dividend payments continued to grow, although somewhat unevenly from one quarter to the next. Dividends resumed their more relentless upward movement beginning in January 1972. With earnings below the levels of 1969, CEOs found it necessary to keep the unemployment rate historically high in order to amplify profits during 1970 and 1971.

17. Federal Reserve Bulletin, June 1970, p. A 68.

Chapter Seven

THE NEAR CORPORATE SELF-LIQUIDATION AND THE AGE OF FINANCIAL INEQUALITY

The decade of the 1960s found the inequality gap narrowing between the top 1 percent of the population and the rest of the citizens of the United States. Corporate profits rose during the decade in part because of military spending by the U.S. government on the Vietnam War. Government deficit spending on the conflict created new jobs that otherwise would not have existed, and raised wages beyond what would otherwise have been the case, thereby narrowing the income and wealth gaps. Unfortunately, inequality is what the corporate economic system had been constructed to breed, as well as to thrive on.

Rising financial equality and the corporate economic system cannot coexist for many years even when aided by de facto corporate welfare programs, such as the U.S. military involvement in Southeast Asia. The reason is simple. Corporations can only obtain profits via two methods; one way is to produce goods and services, and the other is by transferring income and wealth from working people to themselves, either directly or indirectly. As any business expansion begins to mature, more profits are gained by producing goods and services than through income transfers. However, at some point, dividends rise faster than earnings, and this compels our heroes to increasingly shift income and wealth from working people to the affluent to offset the difference in the growth rates. In the short term, say a period of about thirty years, this process can be offset by government programs such as unemployment insurance, as well as engaging in corporate welfare wars, such as the conflict in Vietnam and the 2003-09 oil war in Iraq. As the years pass by, however, the demand for ever rising dividends climbs higher than even these large scale corporate welfare programs can offset. At some point the system can no longer support such generous welfare assistance to the wealthy, along with rising standards of living for people who actually work. If corporate earnings are increasingly diverted to wages and other employee compensation during a period of equality, dividends will still need to constantly rise. At some point the system can support only one of these trends, and it will begin to self-liquidate if dividends stagnate or roll downward for too long a period.

Such a life-threatening scenario occurred to the system in the early 1970s, after a period of roughly 30 years of growing income and wealth equality within the United States. Even before combat troops were sent to Vietnam in large numbers during 1965, and despite a wide variety of corporate welfare programs and the New Deal, it had become obvious to many captains of industry and finance that most corporations could not long continue to provide constantly rising earnings to satiate shareholders while the majority of the citizens of the United States were simultaneously experiencing remarkable rises in their standards of living.

As the inequality gap narrowed in the three decades following the end of World War II, the yearly growth of total corporate profits dropped. As can be seen from the graph below, average earnings rose at a rate of 19.2 percent from 1946 to 1956. The growth slowed significantly the following ten years. It was during the final years of The Age of Equality that corporate income grew, but at rates too low to sustain consistently rising dividends, one quarter after another. There was significant growth in average earnings during 1972, but a rapid rise of profits is typical of an economy coming out of recession. The United States probably experienced a near corporate self-liquidation during the years 1973 to 1983.

Average Yearly Increase in Corporate Profits (First Quarter to First Quarter)

Years	Average Annual Percent Increase
1946–56	19.20%
1956–66	7.70%
1966–74	6.00%
1969–71	1.46%
1972	27.70%
1973–75	-8.90%
1976–85	8.20%
1985-95	18.80%

Source: National Income and Product Accounts of the United States, 1927-97, U.S. Department of Commerce

Before 1973, the captains of industry and finance had tried to offset the rising financial equality by inflating prices at progressively higher rates than had normally been the case. The yearly inflation rate had stayed below 2 percent each year from 1959 to 1965. Combat personnel were sent to Vietnam in large numbers beginning in the latter year, accelerating the closing of the inequality gap. In 1966, inflation hit 2.9 percent, struck 3.1 percent the following year, and then climbed to 4.2 percent in 1968. As the income and wealth gap narrowed, the inflation rate bounced even higher to 5.5 percent in 1969 and to 5.7 percent in 1970. The effects of the recession of 1969-70 forced some corporations to pull back price increases so that the yearly inflation rate rose only 4.4 percent in 1971 and 3.2 percent in 1972.[1] Inflation had offset some of the narrowing of the wealth gap by passing on rising costs to consumers, and the proceeds from higher prices were then passed on as dividend payments to the wealthy. Because inflation had increased significantly during each year of the Vietnam War, but it had not sufficiently helped to off-set the narrowing of the wealth gap brought about by the war and by the New Deal reforms, something else had to be done in order to undermine the gains in income and wealth the lower classes had achieved from 1946 to 1973, and especially during the years from 1963 to 1973.

By 1973, either citizens enjoying a rising tide of prosperity or affluent shareholders needed to experience reductions in their standards of living because the system could not support both. Rich consumers did not want to endure reductions of dividends one quarter after the next for years to come, which would have led the system down the road to self-liquidation. These persons included (and still consist of) wealthy people, politicians, CEOs and others with political and economic power. They were the people with the financial punch to purchase the legislation in the political markets necessary to save their income transfer scheme. Therefore, within government and business, a relatively small number of people with financial stakes in the system, sometimes working together and sometimes not, and over a period of several years, made the decisions that put an end to the rising tide of prosperity for all citizens, enabling the corporate system to survive, while continuing to provide politically and economically powerful shareholders with ever-rising dividends and share prices.

Therefore, the year 1973 marked the beginning of the end of the Age of Equality, and gave birth to the Age of Inequality. The end of direct U.S. involvement in the Vietnam conflict in 1973 terminated a sizable de facto corporate welfare program and left the system gasping for earnings. The economy had reached a stage at which corporate earnings could escalate in the long-term, but not always enough to keep the stock markets flying upward. Given the inefficiencies throughout publicly traded corporations, reducing wages, salaries and benefits were the only ways to enhance profits to the degree necessary to keep dividends perpetually on the rise. In January 1973, private sector real hourly wages peaked at $9.08 per hour, and then downward pressure by corporations and their allies in government sent them tumbling downhill ever since. Real wages had risen nearly 80 percent from 1946 to 1973, raising the standard of living for tens of millions of U.S. citizens. That era was over.

Over the next three decades, U.S. business and political leaders made the decisions to weaken and or eliminate labor unions, environmental laws, health and safety regulations, and New Deal reforms. These vested interests also decided that the super-rich and corporations needed more and more tax cuts, while corporations needed less government regulation in order to enhance earnings, and additional free trade policies were needed to allow for U.S. corporate penetration of lesser developed nations. Furthermore, the free trade argument was continuously used to justify negotiating with lesser developed countries to make it easier to ship jobs from the United States to them. This had already been tried successfully as early as 1965 and before. The electronics industry had exported tens of thousands of jobs from the United States, including the production of radios and televisions. Much of the machine tool industry had shipped thousands of jobs to overseas locations beginning as early as the 1950s. However, a trickle of exported jobs soon became a rising tidal wave as the corporate system moved gradually through the years towards another self-liquidation (that has yet to be achieved). Along with other trends discussed below, such policies resulted, as no doubt intended, in downward pressures on wages, salaries and benefits, and this allowed more room for the continuous escalation of corporate earnings, dividends and share prices for decades.

The Standard Rationales By The Alleged Experts For The Recessions Of 1973, 1980 And 1981

More or less, economists assume that the economy consists of people and businesses who demand goods and services, and those who produce the things necessary to meet those demands. Anything else is considered to be external to the economic system. Many times, economists have credited factors outside of the economy with bringing about recessions on their own. External factors, however, do not determine whether or not an economy moves in or out of recession, unless they alter the prevailing distribution of income by reducing corporate profits and dividends; and this often forces CEOs to cut the jobs and wages of employees, and the lost income of workers is then transferred to the wealthy via constantly rising dividends, at least for as long as possible.

Conservative economists insist the Federal Reserve Bank caused the Great Depression because it lowered the money supply. As was demonstrated earlier, however, the Federal Reserve did the correct thing since the money supply was not an issue at all in that contraction, especially considering that interest rates dropped during the years 1929-33. Likewise, the second recession of the 1970s was considered to be a product of an Arab Oil Embargo, as was the next recession in 1980. The Federal Reserve was considered to be the culprit in the recession of 1981. On the other hand, sometimes outside events raised corporate earnings and carried us out of recessions or otherwise strengthened the economy, such as when the New Deal was enacted, and when money was spent to win World War Two. Government transfer payments, such as unemployment insurance, can certainly be considered an external factor, especially if the actions of another governmental agency (the Federal Reserve Bank) are considered to be an outside factor. There are an infinite number of things that can be considered as being factors outside of an economy: new laws, military conflicts, trade wars, just about anything—even the publication of a single book.

In 1962, Rachel Carson published her environmental masterpiece, *Silent Spring*, the seminal work about the damage to the environment and human health caused by pesticides and other chemicals. Lambasted by the chemical industry and government officials because of the honesty of her arguments, the book was credited with giving birth to the environmental movement, as well as to several acts of congress that banished the use of such pesticides in the United States.[2] Carson's work has been credited with compelling the government to enact laws curbing the pollution of the air, land, and water. A new government bureaucracy, the Environmental Protection Agency (EPA), was created in 1973 to ensure corporations complied with these new laws, which were often expensive to conform with. Therefore, they had an impact on corporate profits. Thus, something as simple as a book can be considered as being an external economic factor.

Because they are bedfellows, most things that are economic, political, cultural and social are typically interrelated. Therefore, there really are no external economic factors. The economy continuously evolves and adjusts, although the basic business cycle remains the same.

The Recession Of 1973-75

The Arab oil embargo began in October 1973, although the captains of Big Oil had already ensured that prices at the pump had begun to rise during the summer. Much like the big petroleum corporations, many oil producing countries worked together as a single price setting cartel called the Organization of Petroleum Exporting Countries (OPEC). By charging higher prices than would have otherwise been the case in the absence of a monopoly, the vested interests of these nations transferred income from working citizens throughout the world to themselves. Many economists have argued that the Arab oil embargo pushed the United States into a recession.

The economy, however, had already entered the last phase of the business expansion several months before the embargo struck. Dividend growth raced ahead of corporate earnings from the second to the third quarter of 1973. Job growth slowed significantly from April to November as CEOs began to lay off workers, as well as cut pay rates and hours at work in great enough numbers to bring about a drop in demand. Workers in the durable goods industries experienced a slow reduction in their number of weekly hours from forty-one and seven-tenths in April 1973 to forty-one and four-tenths in November—the peak of the boom cycle. The unemployment rate hit a low of 4.6 percent in October, and then jumped to 4.8 in November. Real wage rates in the private sector began to precipitously and permanently drop beginning in January of 1973 from $9.08 to $8.87 per hour in November, which was an income transfer mechanism not used by our corporate heroes since the Great Depression. This helped them to provide historically high dividends during the third and fourth quarters of that year, despite drops in profits.[3] All of the above led to weakened demand throughout the economy, and this forced CEOs to lay-off more employees, reduce wage rates, and clip more employee hours.

The manufacturing sector continued to add jobs through December 1973, an historic anomaly. Declining employment in manufacturing occurred prior to the start of every recession for which I could find statistics, except for the economic contraction of 1973-75. It could be these businesses were less likely to lay employees off since they could achieve rising dividends and profits when they slashed wages. Or it could be the economy wasn't quite ready to move into recession, although it was knocking at the door having begun the final stage of the economic expansion many months earlier. This suggests the oil embargo may have been the catalyst that lit the fuse igniting the economic downturn a few months prematurely.

Rapidly rising oil prices have occurred every now and then, and the economy has not necessarily moved into recession. The incredibly weak expansion that began in 2001 is a case in point. Oil prices and short-term interest rates rose dramatically starting in the summer of 2004 and still the economy continued to grow. In 1973, the economy was already headed toward recession, while the business expansion of 2004 had not, and that is the difference between the two, and why rising oil prices may have played a role in one and not the other.

Corporate earnings rose dramatically during the first three quarters of 1974, and dividends rose to historic heights during each. These achievements were fueled by transfers of income and wealth from working people. The unemployment rate rose to 5.9 percent by September from 4.8 percent a year earlier. The real wages of those who still had jobs plummeted from $8.87 per hour in November 1973 to $8.63 per hour in September of the next year.

Tragedy struck our corporate captains in the fourth quarter of 1974 when average earnings nose-dived over -16 percent, and then another -35.4 percent the following three months.[4] You can't keep dividends constantly rolling upward with those numbers. CEOs still hadn't figured out that if you lay enough people off and slice the wages of those who are still employed, the demand for their own goods and services will drop, and profits will correspondingly fall. Naturally, faced with such a dilemma, our heroes decided to repeat this self destructive behavior. To feed the system's unquenchable thirst for ever rising dividends, the employed were sacrificed on an economic altar constructed of greed. The unemployment rate exploded skyward from 5.9 percent in September 1974 to 8.6 percent in March of the following year, a 45.7 percent rise in only six months. Real wages were also rolled back to help ensure the safety of ever increasing earnings and dividends.[5] Thanks to these cutbacks, profits and dividends began moving upward once more, helped along by another factor created by the captains of industry and finance.

Corporations rolled prices upward, defiant to any market mechanisms so sound was their control over the markets for goods and services. The inflation rate jumped to 11.0 percent in 1974 and 9.1 percent in 1975 in spite of weakened demand due to the layoffs and wage reductions. This income transfer program also helped to raise dividends every quarter of the recession.

The recession of 1973-75 marked a turning point in U.S. political and economic history. In order to ensure higher corporate earnings, jobs, poverty, pollution and other social ills were exported to other countries more so than ever before, and at accelerating rates as the years unfolded. Backed by power purchased in the political markets, this process allowed corporations to put continuous downward pressures on wages in the United States and throughout the world for decades to come.

The Economic Expansion Of 1975-80

There were several developing factors that contributed to the rapid rise of corporate earnings from 1975 to 1980, and they also provided momentum to the business expansion that took place. For example, oil prices stabilized. Also, beginning in the 1950s, European countries had begun to withdraw from their geographical areas of military conquest in Africa and Asia, and doing so removed political barriers that had inhibited U.S. corporate penetration into these countries. In 1975, Portugal, for example, withdrew from the mineral rich African nation of Angola. Along with continued trade liberalization, such political events helped our captains in their quest for natural resources to exploit, low-cost labor to take advantage of, and overly generous government contracts that were easily bought on the cheap in the newly created political markets of these newly independent nations. Of course, such economic infiltration usually amounted to income transfers from working citizens of these countries to foreign corporations and their shareholders. These political trends also made it easier for CEOs to transfer jobs from U.S. citizens to people in low wage countries at faster rates than previous, and this provided more leverage with which to reduce real wages in the United States. In addition, advances in communications technologies made it appear easier to monitor and control production facilities across international frontiers during the sixties and seventies, and this also helped to fuel the movement of jobs from the USA.

The boom period of 1975-80 came about because the affluent and their corporations had unofficially declared war against the working citizens of the United States. Since the economy could no longer support relentlessly rising dividends and escalating standards of living for most Americans, one of these trends had to be reversed in order for the other to continue. Only one side understood the decisions that had to be made. Consequently, real average wage rates slid from their peak of $9.08 per hour in January 1973 to $8.22 an hour in December 1979, a level not seen since January 1970. The difference between the old and new wages was transfused into higher dividends, just like the passage of blood between a vampire and its victim, a predatory act that weakens the prey while strengthening the bloodsucker. Meanwhile, a rising tide of corporate controlled inflation was used to transfer even more income and wealth from working people, who were made to pay continuously escalating prices for corporate produced goods and services that were then passed on to super-rich consumers in the form of higher dividends. Corporate profits dramatically climbed 225 percent from the beginning of the boom period in 1975 until the first quarter of 1980 due largely to these income transfers. The race to the bottom through publicly traded limited liability companies had begun in earnest.

The Recession Of 1980

Another oil embargo occurred in 1978 and 1979. Problems in Iraq and the counter-revolution against the U.S. installed a puppet government in Iran once again brought about a drop in Middle Eastern oil supplies to the United States. This resulted in rising oil and gasoline prices. Some experts think this caused a short recession beginning in January 1980. Others contend the money supply increased too rapidly. Still, others thought "…the combination of high interest rates and credit controls had forced the economy into a sharp but brief contraction."[6] None of these explanations were accurate.

You must have the story memorized by now. The next recession officially began in January 1980, but the forces that brought it about developed many months earlier. Dividend growth surpassed the rise in profits during the last quarter of 1978 and the first quarter of 1979. A rapid slowdown in job growth was the result as CEOs reacted to the dividend race by slicing jobs, employee hours, and reducing worker pay. These actions pushed the growth rate of corporate income more in harmony with the upward rise of dividends, but they also gradually curtailed the demand for their own goods and services. Beginning in March, employees in durable goods began to experience shorter hours. Between June 1979 and January 1980, the unemployment rate rose from 5.6 percent to 6.3 percent, a 12.5 percent rise in eight months. This was stimulated in part by the elimination of 271 thousand jobs from the manufacturing sector during the same period, which further depressed the demand sector, and put even more pressure on our heroes to layoff even more employees and or reduce their hours.

Eventually, the deterioration of purchasing power brought about a steep -27 percent drop in corporate profits during the second quarter of 1980. Although they grew with each successive quarter for the remainder of the year, average corporate earnings stayed below their peak. Meanwhile, dividends rose to historic levels during each successive quarter of 1980, fed by double digit inflation, reduced real wages and the rising numbers of unemployed people. Real wages were rolled back to their 1967 level. The rate of unemployment surged from 6.3 percent in January to 7.8 percent in July, an increase of nearly 20 percent. The recession ended in July 1980.

The economic boom that followed lasted only until July 1981 when the economy plunged into its most severe recession since the Great Depression. Our corporate heroes had managed their companies so well they had to produce double-digit inflation during 1980 and 1981 in order to ensure constantly growing profits at a time when demand for goods and services was slack due to the recession of 1980 and its lingering high unemployment.

The Corporate Public Relations Campaign

By the early 1980s, numerous studies had been written proving U.S. corporations had relied too heavily on raising their prices to produce higher earnings beginning in the 1960s.[7] The rapid swelling of prices had put them at a competitive disadvantage vis-à-vis their foreign competitors who had relied more heavily on improving worker productivity by investing in more advanced technologies. Meanwhile, our corporate heroes decided not to invest sufficiently in new equipment for their older facilities in the United States. Instead, they preferred to erect new factories with new equipment in foreign countries where the price of labor was cheaper. The result of such corporate neglect and mismanagement in their home country was lower increases in worker productivity, which resulted in U.S. economic decline. This failure was exemplified by the loss of market shares throughout the world to foreign competitors in such industries as machine tools, automobiles, motorcycles, steel and electronics.

Grumblings of discontent among the vast majority of citizens were clear with regard to inflation, as well as to the declining standards of living offered by the captains of industry and finance, and to U.S. economic deterioration vis-à-vis foreign competitors. In response, the captains of industry and their political allies devised fairy tales that placed the blame for the sad U.S. economic performance on labor unions, the educational system, Roosevelt's New Deal Reforms, slow increases in worker productivity, and just about anything but the economic system, corporate driven inflation, CEOs and wealthy shareholders. Conservatives, recollect from chapter four, consider the economic system to be perfect. Back in 1980, they assumed any problems that existed within the economy must be the fault of government or people, but never the system. The solution, therefore, was only to be found by freeing it from government taxation and regulations, improving public education by eliminating or weakening it if possible, and undermining labor unions and the New Deal reforms.

One of these ridiculous fairy tales was provided by Stanford University economist Arthur Laffer. He claimed jobs would be created if the super-rich simply were given more money than they already possessed. His fable, which you certainly wouldn't want to call a theory, was that investors would create jobs if they were simply allowed to retain more of their income. This notion was preposterous since there already existed a super-rich group of investors in the United States and unemployment often reached very high levels anyway. In 1969, the most affluent consumers in the United States held just 24.9 percent of the total wealth. By 1983, the figure had risen to 34.3 percent, yet the unemployment rate was far higher in 1983 than in 1969.[8] Real wage rates were also higher in 1969 than in 1983. Recollect also that providing the affluent more income via tax reductions and enormously rising dividends had resulted in the Great Corporate Self-Liquidation. Therefore, the fairy tale that wealthy people would create more jobs if only they had more money was an outright lie, and an absurdity cruelly perpetrated on the American public, aided and abetted by the corporate news media, also known as the conservative news media. Nonetheless, Laffer's whimsical fantasy became the centerpiece of the economic program of Republican presidential candidate Ronald Reagan in 1980.

As this study shows, the affluent must destroy jobs and reduce the real wages, salaries and benefits of working citizens in order to increase their unearned income payments via publicly traded, limited liability corporations and the interrelated financial markets.[9] The current economic structure is designed to progressively achieve this outcome, and must therefore continuously lower the standard of living of most everybody else, although it can be offset by government actions for many years. The Reagan proposals could only achieve growing economic inequality, which also just happened to coincide with the needs and purposes of the system.

In 1981, the president enacted a 30 percent federal tax cut spread over three years with the benefits mainly going to the rich. Reagan also proposed reducing business regulations and providing more tax relief for corporations, another public welfare program.[10] If rising standards of living among the great body of citizens was the criteria, the policy was a complete failure at achieving a more healthy economy for the majority of Americans. It only brought about growing financial inequality throughout the world, because it provided already wealthy shareholders with even more cash to demand even higher dividend payments and share prices from our corporate heroes. With the extra cash, wealthy investors were able to apply more pressure on the captains of industry and finance to push real wages and other employee compensation downward in order to provide higher dividends and stock prices. Consequently, the president's tax cuts to some degree suppressed job growth and brought downward pressure on employee compensation throughout the decade, but this reaction by the economy was offset by other factors.

The president, for example, did enact a more useful Keynesian economic program by escalating military spending significantly, although this was only a continuation of the buildup begun earlier under President Carter. Relatively high paying jobs were created in this industry, and they had a ripple effect in other areas of business.

Reagan's tax cuts, coupled with his massive military buildup, resulted in large increases in the federal deficit, and this should have theoretically exerted upward pressure on interest rates and inflation. On the other hand, as explained above, the president's tax cuts resulted in reductions of real wages for over ten years, thereby gradually weakening the demand for goods and services, giving corporations less room to jack up prices.

Meanwhile, the Federal Reserve Bank significantly raised interest rates from 1980 to 1982 in order to suppress the corporate driven inflation of the previous seventeen years. This action severely crimped the demand sector, but it did eventually limit the annual corporate driven spikes of inflation. The yearly rise of the consumer price index remained relatively low from 1983 to 2005, while interest rates slowly continued downward starting in 1983. These two factors added fuel to the economic expansion that, with but one momentary pause, lasted for the nineteen years after 1982. Before this expansion occurred, however, the economy plunged into the worst recession since the Great Corporate Self-Liquidation of fifty years before.

The rapid rise of interest rates during 1981 took our corporate heroes by surprise, much as they had been unprepared for the Arab oil embargo nearly a decade earlier. The Federal Reserve had attempted to arrest inflation with rate hikes before, and during the 1970s failure had been the result. This time rates were going up until inflation was tamed. The economy was not in that great of shape either having just come out of recession.

The Recession Of 1981-1982

The next economic bust cycle officially began in July 1981, which meant that the boom period was tied for the second shortest in history, only twelve months! Corporate earnings had never recovered from their historic high in the first quarter of 1980, but they had begun rolling back upwards through the opening quarter of 1981, and then they sank through the next twelve months. Just imagine; from that lofty pedestal during the first quarter of 1980, average corporate income was down -38.5 percent exactly two years later. Earnings were still very high, but not towering enough to support dividends that had to surge up and away one quarter after the next. During this period, they soared nearly 26 percent, and that is why these unearned income payments reached historic heights during every quarter of 1980 through 1982. The only way to accomplish this miracle of mathematics was to liquidate jobs and transfer the lost wages into dividends. Even before the economy had entered the recession, in order to bring the growth of earnings more in line with dividends, CEOs began to lay off employees, cut pay rates and hours at work. Of course, people working fewer hours per week usually can't purchase as many things as before, and so the demand for goods and services got a little slack. People working in durable goods saw their hour's drop slowly beginning in May 1981. The manufacturing sector began its usual month by month hemorrhage of jobs as eight thousand were eliminated or exported during June and July. The unemployment rate rose steadily from April to June, before dropping momentarily in July. In August, it resumed its upward push.[11] You know the story. As profits stumbled, so too did the demand for goods and services, and so in order to keep dividends moving upward, throughout the economy, the captains of industry laid-off more employees, reduced wage rates, or cut more worker hours. These collective actions further depressed the demand sector, making it impossible for our heroes to jack-up earnings, and this put additional pressure on corporations to continue the labor liquidation process.

To fuel the rising dividends, the sacrificial lay-off victims numbered in the millions, and the unemployment rate jumped over 33 percent from 7.2 percent in July 1981 to 10.8 percent in the last month of the bust cycle, November 1982. Real wage rates bottomed out during that year when they hit $7.81 an hour, a low not seen since March 1964. Working people also saw much of their diminished income transferred to rich shareholders through double digit inflation in 1980 and 1981.

The Federal Reserve brought corporate driven inflation under control through the use of double digit interest rates by 1982. Corporations still continued to use inflation as a tool by which to transfer income and wealth from working people to rich shareholders, but not to the extent of the previous seventeen years. Remember that when jobs are exported to low wage countries, profits can be increased even as the price of goods and services are reduced or held to small increases. After 1982, the exportation of jobs to low wage countries increasingly became more important than inflation as an income transfer mechanism.

From 1982 onward, financial progress for most Americans was now permanently in reverse with the pedal on the metal so that rich shareholders could reap booming dividends during both good financial periods, and most noticeably during times of plunging profits. Working citizens as usual always paid the price, while corporations and the wealthy reaped all of the benefits. The period 1973 to 1982 revealed that the corporate economic system could no longer provide rising standards of living for the majority of U.S. citizens anymore, despite the significant corporate welfare programs intended to prop up the system outlined in Chapter Six. Corporations were established in order to provide the members of the wealthy class with ever-rising unearned income at the expense of everyone else. Contrary to what the apologists and the spokespeople of corporations claim, either individually or as an economic system, business corporations were never created to provide higher standards of living for the majority of the citizens of any country, or of the world, and in the long-term it is highly doubtful such an outcome can occur. By 1982, corporations had to gradually seize wealth and income from more and more of the working citizens of the world in order to provide those always rising dividend payments. This is why a huge shift in income and wealth had to take place in favor of the affluent during those previous ten years, as well as for decades afterwards.

The Reagan Boom Years

The 1980s economic expansion saw the stock markets explode upward, fed at least in part by more income transfers from employed citizens. Real average wages hit a high of $7.99 per hour in April and May of 1986, and then dropped during the last three years of the decade. By the end of 1989, despite large increases in worker productivity, real wages had returned to the level of 1966. Reagan and his cronies considered this to be progress! Corporations were able to put downward pressure on wages by increasingly moving production and service jobs from the United States to lesser paying countries. Pay rates in these nations were (and are) often one-tenth of the U.S. level or less. There are generally no benefits, such as medical, dental or retirement. The use of child labor was (and is) common, and the use of children depressed adult wages even more. The exportation of good paying jobs during the decade kept the unemployment rate higher than would otherwise have been the case, applied downward pressure on salaries, wages and benefits, and brought many labor unions to their knees, forcing them to give their corporate masters wage and benefit concessions in order to save jobs still in the United States. The stock markets had risen in part because of these income transfer schemes, which were supported in large part by purchases made by corporations in the political markets of the federal government. Such policies included weakening trade barriers between nations which made it easier for CEOs to export jobs.

In the face of reduced real wages, the standards for receiving credit were gradually loosened and this helped to fuel the economic fire of the 1980s and the 1990s. Mike Sloan, for example, purchased his own home in 1976, held a respectable job, and possessed an exceptional credit history. For several years he applied for credit cards and was turned down until out of frustration, he wrote a company and outlined ten reasons why he should be awarded a card. Sloan listed all of his accounts he had been paying and provided his mortgage loan information. Mike also mentioned that he had never missed a payment on anything. Because of the letter, he finally received a Visa card, but it had taken more than two years to get it after having first applied. Twelve years later, Sloan's two year old nephew, Michael, received an unsolicited pre-approved credit card offer despite not being employed, or even being old enough to attend school, and he wasn't quite out of diapers either, but he did possess a clean credit history. Standards were relaxed so much that even Fluff, a particularly cantankerous and ill mannered cat, received an unsolicited pre-approved credit card offer just a few years later. Things really had changed! Along with the military buildup and the massive federal deficits, continuously dropping credit standards, declining inflation and lower interest rates were all factors that stimulated the economy and allowed for the prosperity that unfolded during these years.

On the surface, the beginning of the 1990s looked somewhat more promising for working Americans than the previous decade. Unemployment shriveled to 5.0 percent by March 1989, and stayed near that level into the early months of the new decade. Unfortunately for working citizens, the mal-distribution of income and wealth had become so one-sided by then that, even though there were more wage earners per family compared to a few decades earlier, demand for goods and services could not be maintained to an adequate degree, and at satisfactory prices, to sustain the constantly growing obesity of corporate earnings.

The Recession Of 1990-91

The next recession officially began in July 1990. However, long before then, during the last three months of 1987 and the first three months of 1988, the growth of dividends had raced past the rate of increase of corporate profits.[12] In order to correct this imbalance, CEOs began to transfer wages into dividend payments right away. They dropped already low real wages even more throughout the economy, from an average of $7.88 an hour in May 1987 to $7.70 per hour in June 1990. By the middle of 1988, job growth began to slow as our heroes cut jobs and reduced employee hours of work. Profits recovered and moved upward, but once again the captains of industry had clipped the wings of the demand sector because people without jobs and those with reduced hours and pay are not too likely to demand more goods and services, at least not in sufficient quantities and at prices necessary to keep the economy rolling forward. With demand sagging, corporate earnings dropped in every quarter of 1989, but as usual average dividends hit historic highs all through the year. CEOs engineered more layoffs and reduced more employee hours and pay in response to the depressed profits.[13] The captains of manufacturing slashed, burned and exported to lesser paying countries more than 360 thousand jobs from March 1989 though July 1990. In the 17 months prior to the beginning of the recession, the unemployment rate crept upward from 5.0 percent in March 1989 to 5.5 percent in July 1990, fueled in part by the loss of manufacturing jobs. Profits recovered throughout the first nine months of 1990 thanks to the constant transfer of jobs into dividends. Of course, this weakened the demand for goods and services even more. The boom period peaked during July and then the economy finally plunged into recession. Earnings plummeted during the final three months of the year, and stayed at low levels all through 1991. Oh yes, dividend payments rocketed to historic heights in seven of the eight quarters of 1990-91, nicely sparked by the loses of the sacrificial lay-off victims.

The Clinton Boom Years

Although the recession officially hit bottom in March 1991, the unemployment rate continued to explode, peaking at 7.8 percent of the workforce in June 1992. Meanwhile, average real wage rates plummeted to $7.50 per hour in August 1994, a level not seen since sometime before 1964. The difference between the old wages and the new, as well as the employee compensation from the lost jobs, had been transferred into dividends. Therefore, the beginning of the 1990's boom period, which included a massive rise in the value of the various stock markets in the U.S., had been engineered in part by transferring income from working citizens to politically and economically powerful shareholders.

During the decade, corporations continued to export production and service jobs from the United States to low wage countries. However, U.S. corporations increasingly also exported jobs from low wage countries to countries with even lower wages. Therefore, much of the U.S. stock market boom of this decade was also brought about because income was transferred from working citizens throughout the world, such as those of Mexico, to politically powerful and affluent shareholders who produced nothing of substance except political and economic power. During the last fifty-six years, it is probably not an exaggeration to suggest that 25 to 60 million manufacturing jobs have been shipped from the United States to other countries.[14] This has allowed corporations to lower wages from $10+ per hour in the United States, to $1 per hour or less in Mexico, to .25 cents per hour or less in Vietnam and China. Many of these jobs still exist. Thus, because of the enormous number of jobs involved, the shipping of work from low wage to even lower wage countries likely wielded a sizeable influence on dividend payments despite the paucity of the wages of the workers of these factories.

In the United States, high skill jobs in technology, requiring years of college education, were also increasingly exported to low wage countries during the decade. People with master's degrees in engineering and computer programming, for example, saw jobs that paid in the $60-120,000 range shipped to India and China where high tech workers generally earn less than $20,000 per year.

Not everything went badly for working people during Clinton's eight years in office. They were a big winner when the president passed an income tax increase on wealthy consumers. This gave these people less money and less leverage with which to extract higher dividends and share prices from the captains of industry and finance, and relieved some of the pressures to lower wages and export jobs. This is why real wages reversed their slide and rose to their 1971 level. The unemployment rate dropped under 4.0 percent for the first time in several decades. Nonetheless, the mal-distribution of wealth and income had gotten worse for the vast majority of the world's people, including those in the United States. There were several other trends, however, that pushed the booming decade of the 1990s forward.

Interest rates continued to drop throughout those ten years, a trend that began in 1983, and this enhanced the abilities of working people who suffered from historically low real wages to purchase things they otherwise could not. Credit worthiness was loosened even more during the decade, and this expanded the purchasing power of people suffering from some of lowest real wages in history. Fluff the cat and others like him were offered pre-approved credit cards during the latter half of the decade. That's how desperate credit card companies were to loan money. Had he been able to sign his name on the form, the cat toy and catnip markets would have exploded upward and stimulated the economy even more.

Citizens were compelled to save less and spend more during the 1990s. Personal savings peaked in 1982 at $480 billion, but then began a precipitous slide of nearly 80 percent to $103 billion by 2004.[15] Less money saved meant more money spent, and this helped energize the economy.

Housing prices rose rapidly throughout the decade, but families lived off of most of the equity in their homes during the boom period. For example, the price of family houses rose in value by $3.3 trillion in just the four years from 1999 to 2003, but the equity in those properties changed very little because people purchased consumer goods by borrowing against the enhanced values, and this helped to keep the economy booming during the nineties, while it also assisted in keeping the recession of 2001 from being more severe than would have otherwise been the case.

Two earner households also increased in number, and this provided fuel to the economic expansion by helping to keep the demand for goods and services relatively strong. It also gave impetus to the growth of the child care industry since many moms and dads could no longer stay home and raise their children while only one spouse worked. Therefore, the mal-distribution of income and wealth may have frayed the American family structure. Since more people needed to work in order to support themselves and their families, it might be argued that the bond between church and parishioners, as well as the values represented by religion and held dear by much of the public, were also undermined to one degree or another due to the mal-distribution of income that had been unfolding for thirty years.

Expanding immigration into the United States possessed the appearance of a deliberate corporate welfare program because it helped to keep dividends racing upward during the period from 1986 to 2004. In the former year, President Reagan signed legislation granting amnesty to three million illegal immigrants. This was supposed to solve the problem of illegal aliens in the United States. When President George W. Bush proposed enacting similar legislation in 2003, it was estimated that eleven to sixteen million illegal immigrants resided in the United States. In addition, during the period between 1986 and 2003, millions of legal immigrants moved to this country. Although the majority of these people worked and paid taxes, immigration on this scale, legal and illegal, depressed salaries and wages for long-time U.S. citizens, a profitable income transfer mechanism for U.S. corporations. The typical argument for allowing virtually unrestricted immigration has been that U.S. citizens will not take jobs that immigrants are willing to do. However, what this really has meant is that citizens have been unable to perform these jobs at wages that are seriously depressed, a situation created by the influx of millions of immigrants into this country. Furthermore, illegal immigrants normally are not in very good positions to complain about inferior and perhaps legally banned working conditions, which along with subsistence or lower wages, tends to keep citizens of all creeds, nationalities and colors from even applying for these jobs.

Low wage rates are a bonanza to the corporate system, because the savings from declining wages can be morphed into dividends. Meanwhile, millions of new immigrants expand the demand for goods and services even if individually they earn very little. For example, four illegal immigrants earning five dollars per hour each can demand roughly the same amount of goods and services as a citizen earning twenty dollars an hour, more or less. By allowing such rampant immigration on behalf of the corporate system, officials of the federal government lower wages beyond what they would otherwise be, while simultaneously stimulating demand for goods and services, a bonanza to the wealthy via enhanced corporate earnings and dividend payments. The working citizens of this country pay the price for this corporate welfare scheme with higher taxes necessary to pay for overcrowding in the cities, increased crime beyond what it would normally be, enhanced financial stress on our public institutions such as schools, police and medical facilities, the degradation of the environment due to over population, and the use of more natural resources than would otherwise be the case. Worst yet, many immigrants remain mired in poverty for generations because they work too many hours in order to support their families, giving them little if any time to learn English and develop other skills necessary to rise out of poverty. Whole generations remain financially bogged down, and ghettos composed primarily of immigrants rise up out of formerly middle class neighborhoods. Increased immigration simply puts more downward financial pressure on both old and new arrivals, legal or illegal. Such a policy also helps to create a permanent class of renters, which has been pivotal in keeping the housing market from collapsing. Consequently, the immigration policy of the United States government serves to create a permanent underclass of working people that depresses the wage rates of its citizens, including new arrivals, and this happens to help corporations provide ever rising dividends to affluent shareholders.

The 2001 Recession

The next recession officially began in March 2001. However, the growth of dividends surged beyond the rise of corporate profits beginning in the last three months of 1997, and with the exception of one quarter, this continued all through 1998. In order to boost the rate of profit growth sufficiently to catch up with and sustain those always fast rising dividend payments, CEOs began their cutbacks in jobs and employee hours. Only this time the income transfer process wasn't all that statistically subtle. Job growth began to slow significantly beginning in October 1997. Citizens who worked in the durable goods industries experienced a gradual decline in the hours they worked starting as early as January 1998. The manufacturing sector followed shortly when it began its usual hemorrhage of jobs as 706 thousand of them were eliminated or exported from March 1998 through March 2001. Thanks to all of those employee cutbacks, and in spite of earnings that dropped in twelve of the next fifteen months starting in October 1997, dividends reached historic highs in every quarter of 1997 and 1998.[16] Profits rebounded for the first nine months of 2000, which is what the reduced employee hours and job liquidations that had been taking place during the two previous years were supposed to achieve. The unemployment rate finally began to steadily rise from a low of 3.9 percent in October 2000 until hitting 4.3 percent at the peak of the expansion in March 2001. Once again CEOs had punctured the demand sector by transferring jobs into dividends. Slack demand sent profits skidding in the last quarter of 2000, and in every quarterly period of 2001, but thanks to the continued liquidation of jobs, dividends reached historic heights all through this period.

For U.S. citizens, the times were bad, but not as much as they could have been. Much of the American manufacturing sector had already been exported to other countries, and it was in other nations that people truly suffered when their already low paying U.S. corporate jobs were exported to even lower paying areas of the world. For example, in the months leading up to the recession, as well as after it began, hundreds of thousands of jobs that U.S. corporations had gradually exported through the years to Mexico's northern free trade zone were shipped to Vietnam, China and other countries where the wages and working conditions were even worse. No doubt, whenever convenient, this transfer of jobs occurred throughout lesser developed nations as part of the world-wide income transfer scheme that is rigged into the corporate economic system.

The recession officially ended in November 2001, but the effects of it lingered for years afterwards. Private sector job growth remained below pre-recession levels until June 2005. Manufacturing CEOs had exported another three million jobs that still have not been replaced to this day (December 2005). Considering the population grew by eleven million people since the end of the recession, this represented a tremendous failure of the economy. Part of this was due to the burgeoning mal-distribution of income and wealth that had sabotaged the demand sector during the previous thirty years, and part was due to other factors.

In 2001, President Bush and Congress attempted to reverse the economic downturn through tax cuts. In the past, this was done to stimulate the demand for goods and services. However, Bush's tax cuts were primarily directed toward the more affluent members of society, those millionaires the president once referred to as his "base."[17] Consequently, they had little or no impact on stimulating the demand sector since wealthy people were more likely to invest in assets that provided returns on investments, such as stocks and bonds, rather than purchase the goods and services necessary to create jobs. Because of this, some economists, such as Paul Krugman, conceded the tax cuts would not invigorate the economy at all. Few politicians, academics, business people and economists, including Krugman, understood that tax cuts primarily benefiting the wealthy would weaken the demand for goods and services, thereby prolonging the effects of the recession.

Historically, reducing the tax liabilities of the wealthy investor class during economic downturns or slow growth periods have been analogous to pouring gasoline on burning buildings in order to put out fires. President Coolidge showed that such policies were foolhardy during the Roaring Twenties. He proved that providing already rich investors with more money only gave them more leverage to extract higher dividends from our corporate heroes. As demonstrated in chapter five, Coolidge gave a tax cut to the wealthy in 1926. In order to attract the newly available cash, the captains of industry and finance had to offer higher dividend payments. In 1927 average monthly dividends rose almost 80 percent from their levels of 1926. This was only achieved by eliminating jobs and reducing wages. The rapid rise of dividends crippled the economic system in 1926 by transferring income and wealth from working citizens to wealthy shareholders, and resulted in a short, but mild, recession. A tax cut for the wealthy set in motion the same process of redistributing income and wealth again in 1928. And this legislative action pushed the economy into the Great Depression the following year.

Earlier in this chapter we saw how President Ronald Reagan also provided tax cuts to the wealthy during the early 1980s, a period of three or four years known for its two recessions and historically high rates of inflation and unemployment. CEOs sought to entice investors to purchase their stocks with the newly available cash. The results for the next thirteen years were unprecedented drops in real wages, massive rises in dividend payments, and the upward explosions in the values of the various stock markets.

During the first year of the Bush presidency, the financial markets had experienced drops in their values. Money was bleeding from the markets and flowing elsewhere into other countries or other areas of investment to provide higher or safer returns. When the president provided tax cuts to the wealthy, CEOs tried to entice these people into buying corporate shares by providing higher dividend payments. Otherwise, if they did nothing, the price of their stocks might have remained the same or maybe even have dropped, and our corporate captains could have watched the newly available money flow into other areas of investment, and lead to speculative increases in those assets. Rising returns in these other areas would have potentially coaxed even more dollars out of the moribund financial markets, depressed stock prices even further, and jeopardized the jobs of CEOs.

Higher dividends were achieved by laying-off employees, reducing salaries, wages and benefits, and shipping jobs to low wage countries, otherwise known as outsourcing. For these reasons, the president's tax cut for the wealthy in 2001 ensured a nearly jobless economic recovery. So many manufacturing jobs were outsourced, thanks in part to these tax reductions, that Bush became sufficiently concerned about the negative publicity so as to foolishly propose that jobs flipping hamburgers be reclassified from service to manufacturing jobs, which would have allowed him to preside over a dubious expansion of industrial positions. Bush's additional income tax cut in 2003, along with the elimination of taxes on dividends, provided income tax relief chiefly to the rich and gutted jobs and redistributed income and wealth from working people to affluent shareholders for the same reasons as the 2001 tax cut. In 2004, the president made another mistake when he signed a bill giving tax cuts primarily to corporations and the wealthy. By the end of 2004, the economy had lost over 1.2 million private sector jobs, something unheard of since shortly after the Coolidge tax cuts of the mid to late 1920s. The president's perverse tax policies had compelled corporations to outsource millions upon millions of jobs from the United States, and the negative impacts of the recession festered and grew far more than what would otherwise have been the case.

The tax cuts transferred income and wealth from working people to rich people, so it should come as no surprise that the poverty rate and the number of people without health insurance increased under Bush. Labor's share of the national income was worse than any post-World War II recession. But dividend payments and corporate earnings grew, although at historically lackluster rates. These trends suggested the president's tax cuts weakened the demand sector far too much.

Had the president done the right thing, he would have provided sizable tax breaks to the lowest 90 percent of income earners. Since the president had demonstrated enthusiasm for the idea that corporations should receive rebates on taxes they never paid, and since much of that money has been given to wealthy shareholders and CEOs in the form of dividends, it seems fair that less well off citizens should also have received rebates on taxes they never paid. This would have stimulated job growth by strengthening the demand sector, especially if the rebates had amounted to $500 to $2,000 per working person.

The president should also have signed legislation that would have progressively raised the federal income tax rate beginning with those earning over $250 thousand per year. This would have erased much of the leverage investors possess over corporate managers. CEOs would have been relieved of the pressure to produce higher dividends than would have been the case under the lower tax rate, and jobs possibly could have then been created in the USA at greater rates. In addition, the president should have signed into law a very high tax on corporate stocks held only for short-term speculative purposes. This may have given investors second thoughts about selling their shares and stabilized the financial markets in the short-term, and relieved some of the pressures for CEOs to outsource jobs. Instead, the president made all the wrong moves.

Just like the tax breaks on the federal level favoring corporations and the affluent, the tax burdens on state levels had shifted from corporations to working citizens during the last thirty years, and allowed the former to pay the affluent higher dividends. When the economy began its inevitable downturn in 2001, throughout the states, shortages of tax dollars fueled lay-offs of local and state government employees and reduced services for middle class, working and poor citizens. President Bush made the negative impacts of the recession worse when he refused to provide federal aid to the states to stop this hemorrhage of jobs and services.[18] It was highly unlikely that laid-off former government employees were going to boost their demands for goods and services, an idea that apparently never occurred to the president. In order to stop the loss of services provided by state and local agencies, taxes and fees were raised primarily on the financial backs of working citizens and small business owners at some state and local levels, which further depressed the demands for goods and services.

President Bush also signed into law "The No-Child Left Behind Act." This legislation compelled state taxpayers to spend even more state and local tax funds on public education, because very little federal money had been allocated to implement this new federally mandated program. Tax dollars were expropriated throughout the states by the publishing corporations because of the need to purchase tests and test taking materials. These dollars were then (in part) transferred into dividends, making the "No Child Left Behind Act" just another of the president's pet corporate welfare programs, which is more fully discussed in Chapter Nine. In order to fund the president's newest transfer of income scheme, state taxpayers had only two choices; Taxes on the state and local levels had to be increased for working citizens, or services provided by state and local governments had to be reduced. This often equated to lay-offs and reductions of hours worked by government employees, which resulted in decreases of demands for goods and services throughout state and local levels. The financial strains on working citizens of the "No Millionaire Publisher Left Behind Scheme" was relatively minor compared to some of the more sinister income transfer programs planned and carried out by the president and his White House co-conspirators.

Conspiracy Of The Devil

Perhaps the biggest scandal and most heinous crime committed in U.S. presidential history was a deceitful corporate welfare conspiracy carried out by President George W. Bush and several close advisors. As early as January 2001, upon taking office, the president began his search for any plausible reason to send U.S. troops into a war with Iraq. This was nine months prior to the suicide attacks on the World Trade Center buildings in New York City, as well as on the Pentagon in Washington D.C. Vice President Dick Cheney, Secretary of Defense Donald Rumsfield and his undersecretary, Paul Wolfowitz, also supported the president's desire to occupy the Arab nation.[19]

Although it's still unknown, there were a number of probable reasons why the president wanted to go to war. For starters, the world's second biggest oil reserves were thought to be under Iraq. And thanks to a ten year long U.S. led embargo against that nation, it had become economically and militarily weak. Iraq's frailties and massive oil reserves made it a tempting target. Bush and Cheney had both been active for years in the oil industry, although the former was extremely unsuccessful, if not thoroughly incompetent, while the latter had been able to get into the industry only because he had the political connections that made it easier for his corporation to obtain public welfare. Both men had friends and supporters in the industry. Stealing Iraq's oil was consistent with the president's economic policies of rewarding his supporters, "the haves and the have mores," while ensuring that the price of his ambitions was paid by everyone else.

Of course, it is possible the president and his advisors were more ambitious than this. Perhaps they thought the complete financial rape and pillage of Iraq, along with the oil and a never ending war, would enrich his appreciative "base" to unimaginable heights. As will be shown in chapter eight, privatization of public services has always been used as a political deception to disguise the transfer of income and wealth from working people to the rich via higher prices and less service, lower wage rates and less compensation. But such policies have always helped to ensure constantly rising dividends and share prices. If Iraq's government services were to be privatized and taken over by U.S. corporations, a tremendous windfall of billions of dollars would be stolen from the people of Iraq and transferred to the president's "base." Heck, why not just take over the entire economy of Iraq on behalf of corporate America? Now that would be really profitable.

Try as he might, Bush could not find even one good reason to inspire the people of the United States to go to war with Iraq. Then his prayers were answered, helped of course when he and Condoleezza Rice, the president's National Security Advisor, conveniently ignored intelligence warnings that an Islamic terrorist group was planning to launch a strike against the U.S. sometime during the summer of 2001. On August 6th of that year, the president was handed a CIA document titled, "Bin Laden Determined to Attack Inside the United States." The article provided details of the terrorist's plans for hijacking planes and flying them into buildings. Bush and Rice chose not to act on this very serious information. The attacks against the World Trade Center buildings and the Pentagon provided Bush with all the ammunition he needed to achieve his desires of going to war against Iraq. The day after September 11th, Bush demanded members of his administration unearth evidence that Iraq was involved in the attacks, although the CIA and National Security Council members had already concluded and told him that Al Queda, an Arab terrorist group headquartered in Afghanistan, and given aid by Yemen, Saudi Arabia and Iran, had committed the atrocity.[20] No evidence was ever uncovered linking the nation of Iraq and Al Qaeda, much less that they somehow had cooperated in the attack. No plans were ever made to retaliate against the nations of Iran, Yemen or Saudi Arabia for providing aid and comfort to our enemies.

Osama bin Laden was the leader of Al Qaeda. He and much of his organization had long been identified as being located in Afghanistan, which was then governed by a group known as the Taliban. Reluctantly, and somewhat tardily, the president authorized an attack on that country when its leaders refused to hand bin Laden over to the United States. However, in a sinister move, with both bin Laden and the Taliban on the run early in 2002, but before complete success had been achieved, military resources were diverted to the president's pet project

of conquering Iraq. But first he had to convince the public to support the up-
coming corporate welfare war.

Throughout the year 2002 and up until March 2003, the president spoke
often and eloquently when declaring that war with Iraq was not imminent. He
always appeared to be sincerely worried that it had weapons of mass destruction
(WMD), and that they might be given to terrorists to use against the United
States. His sincerity, however, was completely fabricated. At least as early as
July 2002, according to a leaked top secret British document known as the
Downing Street Memo, in the White House, "Military action was now seen as
inevitable. Bush wanted to remove Saddam, through military action, justified
by the conjunction of terrorism and WMD." The case for war was "thin" since
Iraq "was not threatening" its "neighbours (sic)," and its "WMD capability was
less than that of Libya, North Korea or Iran." If the British knew this, then Bush
certainly knew all of this as well. Since he lacked any evidence whatsoever con-
necting Iraq to WMD, but he apparently desired the profits the war would bring
to his "base," Bush and other members of his administration made the decision
to manufacture public opinion in favor of war, by making sure "the intelligence
and facts were being fixed around the policy."[21] So nobody should be surprised
that all the alleged evidence used by the president to support going to war turned
out to be wrong, especially since the plans for manufacturing these lies were being fabricated inside the Bush White House.

At some point, possibly prior to March 2002, but definitely by April of that
year, Bush convinced British Prime Minister Tony Blair to support him in his
quest for regime change in Iraq. Blair also lied to his people and the British Parliament by continuously denying they he had any intention of going to war against
the Arab nation. By now it shouldn't come as a great big shock that the intelligence agencies of both countries transformed themselves into propaganda machines, and ridiculous assertions were made that had nothing to do with reality.[22]

Some of Iraq's aluminum artillery tubes mysteriously became "nuclear related," and were touted as being proof positive that it was developing such
weapons. Despite the objections of the Department of Energy, high officials in
the Bush administration repeated over and over again that "'the tubes could be
used only in centrifuges to create nukes.'" Vice President Dick Cheney even declared on the television show "Meet the Press," that "'It's now public that, in
fact, (Saddam) has been seeking to acquire…the kinds of tubes that are necessary
to build a centrifuge' to enrich uranium for nuclear weapons."[23] We now know

the vice president was not telling the truth, for he was simply manufacturing public consent for going to war by fixing "the intelligence and the facts around the policy." It turns out the tubes were in fact for artillery.

In another case of lies, fraud and deceit, the British accused Iraq of endeavoring to purchase uranium in the African country of Niger. This assertion was apparently intended to strengthen the lie that Iraq's leader, Saddam Hussein, was attempting to build nuclear weapons, the insinuation being that he might supply such armaments to terrorists to use against the United States, or so the president worried over and over again in well choreographed public appearances.[24] Of course, the documents that served as proof of such claims turned out to be forgeries. Who could have been motivated to give the British forged documents? Could those people have forged them? It wouldn't shock too many people if you cast your angry gaze at Bush his fellow conspirators in the White House or at Tony Blair and his minions. In February 2002, CIA officials asked former U.S. ambassador Joseph C. Wilson to investigate these charges. Once in Niger, he quickly concluded that it was "highly doubtful that any such transaction had ever taken place." However, despite Wilson's assertion to the contrary, the British repeated the same charges against Iraq in September 2002. This gave Bush the fuel he needed to charge in January 2003 that Iraq was trying to purchase uranium from Niger in order to develop their nuclear weapons program, which the president knew did not exist, since he appears to have been the conspirator-in-charge of fixing the evidence.[25]

In the continuing efforts to support these White House lies, an alleged major in Iraqi intelligence was unearthed who claimed it possessed mobile biological weapons laboratories. In May 2002 the accuser failed his second lie detector test and some intelligence officials, apparently not in the conspiracy-of-fabrication-loop, warned that his testimony was unreliable, and that it appeared as though his answers had been "coached."[26] And still the president continued to incite fear among citizens that Iraq was armed with biological and nuclear weapons, and that Saddam could give them to terrorists, even though each warning was based on the fabricated intelligence originating from the White House.

In August 2002, Secretary of Defense Donald Rumsfeld played his role quite well when he declared that Iraq was harboring Al Queda members, although just nine months earlier, the president had personally been told by Richard Clarke, his own leader of counterterrorism, as well as CIA Director George Tenet, that such links did not exist.[27] Other claims that were conveniently leaked from the White House to the press trying to link Iraq with WMD and Al Queda turned out to be false, but the corporate press, also known as the conservative press, dutifully continued to report these claims as if they were reality.

In the summer of 2002, the British and the U.S. began the war by bombing Iraq in an attempt to get them to shoot back. Such a reaction on the part of the Iraqis would have provided Bush with a rationale to go to war, although Iraq would only have been defending itself from an aggressive, dishonest president. Had the Iraqis defended themselves, given its history of deceitfulness, the Bush regime would likely have painted a distorted picture of reality in order to convince U.S. citizens that forces of Iraq had been the aggressors. The Iraqis refused to take the bait and return fire, even after the bombing was escalated for months afterwards. After the start of the air war, both Bush and Blair, as well as their co-conspirators, continued to deny that war with Iraq was imminent. They always lied. The newest corporate welfare war had already begun from the sky.

On March 20, 2003, U.S. and British ground forces invaded Iraq, along with a smattering of military personnel from other countries. The invaders quickly swept aside the Iraqi army, and just outside the capital of Baghdad, just prior to the initial assault on the city, two bases were established named Camp Exxon and Camp Shell. The people who contributed the titles of the camps apparently knew the name of the game—oil. Of course, they could just as easily have named one of the two Camp Halliburton, or maybe Camp Cheney after the former CEO of that corporation. Just prior to the beginning of the invasion, a subsidiary of Halliburton received a no-bid multi-billion dollar contract to repair oil fields and provide fuel for U.S. forces in Iraq.[28] Pentagon auditors later discovered that the company had over-billed the military more than $100 million. Iraqi businesses could have provided the fuel for considerably less money, and that would have provided stimulus to their economy. However, that was never the president's plan.

As soon as the major fighting between the two armies was over, the Bush regime quickly moved to consolidate control over the natural resources of Iraq when the president signed Executive Order 13303. This granted legal immunity to U.S. oil corporations dealing with Iraqi oil. Among other things, they could use slave labor in their operations, they could spill millions of gallons of oil and destroy hundreds of miles of shoreline, their corporate security people could murder anyone they desired, and the victims could never sue U.S. corporations in U.S. courts under the president's order. Some claimed that Bush's directive ensured that the oil of Iraq became "the unassailable province of U.S. corporations."[29] Since the conquest of Iraq, there has been a big push to privatize its national oil company, meaning U.S. corporations will be able to own the oil of Iraq on the cheap if this income transfer scheme succeeds, a policy guaranteed to create more misery for the citizens of that country.

Shortly after the major fighting ended, the U.S. Congress authorized $18.4 billion to aid in the reconstruction of the conquered nation. However, by January 2005, it was reported that only $1.5 billion had actually been spent. Reinoud Leenders, a Middle analyst with the International Crisis Group (ICG), a Belgium based think tank, estimated that "40 percent or more of the $1.5 billion was spent by foreign companies on insurance and security. And this means only about $900 million of the over $18.4 billion had been spent on reconstruction in the two years after the end of the war. And what became of all of that oil under the land of Iraq and all of the income and wealth it could have brought to the citizens of that nation? Alas, Iraq's oil was under the control of the U.S. occupation authorities, officially known as the Coalition Provisional Authority (CPA). According to a charity organization called Christian Aid, it was impossible "to tell with any accuracy what the CPA has been doing with Iraq's money," which was chiefly raised by the sale of oil. An estimated $20 billion of it had disappeared, and most of it had not been used to rebuild Iraq. Had is been, it would not have mattered to Iraqis anyway since very few of them benefited from what little reconstruction was occurring. Of the $1.5 billion of Iraq's oil money that was actually known to be used to finance reconstruction, Iraqi companies received only about 2 percent of the contracts, meaning that the profits were being transferred out of the country, which left the people more impoverished than before the war. British and U.S. companies received 85 percent of these contracts. Of the total, Halliburton subsidiary Kellogg, Brown and Root (KBR) received 51 percent of the contracts. Worse yet for Iraq's citizens, the foreign companies receiving contracts preferred to import less expensive workers, which left plenty of unemployed and unhappy Iraqis.[30] Indians imported to serve as cooks for KBR reported they were paid only three dollars a day.[31] Somebody was making big money, and it wasn't the people of Iraq or India. It should not surprise anybody that the standards of living for the citizens of Iraq were shoddier in 2005, and worsening everyday, than prior to the invasion. As of 2005, electricity was less available, and 27 percent of all children less than five years of age were malnourished. Some Iraqi official's stated that the unemployment rate was 27 percent as of December 2004, although other sources claimed that it was closer to 50 percent.[32]

The American occupation officially ended on June 28, 2004 with the establishment of an interim government, although over 100 thousand U.S. military personnel and allies still occupied the country. But U.S. corporate economic dominion over the economy had already been established by the U.S. provisional occupation government under Paul Bremer. He had initiated a policy known as the 100 orders, and the final order did not allow the interim government to terminate them. An examination of some of the orders reveals how U.S. corporate friendly they are. Number thirty-nine ordered the shift from a "'centrally planned economy to a market economy.'" Iraqis had no say in the matter. BearingPoint, Inc., a U.S. corporation "received a $250 million contract" to ensure this transition, which included the "privatization of Iraq's 200 state-owned businesses." Number thirty-nine also calls for "100 percent foreign ownership of Iraq's businesses," "unrestricted, tax-free remittance of all profits and other funds," and "40-year ownership licenses." This means that U.S. corporations can own all of the businesses in Iraq, import workers from India to do all of the work cheaply, and all of the profits can be taken back to the U.S. and placed into the hands of CEOs and the already fat wallets of President Bush's "base." Not a cent of money stolen from Iraquis needs to be reinvested in Iraq. Order number twelve suspended all tariffs and other impediments to the flow of goods entering and leaving Iraq. In 2003, when it was enacted, cheap imported goods swept into the country and wiped out many local businesses, creating a large pool of unemployed people, which helped to feed the growing forces fighting the invading army. Order seventeen "grants foreign contractors, including private security firms," immunity from the laws of Iraq. So if an employee kills a "third-party," or the firm does environmental harm that kills or injures thousands of people, the victims cannot sue the perpetrators in Iraq's legal system. They need to file their lawsuit in the United States, a process likely to be far too expensive to undertake for most Iraqis. Of course, if the foreign business is a U.S. oil corporation, the citizens of Iraq cannot even file a lawsuit in the United States, for under Executive Order 13303 victims cannot sue their tormentors in the USA; and this means such corporations and their employees are completely immune from lawsuits anywhere since there are no legal remedies in either nation with which their victims can fight back. The United States appointed friendly people to the interim government, and they were not likely to do anything about this situation. Prime Minister Iyad Allawi, a thirty year exile with close ties to the CIA and British Intelligence, was the man in charge of the new government.

And every important government ministry had been stacked with U.S. appointees, each with five year terms. So nobody in the new government was likely to reverse Bush's economic rape and pillage of Iraq.[33]

As the occupation persisted, a resistance movement gained recruits and momentum among many of the citizens of the conquered nation, fueled by the transfers of income and wealth that had provided Bush with the desire to invade. As of December 2005, the cost of this corporate welfare war could be tabulated in the dead and the dying: the 100,000 Iraqis killed, the more than 2,000 dead U.S. military personnel, and the nearly 15,000 U.S. military personnel who had been wounded, many permanently without limbs and eyes, and all based on a "pack of lies" and manufactured evidence.

As of December 2005, the fabricators of war had gone unpunished. In fact, some had even been promoted. Before the actual ground invasion had begun, some of these White House conspirators had painted rosy pictures to the citizens of the United States of what war with Iraq would look like. One bogus fantasy was that the conflict would be won with a small military force, and another fabrication was that we would be welcomed as liberators by the bulk of the citizens of Iraq. It turns out these rosy scenarios, as well as the falsehoods of Iraqi WMD and Al Queda links created inside the White House, were only deceptions intended to alleviate the legitimate worries of the citizens of the U.S. as to the reasons for going to war, as well as the duration, expense and the outcome of the hostilities. For successfully dreaming up these fantasies, and for acting with all sincerity in public forums about these fabricated issues, the conspirators retained their positions, or they were promoted. It has yet to occur to more than a few citizens that allowing these people to get away scot-free with these high crimes and misdemeanors only opens the door for even more immoral acts to be committed by the highest government officials on behalf of always rising profits, dividends and share prices.

The Calculable Future

Publicly traded limited liability corporations have yet to strip the common people of the world of sufficient wealth and income to bring about the inevitable collapse of the corporate economic system. It is difficult to guess when such a situation might occur. However, the recession of 2001 suggests we are more than halfway through the life of the system, but more than likely we are closer than that. The starting point would have been somewhere between 1933, when

President Roosevelt initiated the first of his New Deal policies, and the end of World War II in 1945. Thus, perhaps within the calculable future, say between five and fifty years, the system should begin to collapse with massive repercussions. The evidence is very strong on this matter.

During the last thirty years, more and more income and wealth have gradually been transferred from working people to the affluent. This has seriously weakened the demand for goods and services per capita. This trend, however, has been offset to some degree by other factors, such as the federal deficit, immigration, lower credit standards and historically low interest rates.

As of August 2005, while short term interest rates had risen modestly from record lows fourteen months before, long-term rates needed to remain at or near forty year lows in order to keep demand relatively high. The results were the rapid rise of home prices, resulting in housing bubbles in areas throughout the nation, and this helped to keep the economy afloat. As mentioned earlier, homes in the United States gained roughly $3 trillion of equity from 1999 to 2003, but almost all of it was spent. This propped up consumer demand higher than would otherwise have been the case, and also diverted significant money away from the financial markets. If the bubbles burst or even sag anywhere near simultaneously, the economy will be weakened. If long-term interest rates rise to a fair degree, this could prove to be the catalyst puncturing the bubbles, but it is difficult yet to suggest how modest or severe of an impact such a scenario would have on the overall economy, but it would not be a good thing.

The Federal Reserve regulates the demand for goods and services through the manipulation of short-term interest rates. When inflation begins to tick upward too rapidly, the Fed raises rates, thereby restraining demand, and compelling corporations to hold price increases to relatively low levels. During the previous recession (March-November 2001) and for three years afterwards, the Fed discovered it was necessary to push short-term interest rates to forty-year record lows to stimulate demand, but these rates did not really spark the demand sector all that much. They helped some, but the reality is that rates needed to remain historically low for three years after the end of the recession, and this indicates that the Fed may have lost much of its abilities.

As the economy staggered forward from the recession of 2001, the maldistribution of income and wealth continued to favor the rich shareholder class, and this kept the demand for goods and services at lower levels than would otherwise be the case. In order to keep the system buoyant, as the not-so-brisk economic good times continues, more and more income and wealth from around the world will need to be transferred from those productive people who purchase the goods and services necessary to keep the economy chugging along to those unproductive people that make up the investor class. This suggests that when the next bust cycle occurs, the Federal Reserve will need to lower short-term interest rates to somewhere in the vicinity of zero or into the negative range in order to offset the continuous weakening of the demand sector. And this conjures up the scary possibility that the Fed will have no influence whatsoever in the battle to reverse the next recession, just as when reducing interest rates were acts of futility during the opening years of the Great Corporate Self-liquidation (1929-1940). Without a quick and significant reversal of the mal-distribution of income and wealth, there is also the increasing likelihood that each boom cycle will be less robust than each previous expansion, and the negative impacts of each bust cycle will linger longer and longer after they end.

Given the continuous weakening of demand for goods and services per capita, immigration into the U.S. must continuously rise (and at increasingly higher rates than previously) in order to help keep the demand sector sufficiently high to ensure the unremitting rise in corporate earnings from one quarter to the next. However, immigration can only hold off the potential economic disaster for so long. It cannot delay the inevitable forever. Consequently, unrelenting immigration is not a good sign for the future of the corporate economy (nor the ecology).

It is difficult to ascertain just when a corporate collapse is likely to occur, or how it will unfold. Will the system dissolve quickly or slowly? Will we engage in endless wars in order to stave off the coming depression? Will there be other ways in which to slow the inevitable? It matters not, because it is only a matter of time. It will happen sooner or later. My best guess is that within ten to twenty years the system will begin to collapse. The only question is how it will unfold.

Notes

1. The long-term existence of inflation usually cannot occur without a corporate system, or something like it. In a truly competitive environment, prices generally go down. Farm prices during the second half of the 19th century are a prime example. There are some situations in which inflation can occur without a corporate economic system. A time of war, for example, or a period of speculation, can cause inflation. A rapid rise in the money supply can bring about inflation, but only if the distribution of it goes, in large part, to the great body of citizens, as in the case of Germany after World War I. However, these are generally short-lived episodes of inflation—not continuous and forever.

2. Unfortunately, U.S. chemical corporations still sell pesticides such as DDT to other countries, although such substances are illegal in the United States. The crops of those non-U.S. farms are imported into the United States and we eat them. Approximately 20,000 farm workers die every year due to exposure to pesticides according to the March 2003 issue of *Ecologist Magazine*, page 59.

3. Federal Reserve Bulletin, May 1974, page A44.

4. Federal Reserve Bulletin, July 1975, p. A54.

5. Dividends rolled upward to historic heights during every quarter of 1974. The massive drop in earnings in late 1974 and early 1975 pushed them down by 3.73 percent in the first quarter of 1975. They began moving upward during the second quarter of that year.

6. Greider, William, *Secrets of the Temple*, Simon and Shuster: New York, 1987, page 361.

7. *Profits Without Production* by Seymour Melman is an excellent study of this phenomenon.

8. Batra, Ravi, *The Great Depression of 1990*, Venus Books: Texas, 1987, p. 118.

9. Sometimes the rich become wealthy because of their abilities and ideas. Bill Gates and Paul Allen of Microsoft are an example of such people. However, it is likely they are far richer because their company became a publicly traded limited liability corporation than they would have been if such legally created business forms did not exist.

10. Greider, William, *Secrets of the Temple*, Simon and Shuster, Inc. 1987, page 353

11. The economy entered the last phase of the business cycle when the hours worked per week in the durable goods industries reached a peak in May 1981 at 40.6, and then began their downward trend striking 40.3 in July. From June to July—the apex of the expansion—the manufacturing industry lost 8 thousand jobs. The unemployment rate went from 7.2 percent in April 1981 to 7.5 percent in May and June before returning to 7.2 percent in July. Thus, from its low point to the peak of the expansion, the unemployment rate had gone up, or stayed stagnant at 7.2 percent, depending on how you choose to view the situation. However, the drop in July was an aberration since the rate grew in May, stayed the same in June, and following July, grew every month thereafter. Possibly many of our corporate heroes were taken by surprise, and maybe unsure of the economic impact on corporate profits the rapid rise of interest rates might have had. This uncertainty may explain why unemployment rose, but then declined momentarily just prior to the onset of a recession, which is abnormal.

12. Federal Reserve Bulletin, July 1989, p. A35.

13. Federal Reserve Bulletin, July 1990, p. A35.

14. In 1947, the ratio of service to production jobs was roughly five to four. In 2003, the ratio was roughly six to one. There were roughly 110 thousand service jobs in the United States in 2003 and only slightly more than 16 million jobs in manufacturing. In 1947, there were roughly 25 million service jobs and roughly 20 million jobs in manufacturing. Had the ratio stayed the same as in 1947, it would suggest that about 80 million manufacturing jobs should exist in the United States. Take into consideration increases in productivity and subtract the current sixteen million still in the USA, and a reasonable guess might be that 25 to 50 million jobs have left the United States since 1947.

15. Greider, William, "Riding into the Sunset," *Nation*, June 27, 2005, p. 13.

16. At first, much of the increase in dividend payments came out of undistributed corporate profits. However, by the final quarter of 2001, total corporate undistributed profits had dropped to –3.5 percent, something not seen since the Great Depression. They stayed at low levels all through 2002 and 2003. In the fourth quarter of 2001, total corporate earnings were nearly -35 percent less that they had been during the third quarter of 2000. Nonetheless, total dividend payments were 7 percent higher during the fourth quarter of 2001 when the two quarters are compared. This was

thanks to those transfer payments from the growing army of the unemployed. The unemployment rate climbed from 5.8 percent in December 2001 to 6.0 percent in December 2002.

17. Actually the president referred to his base as being "the haves and the have mores." No mention of the evangelical right can be found in his comment, although those right-wing Christians with sufficient income would belong to his "base."

18. Pear, Robert, "Governors Get Sympathy From Bush but No More Money," *New York Times*, Feb. 25, 2003, p. A 22.

19. Suskind, Ron, *The Price of Loyalty, George W. Bush, the White House, and the Education of Paul O'Neil*, Simon and Schuster: New York, 2004, pp. 72–75.

20. Clarke, Richard A., Against *All Enemies: Inside America's War on Terror*, Free Press: New York, 2004 pp. 31–33.

21. Manning, David, "The secret Downing Street memo," *Sunday Times*, London, England, May 01, 2005.

22. McGovern, Ray, "Proof Bush Fixed the Facts," TomPaine.com, May 04, 2005.

23. Sarasohn, David, "The rousing rewardings of wrongness," *Oregonian*, June 3, 2005 p. C13.

24. Novak, Robert, "Mission to Niger," townhall.com, July 14, 2003.

25. Wilson, Joseph C., "What I Didn't Find in Africa," www.commondreams.org , originally published by the *New York Times*, July 6, 2003.

26. Fairweather, Jack, "Chalabi stands by faulty intelligence that toppled Saddam's regime," News.Telegraph.co.uk, February 19, 2004.

27. Graham, Bradley, "Al Queda Presence in Iraq Reported Bagdad Knows, Rumsfeld Says," *Washington Post*, August 21, 2002, p. A1.

28. Eckholm, Eric, Now You See It: An Audit of KBR, *New York Times*, March 20, 2005.

29. Kretzmann, Steve and Jim Vallette, "Bush Give Legal Immunity to Transnational Oil Corporations in Iraq," ReclaimDemocracy.org, First published on July 28, 2003 in TomPaine.com.

30. Henderson, Christian, "Iraq rebuilding still a mirage," Aljazeera.net, January 21, 2005.

31. No author listed, "War profiteering exposed," Alternet.org, January 22, 2004.

34. MeKay, Emad, "U.S. to Take Bigger Bite of Iraq's Economic Pie," www.commondreams.org, December 24, 2004.

35. Juhasz, Antonia, "The Handover That Wasn't," www.AlterNet.org, July 20, 2004.

Chapter Eight

THE RACE TO THE BOTTOM
ON THE ROAD TO SERFDOM

And whoever controls all economic activity controls the means for all
our ends and must therefore decide which are to be satisfied and which
are not. —Frederich Hayek, *The Road to Serfdom*

The control of the production of wealth is the control of human life itself. —Hilaire Belloc, quoted in *The Road to Serfdom*

We know the corporate economic system relies heavily, and increasingly,
upon transfers of income from working people to wealthy shareholders and to
the captains of industry and finance. In the United States, however, it is politically palatable to transfer only so much income and wealth from the lower 98
percent or so of the population to the top during any particular year. Therefore,
during the last thirty years or so, as the need for higher profits has accelerated,
U.S. corporations have pushed their federal government to open up the lesser developed world to free trade in order to more rapidly transfer income and wealth
from those people to themselves. Because of this, income transfers from working citizens of the United States to corporations can be performed at slower, less
noticeable, rates than would otherwise be politically acceptable.

To achieve this goal of continuously transferring income and wealth, it has
proven helpful for many corporations to exercise even more political and economic power in lesser developed countries than they do in the United States. Citizens of these nations are generally unable to compete in their own political
markets against multinational corporations because they cannot afford the prices
charged, lack education and or political sophistication. Therefore, it is not a coincidence that trade treaties and laws and regulations enacted by these governments

often favor foreign corporations at the expense of their own people, leaving their citizens financially worse off than ever before. As new laws favoring corporations are enacted throughout the world, and since these organizations can maintain themselves only through escalating transfusions of income and wealth, a growing number of people throughout the planet will continue to experience declining standards of living as their land, labor, income, health and national resources are transferred to the wealthy via multinational corporations.

Mexico

On January 1st, 1994, the Native-Americans of the southern state of Chiapas, Mexico staged an uprising against the central government. These people rebelled because their political leaders had passed measures that brought about the removal of Article 27 of the Mexican Constitution. It had protected Native-American communal lands known as ejidos since Mexico's independence a hundred and seventy years before.[1] The result of this decision by the government was that "tens of thousands of poor peasants and indigenous people in Mexico" lost their "lands, incomes and homes," which not so coincidently happened to fall into the U.S. corporate tactic of transforming communal lands into private property. For decades people had grown corn and other foodstuffs together on their communes, and then sold their goods in local markets. The government action divided the ejidos among the peasants into one to two acre sections. Not long afterwards, the federal regime eliminated Mexican tariffs on imported corn under pressure from the U.S. government.[2] U.S. corporate farmers have been highly subsidized by the federal establishment for decades.[3] The peasants of the former ejidos, operating without federal financial support, with little or no capital, and working on only one or two acres of land, were not able to compete all that well against U.S. corporate agri-businesses' that were and continue to be highly subsidized. The peasants were not fools. Many knew they had been deliberately set up by their own government to lose their land. Why did their government establish an economic climate in Mexico for U.S. corporations to financially wipe out the Mexican citizens of the ejidos? Then as now, the answer was that the distribution of income and wealth was largely determined in the political and financial markets. These impoverished peasant people had little or no capital to successfully compete in the political markets of their own country. This is the golden rule of democracy in action; He who has the gold makes the rules.

On January 1, 2003, the Mexican government decided to make things worse for its citizens when it eliminated tariffs on chickens because of the NAFTA treaty. Chicken ranches in Mexico were very small compared to the corporate chicken ranches of the United States.[4] Many people thought U.S. producers would eventually dominate the entire Mexican industry. It was estimated that as many as 1 million Mexican workers in the industry would lose their jobs. This legislative action was expected to increase poverty for Mexicans, and drive hundreds of thousands more of its citizens into the United States where they will continue the process of lowering real wages there. Such legislative actions acted as a transfer of income scheme on behalf of U.S. corporations, and at the expense of the citizens of Mexico and of the United States.

Burma

Burmese villagers filed a lawsuit in U.S. court against Unocal Corporation in 1996. The plaintiffs charged that the Burmese military forced them to work in "slave like conditions" on a natural gas pipeline in which Unocal was an investor. In some cases, members of the military kidnapped and raped villagers. Human rights organizations reported that whole communities had been forcibly relocated "to make room for the pipeline and its supporting roads."[5] The plaintiffs were among those who had once lived on the land where the pipeline had been laid, mostly along a thirty-nine mile section near the border of Thailand. A Unocal spokesman denied that the corporation had "participated in, condoned or benefited" from the abuses in Burma, now known as Myanmar. However, the presiding judge of California's Court of Appeals for the Ninth Circuit noted that Unocal consultants had repeatedly warned corporate officers as early as 1995 that it was common for forced labor to be used on the project, and that villagers who resisted working for Unocal were either imprisoned, beaten or executed by the military. The judge also "quoted extensively from depositions, company records, consultants reports and State Department cables" to demonstrate that Unocal and "its partners" knew for many years "human-rights abuses" were being committed and that such atrocities had benefited the Unocal project.[6] Unocal and its shareholders profited handsomely from the enslavement of the villagers, and obtained their natural resources, land, labor and lives in the bargain, a nice income and wealth transfer scheme.

The case got the attention of President George W. Bush. Being an old oil man, and sympathetic to the industry, he had Attorney General John Ashcroft file a brief with the court in which the villager's attempt to seek compensation for their sufferings was ridiculed. Ashcroft argued that the case should be dismissed. The judge rejected his line of reasoning.

Despite the intervention of Bush and his attorney general, justice was served when Unocal agreed to settle the case out of court in early 2005. Because of a confidentiality agreement, we may never know exactly what dollar amount the villagers received. Then again it appears Unocal paid the fifteen victims over $15 million. We know this because the oil and gas giant sued its insurance companies and demanded they cover the reimbursement. These companies "only reimburse claims beyond an initial loss of $15 million," suggesting the settlement was at least that much or higher.[7]

Indonesia

In the United States, dirt poor Indonesians sued ExxonMobile over human rights abuses that are taking place over a natural gas field in Indonesia. The government of that country supplied soldiers as guards for the gas field. Represented by the International Labor Relations Fund (ILRF), the suit accused the corporation of aiding and abetting the Indonesian military in acts of "torture and murder" against villagers. In their lawsuit, the plaintiffs insisted that Exxon Mobil had "provided barracks where the military tortured detainees and lent heavy equipment such as excavators" to "dig mass graves."[8] According to at least one witness, the corporation also obtained the land of some villagers very cheaply, while others received no compensation whatsoever, suggesting perhaps that people may have been compelled through strong arm tactics to sell their land on the cheap, or lose it with no compensation. Living near the pipeline is a "60-year-old villager named Abdullah" who lamented, "I used to own land here." "When they built the plant, we had to move. Now I pay rent."[9]

As might be expected, the U.S. government under President George W. Bush went to court to have the case dismissed on the grounds that "it could hamper the war on terrorism by alienating the Indonesian government."[10] Apparently Bush did not understand that supporting acts of terrorism in the name of fighting a war against terrorism is an absurdity and a contradiction, and a lie, but such a political stance benefits his Big Oil buddies and their continuous quest to keep profits rolling upward.

Throughout the world, with globalization legislatively enacted on behalf of publicly traded corporations, an ever-increasing number of people are producing more and earning less. Worldwide poverty is on the increase, and as the years roll by, the trend will continue to grow given the parasitic structure of the corporate economic system. With their stranglehold on the alleged benefits of free trade ideology (which is in theory supposed to benefit the people of the world), and with the power and favors of government officials easily purchased, our corporate heroes will continue to extract more and more income and wealth from the citizens of the world through whatever schemes and rationales they are able to devise. The events outlined above in Mexico, Burma and Indonesia only scratch the surface of what has been occurring throughout the world.

Globalization and Privatization

In theory, globalization is a process whereby goods and services are freely allowed to move across international borders without any legal barriers such as quotas or tariffs or government subsidies provided to producers. Unfortunately for the people of the world, the real impact of globalization is quite different from the theory. There are some naïve people who believe that this policy is all about providing goods and services to consumers who otherwise would not have them. One assumption is that somehow people earning a dollar a day in Africa are going to be able to purchase a $39 blender, or a $50 cell phone with monthly payments. That is a silly assumption. Some alleged experts are actually foolish enough to think that technology is the great driving force behind globalization. Such people believe that somebody on their cell phone in the Artic wants to be able to talk to somebody on their cell phone in South Africa, and the demand for such items, and other services, is what drives corporate leaders to insist on the enactment of free trade policies. These true believers are dead wrong. The quest for always rising corporate profits is what drives the push for globalization, and don't allow anybody to convince you to believe otherwise. The goods and services wouldn't be provided if the earnings weren't there, especially in always increasing amounts, and there would be very few people demanding globalization without sufficient profits. Providing goods and services via free trade policies is simply a necessary burden coincident to achieving the ultimate objective. Such an objective has a very dark side which is rarely ever discussed in public.

In an economy that relies heavily and increasingly on transfers of wealth from people to corporations, embracing the policy of free trade represents the ultimate in these transfer schemes by fitting neatly into how the corporate economic structure operates. CEOs just love it when their companies can freely move jobs from one country to another, because this ability allows them to consistently cut the price of labor and avoid costly environmental and labor regulations in the United States, and this helps our heroes to continuously raise earnings. That's the primary benefit of free trade. On top of that, corporations are rich enough to purchase rules and regulations from governments across international frontiers, and under globalization policies it has become even easier for these businesses to push for laws in foreign countries giving them control over the labor and resources of lesser developed nations, just ask the people of Indonesia, Burma and Mexico.

As mentioned earlier, the International Monetary Fund (IMF) and the World Bank were established to help war-torn nations rise out of the destruction of World War II. However, during the past forty years or so, these organizations have primarily become tools of multinational corporations in their acts of financial genocide against the world's people. When countries borrow funds from them, or receive loans brokered by them, two of the stipulations typically are that the borrowing countries must enact economic reforms that include opening up their markets to free trade and privatizing government services. These two policies coincide with the corporate requirement for always rising profits, but sharply diverge from the needs of people.

Privatization provides ample opportunities for corporations to constantly increase earnings because they are able to raise the prices captive consumers pay for goods and services almost always provided more cheaply and more efficiently by public institutions unencumbered by the desperate need to incessantly jack up earnings. Corporate officers are like rabid dogs foaming at the mouth over privatizing government services, and not because they believe they can provide goods and services better than governments, but because they need this policy enacted throughout the world in order to help keep earnings, dividends and share prices surging upward. For corporations, enactments of such policies are badly needed gold mines.

Argentina, for example, already heavily in debt and under pressure from the IMF, adopted privatization and opened its borders to free trade in 1989. A decade later, the economy lay prostrate in a state of economic depression reminiscent of the Great Depression of the 1930s in the United States. At one time, Argentina had been the most prosperous nation in all of Latin America. By 2002, over half the population was surviving on less than three dollars a day. Officially nearly 20 percent were without jobs.[11] The economic crisis was the worst in its history.[12] By adopting such policies, the government left its citizens, along with the resources of the nation, defenseless against the predations of foreign corporations.

With the economy fair game, foreign investors rapidly purchased Argentine businesses. "From flour mills to car manufacturers" overseas corporations purchased the "commanding heights" of the economy. In 1995, six of the ten biggest banks were owned by citizens of Argentina, but by 2002, only one was locally held. The economy grew 8 percent annually for the first few years, but employment and wages began to crumble almost immediately. Even during the few brisk years, in the officially measured sectors of the economy, net job creation was zero. The reason was simple. Foreign corporations managed to transfer much of the wealth and income of working Argentines to their shareholders back home. Failure to reinvest enough of it in the country acted as a drag on job creation. Output per employee rose dramatically, but in large part, this was brought about because increasing numbers of people were forced to work more while earning less under their new corporate masters. In just a few years, the number of unemployed people began to rise as their jobs and wages were transferred into dividends to be spent by rich shareholders of foreign nations.[13]

The government also privatized and sold electric, water and gas utilities, telephone companies, railroads, airports, airlines and subways. The postal service was also privatized.[14] Almost all of the time, if not always, privatization means lower service, higher rates and less employee compensation, which reduces the demands for goods and services. A French company, for example, purchased a large share of the water systems, and then raised the price of water by 400 percent in some areas.[15] The difference between the old and the new wage and price standards were used to provide higher dividends to rich foreign shareholders than would otherwise have been the case.

From far away, modern day buccaneers spied the easy booty and decided to get in on the lucrative action. Foreign corporations found it easy to cultivate cozy and profitable relationships with government officials by developing an extensive "web of bribes, subsidies, deals and swindles" that enabled them to steal the riches of Argentina from its now helpless citizens. Corporations such as IBM and Citibank were among the brigands that took part in the plundering. A good example of the corruption was provided by Aerolineas Argentinas, a profitable public airline that the government sold to Iberia, a Spanish corporation. In order to complete the sale, the state had to "sweeten the deal" by swallowing "almost $1 billion in debt." How much money may have been used to bribe government officials for such generous terms may never be known. Iberia sold all of the assets of the airline and "gutted the company with dubious accounting tricks." A few years after the purchase, to keep the airline from closing down, the government had to provide Iberia with nearly a billion dollars more, which it obtained from lenders. Not long afterwards, the Spanish company faced trouble again and the public had to come to the rescue by borrowing another $93 million in order to keep the airline operating. Meanwhile, big hunks of public investments and airline profits magically disappeared into a labyrinth of private accounts, foreign banks, higher dividends and share prices, and left the government holding debts amounting to three times the original sale price of the old public airline, a nearly dead carcass it no longer even owned.[16]

As should be expected, the privatization and free trade schemes which are designed to transfer income and wealth from working people to affluent shareholders, also led to rising unemployment and declining demand. As the economy began to implode during the middle to late 1990s, and with tax revenues dropping, the country needed to attract more and more overseas investors in order to pay the principal, as well as the always accumulating interest, on its foreign loans. In order to entice foreigners into purchasing government bonds, interest rates had to be gradually pushed above 16 percent. At such rates, the debt of Argentina was a jackpot of seemingly endless riches for many buyers, such as Citibank and Chase Manhattan.[17] Unfortunately for the people of Argentina, the rising interest rates only served to accelerate the economy's deterioration.

Things got so bad, tax revenues that normally went to schools and other public services were diverted to pay the interest on the debt. The government also reformed the health insurance system in order to find savings that were used to make payments on the interest. Rich foreign shareholders were reaping huge profits by sucking the captive citizens of Argentina dry, including school children and the sick and the aged, but they were by then scrapping the bottom of the barrel, or so it appeared.

By the year 2000, public officials were forced to appeal to the IMF to help it secure loans in order to help pay just the interest on its mushrooming debt. Before it could receive the funds, the organization demanded the government restructure much of its economy.[18] An agreement was reached that forced officials to reduce "salaries under the government's emergency employment program by 20 percent, from $200 a month to $160," slash the salaries of public employees by 12 to 15 percent, and reduce both private and public retirement pensions by 13 percent.[19] Demands were also made on the government to slice the budget deficit from $5.3 billion (in US dollars) in 2000 to $4.1 billion the following year. The demand sector had already been crushed by the privatization and free trade income transfer scams. Common sense suggested that there could only be one result from the economic madness imposed on Argentina by IMF pro-corporate ideologues.[20] In the year 2000, the unemployment rate hovered around 16 percent.[21] Predictably, by March 2001, GDP had dropped more than 2 percent from the previous year.[22] And by September 2002, the official unemployment rate had risen to nearly 20 percent and was likely much higher. The economy had simply collapsed.

Massive protests occurred in Argentina over the dismal results of the failed economic policies. In order to fend off its hungry and unemployed citizens, and to continue with its IMF imposed strategies, the government allegedly engaged in the torture of protesters. Other people were killed.[23]

Typically, the IMF dismisses criticism that its free market policies do not work by blaming "local corruption and lack of financial sophistication."[24] In most cases, the corruption of governments has big business origins, and this is the normal corporate behavior, not the exception.

Political and financial corruption are principal corporate strategies used to persuade government officials to privatize public services, as well as obtaining government business with remarkably high profits, and all at the public expense. In the book *Blue Gold: The Fight to Stop the Corporate Theft of the World's Water*, author's Maude Barlow and Tony Clarke revealed that judges of Grenoble, France came to the conclusion that the city's water service had been privatized in 1989 at a cost of 19 million Francs, generously given "to the campaign of Mayor Alain Caigon" by Suez, the giant French water corporation. Eventually, the mayor and a Suez officer were thrown into prison for their roles in the scam. In another case in France, the former mayor of the city of Angouleme was also convicted of accepting bribes from corporations seeking "public service concessions" from that city. This case involved the giant water-corporation Vivendi, which along with Suez are the two largest water corporations in the world. Also in France, executives of another water corporation were found guilty of "bribing the mayor of St-Denis on the Ile de la Re'union in order to obtain a water contract." Construction units of the water corporations Suez, Bouygues, and Vivendi have been the subject of a major judicial investigation over allegations that they successfully conspired to work together as a cartel from 1989 and 1996 in the construction of public schools in France while excluding other bidders. A report from the World Bank concluded that the process of privatization "can create corrupt incentives." The report also concluded that "...firms that make payoffs may expect not only to win the contract or the privatisation [sic] auction," but they are also able "to obtain sufficient subsidies, monopoly benefits, and regulatory laxness in the future."[25] There are plenty of other examples of corporate corruption.

In Bolivia, under pressure from the International Monetary Fund, the government sold the public water system of the city of Cochabamba to the buccaneers of International Waters Limited (IWL), which calls London, England its home port. However, the company is a subsidiary of a large U.S. construction company —Bechtel.[26] Shortly after taking possession, the folks who managed IWL tried to make a financial killing from their captive market when they raised the price of water by 35 percent. This sparked protests from tens of thousands of victims and then in April 2000, the Bolivian military attacked the protesters, killing at least two, and perhaps up to six, while leaving 175 injured.[27] The national government proclaimed curfews and "suspended civil liberties.[28] Within a few days the government put an end to the scam when it cancelled IWL's contract.[29]

This transfer of income conspiracy was more devious than meets the eye. The *Canberra Times* asked the most important question: "Why did IWL raise water prices?" The rationale was that the captains of Bechtel wanted to pay for a profitable project called the Misicuni Dam, of which it is part owner. Captive customers such as the water users of Cochabamba usually do not finance private capital projects. That job usually goes to investors and corporations who are willing to risk their money in projects in the hopes of obtaining profits.[30] However, our heroes at Bechtel were not telling the truth. According to investigative reporter Greg Palast the project did not even exist. Perhaps the buccaneers at Bechtel decided that it would not be prudent to entice investors to a project that was imaginary. They might become angry at the fraud, and in many countries such schemes are not legal. The IWL also failed to show evidence that it had any funds directed to Bolivia to build the dam.[31] This suggests that this phony story was concocted with an eye toward obtaining something for nothing for the owners of Bechtel and at the expense of the working citizens of the city of Cochabamba, Bolivia.[32]

For Bolivians, according to Palast, the worst part may be that IWL obtained the public water company for nothing, apparently because of the political connections of its partner, former Bolivian president Jaime Pasamora. At the time, he was allied to then President Banza.[33] If these allegations are true, then the people of Bolivia were betrayed by the politicians who stole a water company and allied themselves with Bechtel in an effort to obtain something for nothing. If any money and other perks changed hands to facilitate this arrangement, there's no telling how much might have been involved, but a person can reasonably suspect there was plenty to go around.

Although the IMF has always insisted that private companies will always perform better than public companies, the people of Bolivia know this is not true based on their experience with Bechtel. The mounting evidence is that corporations cannot operate water systems and other utilities better than public institutions any more than rocks can swim across oceans for the simple reason that corporations must find whatever means necessary to ensure ever-increasing profits, dividends and stock prices. The results of privatization schemes are typically reduced supplies, service and maintenance, along with higher prices for customers, and lower pay and benefits for employees. What Bechtel did with the water system to the people of the city of Cochabamba has been replayed, and will continued to be repeated, throughout the world, so long as the corporate business structure is the prime beneficiary of privatization schemes.

The government of England has privatized water services for many years and citizens have had to pay for this transfer of income scam with higher prices. Northumbrian Water, a subsidiary of the water giant Suez, increased water rates by 110 percent from 1989 to 1995. During these years, the salary of its CEO rose by 150 percent and the profits enjoyed by the corporation grew 800 percent. Also in England, the price of water jumped an average of 106 percent between 1989 and 1995 while earnings for private water companies skyrocketed 692 percent. Water disconnection's rose 50 percent during the same period. In France, customer fees have increased 150 percent since water services were privatized. Corporate held water systems also have higher prices than public water systems throughout that country. Some households in India now pay 25 percent of their yearly income for water due to privatization.[34]

Some privatized water corporations have been compelled to scrimp on regulations, most likely due to their need for ever-rising earnings, and this has ensured that the environmental records of many of them are terrible. In England, from 1989 to 1997, a number of private companies, "Anglian, Northumbrian, Severn Trent, Wessex, and Yorkshire Water, were successfully prosecuted 128 times for violations ranging from water leakages to illegal sewage disposals."[35] Both Bechtel and Enron have been involved in the water privatizing industry. According to the U.S. Environmental Protection Agency, Bechtel was blamed for 730 spills of hazardous materials while Enron has been credited with 76 spills, and some of these were very large. Azurix, formerly a subsidiary of Enron, failed to successfully manage its privatized water system for the city of Bahia Blanca, located 420 miles southwest of Buenos Aires in Argentina. Residents complained bitterly about water quality and limited water pressure during the year 2000. Officials warned citizens "that their tap water was contaminated with bacteria due to an algae outbreak in the city's reservoir. For months, the water had a bad odor and taste."[36] From the Philippines to Great Britain, the horror stories about the privatization of public water companies have been hauntingly similar.

Many if not the vast majority of publicly managed companies are generally far superior to their private rivals when comparing the environmental records and efficiencies of utilities. Since 1998, Chile has partially privatized many of its public water companies. Rather than sell these companies to profit seekers, however, they instead sold shares to private corporations. Before implementing the policy, a 1996 study by the World Bank listed Chile's public water companies as being "model examples of efficiency."[37]

The biggest public utility in the world is SABESP. The company serves 22 million citizens living in the Brazilian state of Sao Paulo. Since 1995, it has gone from providing treated water to 84 percent of the region's population to 91 percent, while the number of citizens receiving sewage services rose from 64 to 73 percent. The company also expanded its ecological commitments by participating in the biggest environmental undertaking of its kind in South America when it helped to clean up the much polluted Tiett River. These gains were all achieved during a period when it reduced its operating budget by 45 percent. Now that's efficient![38]

By a wide margin, the results demonstrate that the privatization of government services is all too often bad for citizens, yet great for corporations and their rich shareholders. Privatizing public services hasn't worked very well the vast majority of times it has been attempted. And even many free market ideologues know this to be a fact, or at least they should know. All of which must make people wonder why it is that the policy is still being forced down the throats of so many of the citizens of the world. The answer is simple. Politically and economically powerful corporations, as well as their affluent shareholders, their easily purchased politicians, their corporate news media, and their international organizations such as the IMF and the World Bank, want this policy of disguised piracy implemented wherever possible in order to make it easier to legally rob working people of as much of their income and wealth as is possible. Let's face it.

In a world in which it is getting more and more difficult to expropriate income and wealth from working people because they have already been robbed of so much of it already, and during a period of time when it has become increasingly necessary and difficult to achieve constantly rising earnings, public companies and their captive customers represent another source of easy money.

Since privatization policies mainly act as mechanisms to transfer income and wealth from those who perform labor to wealthy folks, it stands to reason that a policy of globalization should also be designed for the same purpose since the underlying philosophical rationalization of both is the free trade doctrine. Among the principals that serve as the foundation of this theory is a bias toward small governments that do not interfere in the economy, except to provide certain public services. Originally the doctrine had an even stricter anti-corporate bias. Corporations were never permissible except under a few unusual circumstances, such as providing shipping insurance during times of war. No corporations were ever to be allowed in any manufacturing enterprise under the original doctrine, and this was written by the poster boy of conservative economic thinking, Adam Smith. And of course in order for free trade to actually work as a policy there have always been a number of other uncomfortable, unrealistic and totally ridiculous assumptions and caveats that serve as the foundation of the theory, such as manufacturing facilities cannot be moved from one country to another, and each participating country must have full employment. Of course, another principal is that all businesses in each industry operate in much the same way and as efficiently as their rivals, or else they perish! This means that multinational corporate farms are thought to operate under the same conditions as a Mexican corn farmer working his one or two acres with little or no capital to invest in production. In theory, the small time Mexican farmer is considered to be the equal of any multinational corporate farm backed by investors with hundreds of millions, perhaps tens of billions, of dollars, with a home market protected by a corporate friendly U.S. government, and with considerable political and military power purchased in the Mexican political markets to be used in case the farmer is overly obstinate in his desires to stay on his land. Of course, all the Mexican farmer has to do is manage his farm more efficiently and he will put his U.S. rivals out of business if they don't shape up! Oh, and we can't forget the principal that no person possesses any political power anywhere. Government, remember is always small and stays out of economic issues for the most part, and it never takes sides in any struggle. Some of these underlying principals are so comical that it has to make a person wonder how any-body could insist on the enactment of free trade policies, especially given the most recent evidence showing how harmful it really is. However, when preach-ing the virtues of free trade, it is always best for some people to ignore those un-pleasant details that might pose a threat to what is in reality an income and wealth transfer scheme. Many holy persons of the free trade cult preach its vir-tues while ignoring its vices because their wallets and bank accounts some times rely heavily on corporate dollars to stay fat. Not too many well trained dogs bite the hands that feed them. We have already seen what globalization and privat-ization did for the people of Argentina in just a few short years. And still the preachers preach on, perhaps because they too must eat.

IMF officers, U.S. officials, CEOs and international bankers continue to ar-gue that the key to lifting the poor out of their economic misery is to kill infla-tion, implement a policy of free trade, weaken or eliminate government regulations, destroy labor unions, and privatize government services. In effect, un-muzzle and unleash the corporations of the world and let them freely run wild over the citizens of every country, and somehow everybody will be better off than before. Such a policy is like heaven for the rich since they typically per-form no labor, but it is more like a living purgatory for working people. With the exception of curbing inflation, these actions usually have had disastrous consequences. As mentioned earlier, many countries of Latin America adopted some of these reforms back in the late 1980s and early 1990s. These nations ex-perienced a five percent drop in their combined Gross Domestic Product (GDP) from 1998 to 2002.[39] Nowadays, tens of millions of people in these countries have higher productivity rates than just a few years ago, and they are producing more goods and services per capita than ever before. And in spite of this, they are still being pushed into greater poverty, and increasingly so, under the globaliza-tion scheme.

Ernesto Alonzo was a coffee grower in Nicaragua. A successful farmer most of his life, by the year 2000, the 56 year old possessed a ruined farm be-cause of the free trade policies pushed by the IMF. The coffee that he grew was nearly valueless. The bank wanted to seize his farm. A worldwide glut of coffee had reduced prices for his coffee beans, but Alonzo and other coffee growers weren't the only people hit hard by the disaster created by globalization. Twenty-five million families in the region depended on the harvesting of coffee for their livelihoods. Among many coffee related jobs, some people worked on farms, others transported the coffee, while some workers processed it for export. Most of these people lived in poverty even when coffee bean prices were high. As prices dropped, more than 540,000 jobs in the coffee industry were lost in Central America, which forced many former coffee workers to immigrate north to the United States. And nowadays, those who remain are living in shanty towns, in tents along the road side, reduced to begging anyone for food. "'We don't have food. We don't have work. We don't have anything,'" said Marilla Blandia, a seventeen year old. As she said this, she held her eighteen month old son in her arms. He suffered from diarrhea and flies covered his face.[40] By March 2002, 700,000 people of Guatemala, Honduras, El Salvador and Nicaragua faced starvation, while another one million or so suffered from grim food shortages.[41] The price of free trade for the people of Central America was famine.

On the surface, it appeared that part of the problem for those who made their living in the industry was the worldwide glut of coffee due to the emergence of Vietnam and other countries as producers. However, the real problem for these people was that the IMF and the World Bank pressured debtor countries to over-produce cash crops to enhance their export earnings. For example, the World Bank encouraged the "expansion of coffee acreage" in Vietnam and Indonesia.[42] This helped those governments to pay their debts. Corporations benefited from the over-production because they purchased coffee more cheaply, allowing them to enhance their earnings, but this was only achieved by producing absolute misery for the millions of people who actually worked to overproduce the coffee. On the other hand, along with handsomely compensated corporate leaders who somehow got credit for improving their bottom lines, affluent shareholders reaped all of the benefits while working people starved.

Although the price farmers received for their coffee stunningly dropped over 80 percent from 1997 to 2002, the cost to consumers fell considerably less.[43] During the same years, the average retail price of ground roast coffee slid only 27 percent.[44] The difference between the new lower prices paid to farmers and what major corporations actually charged consumers and businesses resulted in greater earnings than would otherwise have been the case. The tea and coffee division of Sara Lee earned $495 million dollars in 2001 on sales of $2.9 billion. According to Sara Lee spokesperson Joost den Haan, this was its best financial result in five or more years. The coffee section of Proctor and Gamble (P & G) garnered about $1 billion in sales in 2001, "a record year." The folks at P & G refused to comment on how much earnings the company gained through coffee sales, and neither did Kraft or Nestle. Nestle did report that "coffee sales by volume hit a record in 2001."[45] These were incredibly high sales and earnings considering that the United States was mired in a recession for most of that year and demand should have been slack. The following year, even as the producers of coffee were dying of starvation along roadsides throughout Central America, the *New York Times* reported that Procter and Gamble expected a nearly 10 percent increase in earnings, resulting in second quarter dividends of $1.10 a share, up from $1.03 a year earlier.[46]

In the early 1960s', a deal had been struck that "imposed strict limits" on coffee exporting nations, which was supported by the United States as a defense against encroaching communism. Allowing people to work and live at subsistence levels was thought to have helped arrest the yearnings of the people of the region for a communist economy. When the Berlin Wall fell in 1989, the United States altered its position and campaigned for greater free trade. Communism had been slain, but this event allowed for the additional growth of unfettered corporate domination in economics and politics—world-wide. Coffee producing nations put an end to their "stockpiling programs" that had helped to control the supply. Nowadays, Procter & Gamble, Nestle and other large corporations use their considerable international knowledge and economic clout to purchase straight from small farmers.[47] This is a huge problem for growers since P&G, Sara Lee, Philip Morris and Nestle control about half of the worldwide coffee market.[48] This gives them considerable leverage over the prices they pay for coffee, as well as what they charge. Given the large number of farmers and the small number of powerful institutional buyers, the IMF demand to overproduce coffee helped these corporations to put even more downward pressure on the prices they paid for it, while maintaining relatively high retail costs, all of which was very helpful at keeping dividends rising, while simultaneously crushing the people who actually produce the crop.[49]

Under IMF and World Bank pressures, Central American farmers who cultivated food crops turned to growing coffee for export, which helped to glut the market even more. But nobody could eat the coffee later when the worldwide market collapsed. The policy of globalization was all wrong for people, but it worked out great for foreign corporations.

The citizens of Central America would have really benefited from an economic development plan that emphasized the growth and nurturing of a sustainable and ecologically sound economy in which people produced food, goods and services for local consumption. One of those nasty stipulations of free trade theory, seemingly always and deliberately left unsaid by the well paid priests of globalization, is that money and production are always immobile. They can't be moved from one country to another, so such a local development plan would have been in harmony with the complete free trade theory. On the other hand, the multi-national corporations of the world would not have benefited from such a strategy for economic progress because they would have been left out of the loop, which isn't very profitable, and therefore not much help at ensuring constantly rising earnings. And this may very well account for why IMF officials and their political and corporate allies reject authentic economic development plans, and continue to cling only to certain parts of a failed and discredited hypothesis developed more than two hundred years ago when the world was much different than it is today.

The continent of Africa provides yet another glaring example of how people are suffering under the expanding globalization of the corporate economic system. The area south of the Sahara desert is perhaps best known for where the fictional character Tarzan lived, of genocides, the AIDS epidemic, corrupt governments and overwhelming poverty. For the most part black Africans seem to have monumental problems that they are unable to solve on their own, or so it appears on the surface. In the good old days, sometime after the European conquest and before the independence movements of the 1960s, the primary problem black Africans had was white people. Nowadays, at least a significant portion of the problems faced by Africans are foreign corporations and international organizations like the IMF and the World Bank, which coincidently are mostly owned and managed by relatively well-to-do white people. Africans also suffer from the notions of free trade, which is a concept developed by white people, and mostly pushed onto others by white folks, as well.

Ivory Coast is one of the world's major producers of cocoa. The people at the World Bank and the IMF pressured the African country to abandon fixed prices for their raw product in favor of free market prices. When this occurred, a European cocoa industry executive remarked, "It is somewhat ironic that while European and American agriculture is protected, we should argue to developing countries that they should be fully exposed to the vagaries of the market."[50] It doesn't take a psychic to figure out who benefited from this action, and in which direction the price of freshly farmed cocoa headed.

In Ivory Coast, most cocoa farms are "small family owned businesses," often located in remote areas, far removed from information pertaining to the price of cocoa. Some farms can be reached "only by driving on flooded and crater-filled dirt roads and hiking for miles through dense forests." Being so remote, as well as poverty stricken, brings many problems. The price of cocoa in London, England or New York City means virtually nothing to the farmer living in Ivory Coast. When news arrives it is more often than not already much too old to be of much use to the farmers. Remote locations are one the reasons why the International Cocoa Organization, with 42 member nations, concluded that cocoa farmers were persistently underpaid. But the group also declared that Ivory Coast's mostly illiterate cultivators simply lacked the basic knowledge of the market to barter with hard-bargaining commodity buyers, and this was another factor that left them persistently underpaid."[51]

That the farmer knows little of international cocoa prices works in favor of exporters and buyers. Also, because of their numbers, it is unlikely that these farmers will ever be able to act in concert when attempting to sell their product. On the other hand, it is possible for a few buyers and exporters to conspire together to obtain the lowest possible price from the farmers. It's even possible for one or more corporations to dominate the market for a while. One London cocoa trade firm, Armajaro, was thought to have purchased somewhere between 150,000 and 200,000 tons of cocoa, which was more than 5 percent of the worldwide total. The company had bought cheaply, and because of a civil war in Ivory Coast that interrupted cocoa production and sent prices higher on the international markets, sold dear and procured a profit of $90 million in a short time. Cocoa farmers, however, did not share in the increased price of cocoa.[52] This is because they lacked the means necessary to work in concert together to purchase, or withhold, 5 percent of the world's cocoa supply. Had they the power to do so, it is the dirt poor farmers who would have been enriched by $90 million, but they did not possess the knowledge, the clout, or the market and political power others possess. And so farmers could obtain fair prices for their cocoa if prices were fixed at relatively high levels. Their standards of living would correspondingly rise.

By Western standards, cocoa farmers and laborers live below all conceivable standards of poverty. One farmer, Mr. Kabore, referring to growers like himself said, "'We hold the cocoa economy in our hands,'" but "'we are forced to live like rats, hidden away in our homes.'"[53]

A laborer on a cocoa farm can do much worse. Some earn only $135 per year. It is not uncommon for adults to receive only 50 cents or less per day. And yes, child labor is normal in the cocoa fields. One child earned only four cents per day. The work is backbreaking, but it keeps them from the bottom rung of the economic ladder in Africa.[54]

On the other hand, intense poverty and backbreaking labor for black Africans ensures higher dividends and rising stock prices for the mostly white shareholder classes. By holding one share of Nestle or the Hershey Foods Corporation for one quarterly period, without expending a single calorie of energy on labor of any kind, anybody could expropriate more money than farmers or laborers earn working in the cocoa fields for two days, sixteen hours per day.

As poverty was laying waste child and adult laborers along with farmers in the cocoa fields of the Ivory Coast, Nestle reported a 79 percent increase in profits for the first half of 2002 compared to the first half of the previous year, on sales of $29.5 billion.[55] On July 23, 2001 the *Wall Street Journal* reported the Hershey Foods Corporation enhanced its net income for the second quarter of the year 2001 by 31 percent. They did this on increased sales of 7.5 percent. In part, this increase in earnings was due to "favorable commodity costs." The result was a transfer of income payment to shareholders of 38 cents per share which was up from 29 cents a year earlier.[56] Remarkably, this run of good fortune occurred during a recession in the United States when demand for goods and services should have been slack. The following year the *New York Times* reported Hershey had enlarged its third quarter 2002 profits by 1.9 percent. This increased the transfer of income payment, or dividend, to "89 cents per share from 88 cents per share" garnered during the third quarter of 2001. However, according to the *Times*, "Excluding one-time items, third quarter earnings were $139.8 million, or $1.01 a share." One analyst expected Hershey to pay 99 cents per share.[57] A child making four cents per day would need to work 25 days, perhaps sixteen hours per day, to earn that kind of money.

The free floating prices demanded of Ivory Coast by the IMF and the World Bank certainly helped corporations and their shareholders achieve higher earnings than would normally have been the case. But this feat was only accomplished by making living conditions worse for those who actually performed the backbreaking labor in the cocoa fields as another free trade policy had once again freely transferred income and wealth from working people to rich shareholders. That's the way the leaders of the corporate world want to continue to guide the rest of the world's people, because such policies are always in favor of the mostly white, rich shareholder class.

In the early summer of 2005, at a meeting of the Organization of American States, even as hundreds of thousands of poverty stricken Bolivians forced the resignation of their latest president and threatened civil war unless the privatization of the country's natural gas supplies was reversed by nationalizing them, no doubt on behalf of his self proclaimed "base," President George W. Bush boldly called for more free trade and privatization throughout the hemisphere. Unless he is a completely brain dead idiot, there can be little doubt that the president already knew that free trade and privatization were failed schemes at ending poverty for many people, and he knew poverty expanded under these policies. As a long-time resident and former governor of Texas, he had a front row seat as these policies enriched his "base" at the expense of working people.

It is in Texas, along the border with Mexico, that hundreds of thousands of the world's most impoverished people live, victims of a failed policy of free trade established just forty years before the president gave his speech in Bolivia. A free trade zone had been established between the United States and Mexico in 1965. The Mexican government promised to supply cheap labor. "The Mexican Minister of Commerce told the *Wall Street Journal* (May 25, 1967): 'Our idea is to offer an alternative to Hong Kong, Japan and Puerto Rico for free enterprise.'"[58] Supplying cheap labor didn't sound much like an economic development plan, at least not for the workers.

The zone, known as Maquiladora, lies in Mexico along the border with the United States. It is twelve and a half miles wide and extends from coast to coast. Any foreign owned company can establish its production facilities there "virtually tax free and tariff free." Corporations have been able to assemble any products there, and then import them into the United States. And they pay only a minor tax on the value added after the products have been assembled, which is the price of that "cheap" Mexican labor.[59] Not so coincidently, establishing the zone created another source of tax revenue for the Mexican government, which is perhaps why these officials agreed to this economic anti-development plan in the first place. Since 1965, additional free trade zones have been erected throughout Latin America most likely with the same purpose in mind.

Right from the start, among many other industries, corporations moved textile, television, radio, aircraft and toy factories from the USA into the zone, enabling them to transfer the difference in employee compensation between the old and the new rates into the wallets of shareholders. These hardy pioneers included "Litton Industries, Transitron, Motorola, Fairchild, Hughes Aircraft, and General Electric." There were seventy-two U.S. factories in the zone in 1967.[60] The number gradually rose to 3,485 thirty-one years later.

The rate of pay for most people working in the zone has always been remarkably low, while benefits have always been largely non-existent. According to at least one survey, in the year 2003, an assembly line worker in Mexico earned $1.47 an hour.[61] Factory wages have dropped 21 percent throughout Mexico since the signing of the North American Free Trade Agreement (NAFTA) in 1994 between Mexico, Canada and the United States, and this has left workers in the zone worse off than before the treaty.

Employees often work up to sixteen hours per day. Despite their labors, they have always received such low wages that it has left them at all times with little choice but to go home to shameful poverty. The houses of these people are typically constructed of trash obtained from the factories. These dwellings are typically made of throwaway wooden pallets, cardboard and corrugated tin. Rocks often hold down the pieces of each house. Gaping holes can be found in the walls. Running water is non-existent.[62] Floors are made of dirt. Electricity does not exist. Their bathrooms consist of communal outhouses that spill over when nearby rivers flood. And their children go to school in buildings made up entirely of cardboard taken from the garbage of the factories.

People who work in the zone live in unincorporated villages. About half of them are located just across the border from Mexico in the United States. In George W. Bush country, otherwise known as the proud state of Texas, there are 400,000 Maquiladora workers, along with hundreds of thousands of family members, who live in the midst of this shameful poverty. Another 200,000 of these workers live in California, New Mexico, and Arizona. Roughly 600,000 live in similar conditions in the north of Mexico.

Most of the people who work in the various free trade zones throughout Latin America are young women sixteen to twenty-four years of age.[63] However, it is common for these factories (known as Maquilas) to hire children as young as twelve.[64] According to the Reverend Philip Wheaton, "For those lucky enough to find jobs, working conditions in the Maquilas are extremely demanding and tedious, requiring the acute dexterity and excellent health which only youth provides."[65] Young women can be more docile than men and easier to order around, and this creates a work climate in which managers have nearly infinite power to be more demanding and abusive of employees than elsewhere. A study by the Committee for the Defense of Human Rights in Honduras, revealed "that 40 percent of the women who work in Maquilas in that country are subject to physical mistreatment like being pushed, slapped, whipped, insulted, screamed at, hit on the head, or forced to stand in the sun."[66] According to the testimony of Lesly Rodriquez, a Maquila worker,

They don't let us talk when we work. If they catch us talking to each other, we are punished. The supervisors shout at us and send us home without pay for four or five days at a time. The supervisors are always screaming that we have to work faster. Sometimes they hit us on the head or on the back.[67]

Sexual harassment can become real when young women are working in a plant and they do not have any legally guaranteed rights. And what can women do about this kind of situation? In the Maquiladora Zone of Mexico, women workers of the National O-Ring factory demonstrated in the streets of Tijuana during the 1990s. They had been laid-off because they had filed "sexual harassment" charges against the company "in courts in Tijuana and Los Angeles."[68] However, the zones hold more horror for workers than just low pay, poverty, terrible working conditions, and sexual harassment.

The free trade zones have also provided U.S. based corporations with wonderful opportunities to freely export pollution on a grand scale. The Environmental Protection Agency (EPA) has proven to be a nuisance to our captains of industry. The EPA was established in 1973 to act as an enforcer to ensure that industries did not exceed federally mandated limits of pollution. Reducing contaminants that threaten the environment and human health by fouling our air, land and water can be expensive and cut into earnings. Sometimes it's just easier to avoid these controls by exporting the pollution to other countries because it often does not need to be neatly and safely tucked away in unpopulated areas once there. Instead, people are made to live and work in it and with dire health results.

Chemicals from a closed battery recycling plant seeped up through the ground in the village of Chilpancingo, Mexico. Along with the pollution produced from factories nearby, the toxic wastes of the pits were generally credited with being the primary reason nineteen children of the village were born without brains in 1993 and 1994.[69] Children in Juarez, Mexico have experienced burned skin on their feet and legs when they came into contact with venomous wastes released from the maquilas into open canals that flow through the city. Toxic pollution from these factories threatens the water supplies of both Mexico and the United States.[70] In both countries industrial and human wastes have contaminated the water to such a degree that the levels of disease are significantly greater than their national averages along both sides of the border. According to U.S. health officials, the incidence of hepatitis A and shigellosis, two water born diseases, are three times the U.S. average along the border with Mexico than elsewhere in the country. However, things are even worse on the Mexican side of the national frontier. The city of Juarez suffers around "650 cases of hepatitis A per year, almost 10 times the rate in El Paso." This is because the "treated sewage" of Juarez drifts through canals and transports water blackened by contamination. The pollution travels fifty miles into the farmlands south of the city. Farmers there have complained that the water is no good for irrigating their crops because the pollution makes it unfit to use for growing produce for human consumption. Disease is also a significant problem in the un-incorporated villages that exist on either side of the U.S./Mexican border. A handful of sewage treatment facilities are in use in some of these places, yet not one of them can match the health standards set by the U.S. government.[71]

Despite being paid so little that they are forced to live in houses made of garbage, as well as work and live in toxic environmental conditions, the citizens of the zone have never possessed any job security. Roughly 240,000 jobs in the zone were sent abroad to lower wage countries during the recession of 2001. This official statistic represented nearly one-fifth of the jobs there.[72] Other estimates have suggested that up to 500,000 jobs were outsourced (out of 1.2 million) during the recession.

China, Indonesia, Pakistan, Guatemala, Vietnam or some other such countries usually gain jobs that Mexico loses.[73] While the average wage for an assembly line worker is $1.47 per hour in the maquilas of Mexico, in China the average hourly earnings for doing the same work is $.59 per hour.[74] But wages can drift even lower in China. In 2005, a twenty-six year old employee named Lu Ling said she works for a contractor that produces goods for Nike. She earned $145 a month by working ten hours a day six days a week, but that's hardly the worst that can be found there.[75] Despite an excessive amount of workers, a labor shortage exists in Guangdong province, an area known as the "world's factory." As of the year 2004, wages had not risen in ten years, remaining a paltry $50 per month, despite the yearly growth of inflation. Living conditions are horrendous with 16 people often living in crowded dormitories provided by the corporations, their contractors and subcontractors. Add to that an abundance of on the job injuries, a lack of regard for labor laws by employers and the government, employees often not being paid, and workers unable to form labor unions in the communist nation, and you can understand why people are leaving their poverty laden corporate jobs and going home.[76] Nonetheless, it is possible that this is not the economic and moral bottom of the corporate system.

In 1999, the *Chicago Tribune* reported that the International Confederation of Free Trade Unions (ICFTU) had filmed children working in Sialkot, Pakistan. Boys as young as eight years old sat on bare floors and hunkered down while they worked in cramped, noisy workshops, grinding, filing, polishing and assembling surgical instruments. The boys labored without any sort of protective gear against the "toxic metal dust or the sharp scalpels and scissors" they were producing for export to other countries, "possibly including the United States." Many earned .75 cents or less for working nine hour days. Children under the age of fourteen accounted for about 15 percent of the roughly 50,000 people who worked in the manufacture of surgical instruments in Sialkot. These people suffered many injuries from machines, such as burns from sizzling metal.[77] They also developed "'respiratory problems from inhaling poisonous metal dust,'" according to a report provided by a labor group based in France, Public Services International (PSI).[78] Most of the children worked for subcontractors that supplied the needs of corporations from other countries.

Despite international efforts to eradicate the practice during the last fifteen years or so, child labor has grown according to a report issued by the International Labor Organization (ILO) in the year 2002.[79] War and AIDS are usually cited as reasons for the persistence of child labor. These maladies leave many adults dead and disabled, and force children to work in their place in order to support themselves and their families. However, war has been common in third world countries for decades and centuries. AIDS has been around for over two decades. It isn't a stretch at all to suggest that the rise in child labor throughout the world is primarily due to the continued expansion and needs of the corporate economic system.

Quite often the wages of children determine the wages of adults. As more and younger children enter the work force, their rising numbers depress wages in general. As the compensation plummets, families need more money just to feed themselves, and so they send even younger children to work, which depresses wages further in a seemingly never ending cycle. Within a corporate dominated economy, as it become more difficult to transfer wealth from working people who have less and less of it, more children at younger ages will need to work in order to put downward pressure on wages, and in order for their families to survive. In the Philippines, for example, a 1995 study showed that the age range of child laborers was nine to seventeen years. By April 2002, the range had widened from five to seventeen. The ILO estimated the number of children in the labor force worldwide at 246 million in 2002, and the number is likely to have risen since then.

Corporations hire contractors and subcontractors, who in turn hire children to produce many of the world's products. Hiring contractors and subcontractors has always been a nifty method by which businesses have been able to hide their involvement in the use of children, and thereby help to evade laws against such practices, as well as avoid negative public opinion in their countries of origin. By keeping children employed and in poverty, along with their families, our corporate heroes conveniently transfer the labor of children into higher income and increased dividends, while maintaining a competitive edge over their rivals that do not resort to such barbaric methods.

Throughout the world, like a sword held at our throats, corporations are wielding more and more political and economic power, and are transferring rising amounts of our salaries, wages and other compensation to an affluent group of largely unproductive people. Our financial, health, food and water, educational, political and environmental needs are increasingly in the hands of the few who control and or obtain their wealth and income from major corporations. As time passes along, they need to expropriate a rising amount of each of the above in order to sustain their system. Therefore, increasingly, we are discovering that control over these factors of our lives is shifting more and more to those who wield political, economic and ideological power. The battle for control over human life itself is being fought throughout the world, and the people of the lower 98 percent or so of income earners are losing their fight against a small minority of people.

Economist Frederich Hayek pointed out that whoever controls the rules, "controls all economic activity" and therefore such people and corporations control "...the means for all our ends and must therefore decide which are to be satisfied and which are not," and these are actions that have been occurring for quite some time. Hayek was referring to government ownership of the means of production in his book, *The Road to Serfdom*. Unlike his far more intellectually gifted contemporary, Thorstein Veblen, Hayek was never able to comprehend that there has always existed financial bonds between governments (which is the tool used by corporations to make the rules), the financial markets, big corporate businesses, and wealthy shareholders. He didn't understand that combined they make the vast majority of rules. Hayek also never understood that the modern corporate economy has been developed for the primary purpose of transferring income from the bottom of the world's population to the top. He also erroneously assumed that a capitalist local baker operated his or her business under the same rules as a multi-national corporation. He did not understand who or what represented the real threats to our freedoms.

Since a powerful corporate class now controls or wields heavy influence among all or nearly all governments throughout the world, Hayek's warnings are as pertinent today when used against the corporate economic system as they were in 1944 when he wrote against socialism and communism. Control over the world's resources and labor is the principal method by which those in power intend to continue to achieve ever-increasing profits and dividend payments. Income and wealth inequality will continue to grow relentlessly throughout the world so long as corporate domination of the world's governments and economies continues to expand. It is becoming increasingly obvious that the corporate economic system is leading us on a race to the bottom on the road to corporate serfdom. This warning should not be taken lightly by the citizens of the United States, many of whom have already been among the victims of this parasitic system.

Notes

1. Wright, Scott, *The Globalization of Hope*, EPICA: Washington D.C., 1998, p. 18.
2. Wheaton, Philip E., *Unmasking the Powers in Mexico: The Zapatista Prophetic Alternative to the New World Order*, EPICA: Washington D.C., 1998, pp. 9-10.
3. Edelman, Marc, "Price of Free Trade: Famine," *Los Angeles Times*, March 22, 2002, p. B17.
4. Jordan, Mary and Sullivan, Kevin, "Mexican farmers fear Nafta's influence," *Oregonian*, December 8, 2002, p. A21.
5. Schrage, Elliot, "A Long Way To Justice: What Are Burmese Villagers Doing in a California Court?" *Washington Post*, July 14, 2002, p. B6.
6. Waldman, Peter, "Unocal To Face Trial Over Link To Forced Labor," *Wall Street Journal*, June 12, 2002 p. B1.
7. Eviatar, Daphne, "A Big Win for Human Rights," *The Nation*, May 9, 2005.
8. Banerjee, Abstract to "Lawsuit Says Exxon Aided Rights Abuses," *New York Times*, June 21, 2001, p. C.1.
9. Perlez, Jane, "Indonesia's Guerilla War Puts Exxon Under Seige," *New York Times*, July 14, 2002, no page cited.
10. McConnell, Carolyn, "Unocal Can Be Sued for Atrocities, says Judge," *Yes!*, Winter 2003, p. 9.
11. Faiola, Anothy, "As Argentina Cries, The Party of Evita Sinks Into Turmoil Ruling Peronists Mired in Infighting While Poverty, Joblessness Worsen," *Washington Post*, September 4, 2002, A14.
12. Associated Press, "IMF Gives Argentina Year Extension on Loans," *Washington Post*, September 6, 2002, E4.
13. Healy, Mark A., Seman, Ernesto, "The Costs of Orthodoxy: Argentina was the poster child for austerity and obedience to the IMF formula," *American Prospect Magazine*, Winter 2002.
14. Healy, Mark A., Seman, Ernesto, "The Costs of Orthodoxy: Argentina was the poster child for austerity and obedience to the IMF formula," *American Prospect Magazine*, Winter 2002.
15. Palast, Greg, *The Best Democracy Money Can Buy*, Pluto Press: Virginia, 2002, p. 61.
16. Healy, Mark A., Seman, Ernesto, "The Costs of Orthodoxy: Argentina was the poster child for austerity and obedience to the IMF formula," *American Prospect Magazine*, Winter 2002.
17. Krebsback, Karen, "Crying for Argentina," *USBanker*, New York, Oct 2002, Volume 112, Issue 10, pp. 66-70.

18. Faiola.

19. Palast, p. 60.

20. According to Palast, Argentina had accepted the medicine of the IMF because the government was offered an $8 billion aid package. It was paying "27 billion dollars" per year in interest on a total budget deficit of $128 billion. None of the "$8 billion loan package" left New York City. Instead, it lingered "to pay interest to US creditors holding the Argentine debt," corporations like Citibank.

21. Palast, p. 59.

22. Palast, p. 60.

23. Palast, p. 61-62.

24. *Canberra Times*, "Privatise the rivers, damn the ecology," Sept. 3, 2002, p. A11.

25. Barlow and Clarke, pp. 126-127.

26. *Canberra Times*.

27. Palast puts the figure at six dead. The *Canberra News* reports two died.

28. *Canberra Times*.

29. Palast, pp. 55-56.

30. *Canberra Times*.

31. Palast, p. 55.

32. In 1997, according to Palast, hydrologists and engineers of the World Bank suggested that there was an alternative to the Misicuni Dam that would cost one sixth of the price of the dam. They also argued that the alternative could be paid off without raising the price of water. Therefore, the dam itself was recognized by the World Bank as a pork barrel project far more absurd than any public agency would dare attempt.

33. Palast, p. 55.

34. Barlow, Maude, Clarke, Tony, *Blue Gold: the Fight to Stop the Corporate Theft of the World's Water*, New Press: New York, 2002, pp. 89-90.

35. Barlow and Clark, pp. 125-126.

36. Barlow, Maude, Clarke, Tony, Blue Gold: "The Battle Against Corporate Theft of the World's Water," Polaris Institute, www.polarisinstitute.org/pubs_blue_gold_ch5.html.

37. Barlow and Clark, Polaris Institute.

38. Barlow and Clark, Polaris Institute.

39. Blustein, Paul, "Globally Disillusioned," *Oregonian*, Sept. 22, 2002, p. D1.

40. Miller, Christian T. and Maharaj, Davan, "Coffee's Bitter Harvest: Farmers from Central America to Africa are struggling to survive as oversupply cripples their earnings. Retail prices have fallen far less," *Los Angeles Times*, October 5, 2002, p. A-1.

41. Edelman, Marc, "Price of Free Trade: Famine," *Los Angeles Times*, March 22, 2002, p. B-17.

42. Edelman.

43. Fritsch, Peter, "Bitter Brew: An Oversupply of Coffee beans Deepens Latin America's Woes—Meanwhile, Corporate Profits Rise, as Retail Prices Fall Far Less Than Wholesale—Growers Try Heroin Poppies," *Wall Street Journal*, July 8, 2002, p. A-1.

44. Miller, Christian T., and Maharaj, Davan, "Coffee's Bitter Harvest: Farmers from Central America to Africa are struggling to survive as oversupply cripples their earnings. Retail prices have fallen far less," *Los Angeles Times*, Oct. 5, 2002, p. A-1.

45. Fritsch.

46. No author, *New York Times*, December 12, 2002, p. C-4.

47. Fritsch.

48. Miller and Maharaj.

49. Maize farmers of Central America are in a similar situation as coffee growers. The push toward free trade in the area is squeezing farmers and those who work on their farms. Tariff protection against low cost imports is largely non-existent nowadays in Central America. This leaves indigenous maize farmers unable to compete with "highly subsidized" U.S. corporate farmers.

50. Cowell, Alan, "War inflates Cocoa Prices But Leaves Africans Poor," *New York Times*, Oct. 31, 2002, p. 1.

51. Cowell.

52. Cowell.

53. Cowell.

54. Onishi, Norimitsu, "The Bondage of Poverty That Produces Chocolate," *New York Times*, July 29, 2001, p. 1.

55. "Nestle Reports 79% Increase In Profit During the First Half," *New York Times*, Aug. 22, 2002, p. 1.

56. "Business Brief—Hershey Foods Corp.: Net Income Rises by 31% On a 7.5% Increase in Sales," *Wall Street Journal*, July 23, 2001, p. B.11.

57. Company News, "Hershey Says Exploration of Sale Cut into Profits," *New York Times*, Oct. 18, 2002, p. 3.

58. Melman, Seymour, *Profits Without Production*, Alfred A. Knopf, New York: 1983, p. 27.

59. Melman, pp. 27-28.

60. Melman, p. 28.

61. Linblad, Cristina, Smith, Geri, "Mexico Was NAFTA Worth It?, *BusinessWeek*, Dec. 22, 2003, p. 66.

62. Moore, Molly, "Nightmare in the City of Dreams," Washington..com.

63. Wheaton, p. 10.

64. Moore, Molly.

65. Wheaton, p. 11.

66. Aguilar, Jose Victor and Cavada, Miguel, *Ten Plagues of Globalization*, EPICA: Washington D.C., 2002, p. 42.

67. Aguilar and Cavada, p. 44.

68. Bacon, David, "Mexico: Rebellion on the Border." There are photographs and descriptions of the people of the maquiladoras and their struggle for a just working and living environment, www.igc.apc.org/dbacon/Mexico/border11.htm.

69. Bacon, David.

70. Jackson, Kevin T., "Spirituality as a Foundation for Freedom and Creative Imagination in International Business Ethics," *Journal of Business Ethics*, March 1999, pp. 61-70.

71. Sullivan, Kevin, "Life Along the Rio Grande Defined by a Lack of Water," *Washington Post*, Nov. 3, 2000, p. A-1.

72. Smith, Geri, "The Decline of the Maquiladora," *BusinessWeek*, April 29, 2002, p. 59.

73. Smith, p. 59.

74. Lindblad and Smith, p. 71.

75. Read, Richard, "At one Nike contract plant, no sweatshop, but plenty of sweat," *Oregonian*, June 18, 2005.

76. Johnson, Tim, "Jobs go begging in China 'factory' region," *Oregonian*, September 13, 2004, p. C1.

77. Branigin, William, "Pakistani Youth Become Focus of a Campaign Against Child Labor: Conditions Cited in *Shops Making Surgical Tools*," *Washington Post*, June 6, 1999, p. A16.

78. Branigin, William, "Pakistani Youth Become Focus of a Campaign Against Child Labor: Conditions Cited in Shops Making Surgical Tools," *Washington Post*, June 6, 1999, p. A16.

79. No author listed, "Despite Global Effort, Child Labor Persists on a Massive Scale," *Chicago Tribune*, May 7, 2002.

Chapter Nine

BETRAYAL OF THE PEOPLE:
THE U.S. CORPORATE PLUTOCRACY

W hen the constitution of the United States was written, no mention was made of corporations. There was a reason for this omission, and no it wasn't because the founding fathers were forgetful. The U.S. government was founded on the simple principal that people should determine public policy. Everybody eligible to vote had equal rights under the law, in theory, if not always in practice. Citizens were given the right to vote for candidates that campaigned for public office, and the winners would then be the agents representing the needs and interests of the people who elected them in the halls of government. This is what representative democracy was supposed to be. Our founding fathers would have been shocked if they knew that creations of legislative fiats would have more rights and more political and economic power than people.

Corporations and their wealthy shareholders and CEOs rule nowadays because of their abilities to make purchases in the political markets. The reason for this situation is simple—money, and lots of it expropriated from working people all over the world, and much of which is then given to elected representatives at all levels of government. In the United States, 83 percent of all campaign contributions in the elections of 2002 came from "less than one-tenth of one percent of the population." These were the people in the top income bracket. In the political markets, these extremely rich people and their corporations purchased billions of dollars in "tax breaks, subsidies and the right to exploit public land at ridiculously low prices."[1] They also purchased legislation and regulations enabling them to rip off working people all over the world, such as free trade treaties, and in turn, their ill-gotten gains were used to buy more of the same items in the political markets.

According to CNN reporter Bill Press, "We've never seen stronger proof that Washington today is a cash-and-carry government: You lay down the cash; you walk away with what you want from elected officials."[2] A "cash and carry government" is not a democracy. It is reminiscent of the wealthy aristocratic government that gave rise to the rebellion that freed the United States from British rule. A "cash and carry government" represents the interests of only those who can afford the prices of the legislative and regulatory goodies for sale. Unfortunately for the vast majority of U.S. citizens, only corporations and the very wealthy have sufficient means to purchase legislation and access to politicians in the political markets. Press also noted the following.

> If there ever was any doubt that campaign contributions buy special access and favors from elected officials, there is no longer. Enron would never have been able to cheat its employees and investors, nor would its accounting firm, Arthur Andersen, have been able to cook Enron's books, without the protection they bought from politicians of both parties.[3]

Prior to the public disclosure of the Enron scandal, Arthur Leavitt, chairman of the Securities and Exchange Commission under President Clinton, on three different occasions tried to convince the U.S. Congress to prohibit accounting firms from acting as consultants as well as auditors to corporations. Leavitt knew this arrangement acted as a conflict of interest. Unfortunately, the five biggest accounting firms paid "$53 million to members of congress" between 1990 and 2002 in order to ensure friendly legislation, including the defeat of Leavitt's proposals. This enabled the accounting firm Arthur Andersen to help Enron officials to cook their own books, as well as assist in the subsequent cover up attempt.[4] Other accounting firms also had their fingerprints on the myriad of accounting scandals that came to light during these years.

Enron gave generously to George W. Bush as a presidential candidate, as well as when he was governor of Texas. As mentioned in Chapter Three, Enron officials purchased six secret meetings with the energy task force of Vice President Dick Cheney, which was determining national energy policy at the time. Enron Chief Executive Officer Kenneth Lay received a one-on-one meeting with the vice president. Lay's company also bought the right to help select candidates for the Federal Energy Regulatory Commission, which regulated Enron's business operations. That sounds like a conflict of interest. In India, Enron also paid for the personal intervention of Cheney on behalf of its natural gas plant. In addition, the company also got "Bush and Cheney's opposition to price caps for electricity sales to California."[5] In other words, Enron purchased quite a number of favors just from Bush and Cheney, and none of them benefited anybody but its CEOs and its eventually bamboozled shareholders and employees. There are, however, plenty of political merchants beyond just Bush and Cheney.

The price paid by Californians for energy skyrocketed hundreds of percent starting during the summer of 2000. This conspiracy lasted for about twelve months. Half way through the scam, in December of that first year, Enron and other energy corporations had purchased enough votes in the U.S. Congress to pass the Commodity Futures Modernization Act. The bill limited government regulation of electronic trading, and this helped to ensure that energy prices continued to rise in California for several months afterwards. As mentioned in Chapter Three, the folks at Enron artificially created the power crisis by trading its energy in California to its facilities in other states, and then purchased the power back from itself at inflated prices, which the company then conveniently passed on to the citizens of California.[6] Enron officials were only able to steal this money, in part if not completely, because of the influence they were able to purchase in the halls of congress.

Enron's abilities to buy political favors were not limited to Republicans. In 1992, the company began negotiations with the government of India to build a power plant. President Clinton took an interest in these discussions. He asked his former chief of staff, Thomas F. McLarty, to keep an eye on the proceedings. McLarty met with Kenneth Lay several times to discuss issues concerning the plant and the on-going negotiations. He was later hired by Enron as a director. In August 1995, Clinton's Treasury Secretary Robert Rubin and Energy Secretary Hazel O'Leary personally urged Indian officials to authorize the building of the facility. In 1996, four days before the Indian government gave its approval, the Houston based corporation donated $100,000 to the Democratic Party.[7] President Clinton also threatened to reduce the foreign aid going to the impoverished nation of Mozambique if it failed to give a pipeline project to Enron.[8]

Common Cause, the public watchdog group, noted on its web site many other examples in which the Enron Corporation purchased the favors of politicians, and may have even influenced the judicial process. From 1993 to 2002, Enron petitioned the Texas Supreme Court to review three cases in which it was involved. The judges twice reversed lower court rulings when they decided in favor of the Texas company. Enron's political action committee (PAC) and its executives gave Texas High Court justices $134,058 during these years, providing an appearance of impropriety, if not a conspicuous conflict of interest. In addition, Texas Governor Rick Perry received $187,000 of Enron money during this period, and he was kind enough to appoint "former Enron de Mexico President Mario Max Yzaguirre as Public Utility Commission chair in June 2001," another apparent conflict of interest. Perry received his check from Enron the day after making the appointment. In 2000, the Houston Astros inaugurated their new Enron Field, which was financed with $180 million in public tax dollars and $100 million from Enron. In return, the company received tax breaks and a $200 million contract to power the stadium.[9] Enron was a major buyer in the political markets throughout the nation, but it was not the only corporation able to purchase the favors of government officials.

After his successful campaign for re-election in 2004, President Bush worked enthusiastically in an attempt to convince the public that diverting payroll contributions going to the Social Security retirement system to private investment accounts would be a good idea. However, it was an excellent proposal only for securities and investment firms because it would transfer income from ordinary citizens to themselves in the form of billions of dollars of commissions, and some of this money would likely be recycled into political contributions. In his intense passion for the scheme, President Bush appeared to dislike mentioning that in Chile, a few decades before, citizens had been given a similar option. Those who decided to stay with the guaranteed pension offered by the state retirement system typically received more income when they retired than those who had opted for privatized accounts. Nonetheless, the president continued for many months to praise the virtues of Social Security privatization. As should be expected, during the 2004 election cycle, seven of the president's top ten biggest contributors were businesses involved in buying and selling corporate stocks. Morgan Stanley gave the president $600,480 during this period. This company was the president's number one contributor overall during the election cycle. Merrill Lynch, another investment firm, was number two. It had given $580,004 to the president's re-election bid. Goldman Sachs ($388,600), Credit Suisse First Boston ($330,040), Lehman Brothers ($327,725), Citigroup Inc. ($320,120), and Bear Sterns ($309,150) were the other investment and securities firms that were among the top ten investors in the president's re-election campaign.[10]

President Bush also supported tougher bankruptcy standards, but only for working people. The Senate and the House of Representatives passed a bankruptcy reform bill early in 2005. The legislation passed through the Senate by a vote of seventy-five to twenty-four. The new law was supported by the banking and credit card industry, which spent an average of $36,600 between 1999 and 2004 on each of the seventy-five senators who voted for it. The twenty-five who voted against the bill received only an average of $20,221 from the industry during these years. This law made it more difficult for working people to declare bankruptcy, but it did provide wealthy people with nice loopholes.[11] Given his consistent record for using government legislation to transfer income from working people to the wealthy, it was highly unlikely the president had any intention whatsoever of defending the majority of his fellow citizens from this attack by the banking and credit card industry. So it came as no surprise when he signed the bill into law in April 2005. MBNA Corporation, a major credit card company, had wisely invested $354,350 toward his re-election bid. The company was a major supporter of the legislation. Citigroup and the Bank of America were also among the top twenty investors bidding for the president's favors during his race to the White House in 2004.[12] They got what they paid for. The citizens and organizations arrayed against the measure possessed insufficient financial clout to outbid proponents of it. The result meant that some working people who file for bankruptcy will be forced to continue paying some of their debts to banks and credit card corporations, even when the burden might prove to be unbearable. A fresh start unencumbered by debt may prove to be impossible for these people. But affluent shareholders of these companies will reap the benefits of these continued payments, and because of the new law, they are also entitled to receive much better terms from lending institutions should they ever need to file for bankruptcy.

According to Public Campaign, a citizen's watchdog group, between 1989 and 2002, coal, gas, mining, oil and timber corporations paid $318.7 million to elected officials in exchange for government handouts. Utilities spent $71.5 million in the political markets during this period. This enabled them to purchase the Clear Skies proposal, which would protect them from mandatory reductions of air pollution. During these same years, the timber industry spent $30.6 million for the Healthy Forests Initiative, a bill that "opens more federal lands to logging."[13]

During the summer of 2005, the federal government enacted what should have been called the Energy Corporate Welfare Act. The oil, natural gas, nuclear, electricity and coal industries had purchased the favors of enough members of congress, as well as the president, to receive $8.5 billion in tax breaks and many more billions of dollars of government welfare, which some people of the news media politely but incorrectly called "subsidies." The oil and nuclear industries also received "regulatory rollbacks." Corporations purchased these taxpayer give-a-ways from members of Congress for only $90 million. The payments had been conveniently spread out over a few years from 2001 to 2005. The new energy policy was little more than a bill of sale that outlined exactly what corporations had purchased. In addition to the taxpayer subsidized welfare provided by the bill, the nuclear industry also bought "unlimited taxpayer-backed loan guarantees for the construction of new reactors" and "extended the industry's limited liability in the case of an accident to new reactors."[14] This legislation was supposed to provide a national energy policy, but what it mostly doled out was public welfare for rich people, with their corporations serving as income and wealth transfer conduits. The rich folks will receive higher dividends and stock prices thanks to all of those billions of dollars of tax breaks, subsidies, and guaranteed loans. Before passing the new law, measures to reduce the reliance of the U.S. on foreign oil, such as requiring improved fuel efficiency in automobiles, were deleted from it. Conservation would have meant reduced sales and demand for energy, and therefore lower profits, dividends and share prices. And that is never included in the plans of President Bush, as well as many members of congress. Failure to include conservation in the energy policy brought a terse reply from the editors of the Oregonian newspaper. They noted such an oversight was "foolhardy" and "a recipe for economic and political disaster."[15] This legislation wasn't passed to help the vast majority of the people of the United States. On the contrary, it was mainly enacted to enrich already wealthy shareholders even more, and at public expense.

The high priced bidding wars in the halls of congress and the White House have left behind those citizens who lack the financial means to be able to compete in the supermarkets of politics, which means roughly 98 percent of the population is not represented at all. Since only the wealthiest members of society are able to successfully bid for legislative favors, this deficiency of representation in government among the poor, working and middle classes has largely eliminated the progressive tax systems in the United States. Remarkably, it appears that most rich people want to pay less and less of their income in taxes, even though they are the prime beneficiaries of a widening array of government welfare that continuously enhances their income and wealth at taxpayer expense, and even as they reap the benefits of an economic system constructed as a conduit to continuously transfer more and more income and wealth from productive people to themselves.

Historically, with a progressive tax system in place, the richest members of society paid a higher percentage of their income in taxes than those with lesser earnings because they benefited more from the system they had constructed. However, the days of progressive taxation in the United States were eliminated many years ago.

In the year 2002, the United States Bureau of Labor Statistics reported that the tax burden was distributed fairly evenly among the tax paying public when all forms of taxation were taken into account, including income, sales, property, excise and payroll taxes. That's not a progressive system; it's regressive. The poorest fifth of the population, which earned less than eight thousand dollars per year, paid a cumulative rate of 18 percent of their income in taxes. The richest fifth paid 19 percent.[16] However, this assessment was before President Bush engineered federal income tax cuts primarily benefiting the wealthy (his self-proclaimed "base") in 2001 and 2003. He also signed a bill into law that reduced the tax on dividends which was paid mainly by the affluent. By 2005, the tax system had become even more regressive than in 2002 as productive people paid a higher percentage of their income in taxes than the politically powerful, but largely unproductive, affluent class.

Corporations also buy tax breaks from the government, and pass on much of the savings to their wealthy shareholders and CEOs. From 1996 to 1998, businesses such as Bristol-Myers Squibb, Microsoft, Pfizer, ExxonMobil, AT&T, Chase Manhattan, Enron, General Electric, and Phillip Morris spent a paltry $150.1 million in campaign contributions to purchase tax breaks of $55 billion. During those years, they also bought legislation that gutted the "alternative minimum tax" and selected corporations received billions of dollars in rebates, often on taxes they never paid.[17] From 1989 to 2002, the railroad corporation CSX invested $5.9 million in the political markets. The company had more than $1 billion in earnings during the four years prior to 2003, and yet paid taxes only in one of those years, and it received $164 million in tax rebates during this period. This means that CSX bought rebates (or more precisely welfare) on taxes it never even paid!![18] Because it was largely tax exempt during this time, the company was able to provide higher dividends and share prices than would normally have been the case if it had been a good corporate citizen and paid its taxes.

The political movement in favor of regressive taxation, which benefits the leisure class while being detrimental to working people, has been also occurring on state and local levels. For example, according to the Institute on Taxation & Economic Policy, the bottom 60 percent of income earners in Oregon paid more in state taxes as a percentage of their income in 2002 than they did in 1989. During this period, the top 20 percent of income earners experienced reduced tax liabilities as a percentage of their income. For corporations, the pattern was the same. In Oregon, corporations paid 14 percent of state tax revenue during 1980, but this share slowly began to drop. State economists expect it to "fall to less than 4 percent" by 2009.[19] In 2005, the Portland Public School District laid off hundreds of employees, including teachers. Class sizes surged. While the district financially imploded, the state legislature granted more tax breaks to corporations.

The cutback of corporate tax liabilities in Oregon became extremely pronounced during and after the recession of 2001. Since it began and ended during the same year, the economic bust cycle was short by any historical standards. Nonetheless, a state fiscal crisis arose as jobs were slashed for several years after the bust cycle ended, and state tax revenue dropped due to the loss of jobs.

Many people, both high and low, placed the blame for the state's fiscal crisis squarely on public employee unions, and especially on their retirement system. Few people mentioned that corporate tax liabilities in Oregon had been consistently dropping for over twenty years compared to what individuals provided the state. Just a few years prior to the recession, corporations purchased tax breaks from the state legislature amounting to 27 percent of their tax liabilities.[20] If corporations had not received such large tax breaks, the fiscal crisis would have been modest, and it might not even have come into existence. During the years 2001-05, the results of the growing inequality of taxation in Oregon were that people worked more and earned less in many cases. For example, as part of their new contract, teachers of the largest state school district, Portland Public, worked ten days for free. To make up for the budget deficit that should never have existed, school days were cut, school activities reduced, class sizes soared, other public employees were laid off, and state and local services to the mentally ill, the aged and the poor were reduced. But the rich received higher dividends and share prices because of the reduced corporate tax burden than would otherwise have been the case.

How Public Education Has Become A Corporate Welfare Program

For 15 decades or more, public school teachers, administrators, parents and locally elected school boards had chosen a variety of methods with which to assess how well students had learned what it was they had been taught in schools. During these years, school boards comprised of local citizens often agreed that district and teacher produced assessments were fine in determining student progress. The corporations of the publishing industry, however, saw the potential profits to be extorted, and decided district and teacher provided evaluations were insufficient to gauge student expertise of educational curriculum. They won their first arguments in the legislatures of many states starting about twenty years ago, beginning a process of undermining citizen control of schools throughout the nation, while enhancing the self-serving corporate influence over the education of everybody else's children.

In 2001, President Bush decided to enhance the profits of his personal friends from among the publishing corporations. These institutions won a captive market of children nationwide when he signed into law the "No Child Left Behind Act." This legislation ordered the standardized testing of all children in public schools throughout the country. The federal government threatened to withhold any federal tax dollars going to the states for public education if they failed to comply with this mandate. The national regime was now in the business of blackmailing the citizens of states on behalf of corporations and the wealthy.

All during his life, President Bush and the publishing industry had been closely linked. His grandfather, Prescott Bush, and James McGraw Jr., had established a close friendship during the 1930s. The strong ties between the families have lasted ever since. McGraw Jr. managed a family business named McGraw-Hill, a publishing firm. As of 2001, Harold McGraw III managed this corporation. A long time friend of George W. Bush, McGraw was a member of the president's "transition advisory team" during Bush's first term in office. So was Edward Rust Jr., a board member of McGraw-Hill.[21] In addition, Harold McGraw Jr. served on the "national grant advisory and founding board of the Barbara Bush Foundation for Family Literacy." Barbara Bush is the mother of the president. In Texas, under Governor Bush, McGraw-Hill gained a "dominant" share of the profitable textbook market.[22] When Bush ascended the presidency, his publishing buddies stood to gain plenty of corporate welfare through the federal government.

When the president called for school report cards and testing all students, an executive of NCS Pearson, a publisher of testing materials, proclaimed, "This almost reads like our business plan."[23] This person had no reason to lie, so his comment was probably true, but a person may be suspicious that the president's proposal may have more exactly resembled the business plan of his pals at McGraw-Hill.

Nowadays, public school districts need to purchase tests and accessories from the president's friends, as well as from other publishing corporations, in order to fulfill the requirements of enriching these businesses at public expense by testing all students. The bill to local and state taxpayers has been in the billions of dollars (and rising) for what should be labeled "The No Publishing Corporation Left Behind Welfare Act," or perhaps "The No Rich Buddies of Mine Left Behind Welfare Act." Working people are paying the bills, and they are forced to deal with the tests, along with their children, teachers and administrators. These examinations don't actually help students learn anything. Some students refer to taking them as "busy work." But the tests do force teachers to teach to the test because they need to keep student achievement rising to satisfy those darn school report cards. This is accomplished by cutting corners or eliminating important aspects of public education, such as critical thinking skills, art, and interpersonal skills. Meanwhile, well heeled shareholders and the CEOs of the publishing corporations are the prime beneficiaries of this intrusion into local public education—not the students, for they were never the intended beneficiaries of this corporate welfare conspiracy.

President Bush provided only "$387 million" of federal corporate welfare money to help the fifty states meet the demands of the misnamed "No Child Left Behind Act." However, it was estimated that $2.7 to $7 billion per year was needed to fund the federal mandate in order to give school personnel any chance of successfully meeting all of the requirements of this conspiracy.[24] Obviously, the president never intended children to be the beneficiaries of this con job since he knew that many states, such as Oregon, had already cut back on education, social services, health care and police because of the effects of the 2001 recession. During this time, the president's pals at Halliburton Corporation received billions of dollars of no-bid federal contracts, and billions of dollars of tax cuts were given to his "base," but the man in the White House couldn't spare much money at all for the children of the nation. Under the circumstances, how could the states implement the new federally mandated corporate welfare scheme? Especially when Bush made it quite clear at a meeting with the governor's of the states that he had no intention of helping them out of their fiscal shortfalls. For many states, the only way to pay for this boondoggle was by cutting other services or by raising taxes, even as the tax liabilities of corporations and wealthy shareholders were declining.

Early in 2005, the largest teachers union in the U.S., the National Education Association, along with nine school districts from three different states, sued the Bush administration in an effort to free school districts, children, parents, teachers and administrators from the tyranny of having to fulfill the requirements of this welfare scam. The rationale for the lawsuit was that the federal government had short changed school districts by $27 billion, which was the difference between what congress had authorized and what the government had actually spent. This violated a provision in the law. Bill Mathis, superintendent of one of the districts suing the administration, perhaps said it best, "It is the cruelest illusion to give the children a promise that we never intended to keep."[25] Mathis was right. Bush never intended children to be the beneficiaries of this program. They were only to be the conduits by which local, state and federal tax money could freely flow to his rich pals of the publishing corporations.

Our Legal And Civil Rights Are Under Siege

The captains of industry and finance are continuously trying to undermine citizen control over local and state governments in order to increase profits at the expense of the public, and they use more than just the federal government to achieve this purpose. For example, several years ago, lobbyists for corporate agribusinesses convinced Pennsylvania policymakers to enact a "weak waste disposal law." A few years later, in 1997, lobbyists for these companies convinced state politicians to enforce it. When they did, this action effectively annulled the stricter "waste-disposal regulations of more than one hundred townships." The new law also prohibited local governments from passing any laws that were stricter than the state regulations.[26]

With the new legislation, corporations were able to override local ordinances regulating the spread of municipal sewage sludge to smaller communities. Corporate haulers of sewage sold the sludge to farmers as fertilizers, and by doing so avoided waste disposal costs. Pennsylvania only required the sludge to be tested every three months, "and only for E. Coli and heavy metals." After two young people died from pathogens in the waste, local officials attempted to pass regulations to put a stop to this practice. Unfortunately, Pennsylvania's less restrictive law overruled the local regulations. Locally elected officials were outraged at the "state's apparent complicity" in this corporate coup d'état.[27] The people in these communities recognized the underlying problems to maintaining their ways of life were corporations and their abilities to purchase legislative and regulatory favors from politicians in the state government.

Rush Township became the first of several to pass an ordinance to control the spread of sludge. This law forced haulers of the substance to test every load of the stuff at their own expense for a wider number of toxic matters than was required by the weaker state law before selling it to farmers in the jurisdiction of the township.[28]

Corporations retaliated quickly. Claiming its constitutional rights had been violated, an international hauler of sludge, Synagro-WTT Inc., sued Rush Township. Page one of the lawsuit declared, "'we the corporations are people and this ordinance violates our personhood rights.'" The company claimed the anti-sludge ordinance unlawfully preempted the weaker state law, and its due process rights had been violated because it was considered to be a person with all of the protections of the constitution of the United States. Synagro-WTT, Inc. also sued each supervisor for one million dollars each. This apparently was intended to discourage other local governmental officials from representing the interests of their citizens against the interests of out-of-town and out-of-state corporations. PennAg Industries Association also filed a suit against a township ordinance in Fulton County.[29]

In response to these lawsuits, two Clarion County townships, Licking and Porter, boldly declared their independence from corporate misrule when they enacted laws announcing that corporations would no longer be considered persons within their jurisdictions. The protections of the Constitution, which were intended only for individual human beings, no longer were legally applied to corporations in these communities. Several other townships were considering enacting similar ordinances.[30] Unlike the Supreme Court of the United States, the supervisors of these townships recognized that the Constitution only gave people civil and legal rights.

In 2002, on behalf of corporations, politicians tried to ram a bill through the state legislature that would have eliminated the rights of townships to regulate agriculture, "including sludge applications." Local citizen control over agriculture and sludge would have been terminated. The supervisors of the townships recognized the dangers this conspiracy held for the citizens they represented. Just as the revolutionary patriots of 1774 were once moved into action against the British government acting on behalf of its favorite corporation, the British East India Company, over 400 communities of modern day patriots quickly rallied against the attempted surrender of their legal rights. They were supported by such organizations as Common Cause, the Sierra Club and the United Mine Workers. Citizen patriots and their allies were arrayed against politically powerful corporations, but the patriots won when the bill became unpopular simply because knowledge of it had spread, and citizens throughout the state recognized that it would have transferred more legal rights of people to corporations acting on behalf of their wealthy shareholders.[31]

Corporations and their politicians never want an angry and politically aroused citizenry. When average citizens recognize the dangers to their constitutional rights, as well as to their livelihoods, large and united groups of them are threats to corporate control over federal, state and local governments.

Enlightenment and subsequent political action have already occurred on behalf of people who work for a living in Pennsylvania. Several other states have also passed laws banning corporate ownership of farms. These states are "Iowa, Kansas, Minnesota, Missouri, Nebraska, Oklahoma, North Dakota, South Dakota, and Wisconsin."[32]

Political action that results in restricting and rolling back corporate rights will lead to healthy non-corporate economies and vibrant democracies for most people. To avoid such an unprofitable outcome, at least from the corporate point of view, the logical thing for the captains of industry to do is to establish governments in which they have all of the legal rights, while ensuring that people have none. This is a process already underway.

International Trade Policy And The Transfer Of Income And Wealth From People To Corporations

In addition to determining federal laws, regulations and tax burdens, corporations and their freeloading shareholder class are driving U.S. trade policies through their purchases in the political markets. These policies are negotiated with the intention of raising corporate earnings through income, wealth and health transfers from human beings to corporations throughout the world.

On-going top-secret negotiations through the World Trade Organization have the potential to open private service jobs to competition from foreign workers right here in the United States; public services will also be privatized. These discussions are expected to be completed by the end of 2006. What is being negotiated is the "General Agreement on Trade and Services" (GATS). According to the Northwest Labor Press, one proposal being discussed will allow "companies to import foreign workers" and permit corporations to pay them "at foreign wage rates and under foreign labor laws, for 'temporary' periods of up to three years."[33] Under this coming law, nurses from the Philippines can be imported to work in U.S. hospitals for whatever they are earning in their home country, which is likely only a fraction of what U.S. citizens make in this profession. Instead of having to ship the jobs of software engineers to India, Intel Corporation will be able to import non-Americans to work in their facilities in the United

States. Rather than paying them wages typically earned in the U.S., or even at any state or federal minimum wage rates, the corporate heroes of Intel can pay these imported employees the $7000 per year or whatever it is that they earn in India or elsewhere. Worse yet, these people will be allowed to work under the same conditions as those that exist in their native countries. They can be forced to work in toxic chemicals right here in the U.S. if that is the situation in their home nations. U.S. labor laws will not apply to these folks. They can be compelled to work overtime without pay if this is their situation in their home countries. Health and safety laws, minimum wage laws and laws governing overtime pay are just a few U.S. statutes that will be usurped by corporations so that they can continue to propel the citizens of every country on a race to the bottom on the road to serfdom. If this proposal is passed, even illegal immigrants working in the United States may find their meager wages undercut by these soon to be legally imported workers. GATS is being negotiated for the single purpose of transferring income, wealth, health and democracy from people who work for a living to CEOs and rich shareholders in the form of higher dividends, stock prices and greater political clout.

A short list of the jobs potentially up for grabs by foreign workers include: legal services; accounting, auditing and bookkeeping; engineering; data processing; advertising; investigation and security; custodian; postal services; couriers; voice telephone services; building completion and finishing work; general construction work for civil engineering; retailing and wholesale trade services; primary and secondary education services; higher education; refuse disposal; banking and financial; air transport services; social services; libraries, archives, museums as well as other cultural services. Remember, this is not a complete list.

Democracy, especially local control of public affairs, is being seriously jeopardized by the GATS negotiations far beyond what has occurred in the past when corporations have pilfered political power from the people. Economist Margaret Gribskov has pointed out that "...authority over and control of vital public services..." will be taken "...away from community and states to distant multinational corporations" if these negotiations are successful.[34] What if you have a complaint about services? What if the customer service representatives cannot speak English very well, if at all? Under the reign of GATS, will citizens have to go to secret tribunals in Switzerland or India, possibly presided over by sympathizers, officers or shareholders of the offending corporations? If NAFTA is any indicator, citizen complainers will not likely even be allowed into the hearings. Imagine having to complain to a corporation in India or France about your garbage service, or about your electricity bill. Local control and accountability, an important component of democracy throughout the history of the United States, is being sold by publicly traded, limited liability corporations through their paid agents in political office in order to ensure ever increasing corporate earnings. The result is the complete political betrayal and financial rape of the majority of the citizens of the United States.

GATS will also serve to gut much of the tax revenue currently going to public services because of its downward push on wages, salaries and benefits. The result will emaciate our already distressed public school systems, social services, police, fire and other local and state government services. Streets, highways, parks, and school buildings, for example, will go into disrepair even more so than nowadays because governments will not be able to afford to repair them. The face of local governments and the services they provide will change forever if these negotiations are ever enacted into law.

NAFTA

NAFTA was the first serious success achieved by corporations to create a governmental body that was unaccountable to any democratic processes. The treaty allows them to override U.S., Canadian and Mexican laws established to protect their citizens.

Chapter eleven is a clause buried deep within the 555 pages of the North American Free Trade Agreement (NAFTA). Under this section, corporations can seek compensation if foreign governments enact regulations or laws that bring about real or imagined drops in their alleged future potential profits. For example, if an additive in gasoline causes cancer in people, and some state government decides to ban it, the corporation producing it can sue that government for the loss of future earnings. When a business sues a government using chapter eleven, a secret tribunal determines innocence or guilt and assesses compensation. No court of appeals exists. Citizens and government representatives may not even know if the judges are linked to the corporation that is responsible for their complaint. In these secret trials, if the corporation wins, something that occurs the vast majority of times, state and local governments must still eliminate the offending law or risk being sued again for up to fifteen years.

Methanex is a Canadian corporation that manufactures a gasoline additive known as MTBE. It reputedly causes cancer in people. In addition, the product has been identified as a danger to water supplies because it makes the fluid taste like turpentine. A few years ago, the city of Santa Monica, California was forced to close most of its municipal wells because MTBE had found its way into them. Subsequently, California's state government decided to prohibit the sale of the product within its borders. Sixteen other states also outlaw it. Under NAFTA's rules, however, Methanex was able to file a suit against the U.S. government for $970 million, which was the amount of the potential loss of alleged future profits that went down the drain with the enactment of California's ban. The case has yet to be decided.

In Mexico, citizens stopped a U.S. corporation from re-opening a toxic waste dump because they were convinced it was the cause of a significant rise in local cancer cases. The corporation sued via one of NAFTA's secret tribunals and won $16 million in compensation. Taxpayers footed the bill. This case, as usual, represented a transfer of income from working citizens to corporate investors via tax dollars. The $16 million might otherwise have gone to such things as education, highway maintenance, fire fighters and police. More importantly, the health of citizens was also transferred to corporations as so much life to be slowly killed in order to earn a higher rate of return on investment. Thus, under NAFTA, you have to pay not to be murdered.

A Canadian corporation could put mad cow infected beef into the food of children in the United States, and if citizens ban the imported product, they might very well need to pay compensation to the tarnished beef suppliers because of the NAFTA treaty. The same process would occur if a U.S. corporation imported a similar product into Canada. Canadian citizens would need to pay the offending company not to be poisoned. You may think of this as being crazy and a highly unlikely scenario, but in May 2003, the U.S. government prohibited the importation of Canadian beef and cattle just because mad cow disease had been discovered in livestock in the province of Alberta. Since then, approximately 500 Canadian cattlemen have filed 121 claims under NAFTA demanding that they be compensated over $300 million because of alleged lost earnings in the U.S. market attributed to the ban.[35] Let's get one key point straight; these claims are really dumb. How much beef suspected of being contaminated by mad cow disease would you or any other relatively sane person purchase? The honest answer is probably fairly close to zero; and this means the future profits of these cattlemen are likely to be big fat losses, making their claims in NAFTA's secret tribunals completely bogus, just a sham really, but they likely will be awarded compensation at taxpayer expense. Nowadays, the threat of a lawsuit under NAFTA is enough to make any governmental body think twice about enacting laws to protect the health of its citizens, or to save taxpayer money.

In California, 32 million old car tires are disposed of every year, which creates a big environmental dilemma. The state assembly passed a bill that allowed the tires to be used in asphalt for building roads. Mexican and Canadian rubber exporters issued complaints about the legislation. Although he supported it, Governor Arnold Schwarzenegger vetoed the bill because he thought it would violate the NAFTA treaty.[36]

In another case, the Canadian government wanted to regulate the packaging of cigarettes. Using the chapter eleven provision as leverage, the tobacco industry threatened a lawsuit and compelled the government to back down.

Carla Hills was the "arm-twister-in-chief" of the tobacco corporations. She had also been the head of the US team that negotiated the NAFTA treaty. Her consulting firm was among twenty-nine corporations that demanded the chapter eleven clause be included as the corporate controlled Bush regime negotiated to expand NAFTA to thirty-one other nations.[37]

Given that investor interests provided the primary input during the negotiations of the NAFTA accord, a person can reasonably expect that chapter eleven was deliberately inserted into it. A claim such as this has merit. Clayton Yeutter, a trade representative to the Uruguay round of the General Agreement on Trade and Tariffs (GATT), "expressed the aim of using GATT to dilute state and local food safety regulations or to place downward international pressures" on US and European standards for food.[38] So it shouldn't come as any big surprise that corporations found a way around local, state and federal laws when negotiating NAFTA; and this shows how badly corporate and shareholders rights have scored a knockout over the democratic rights of people.

The Corporate Bias Of Government Officials

Many politicians and government bureaucrats possess sentimental ties to publicly traded corporations, often because they have achieved considerable standards of living while working for them at some point during their lives. These people bring their knowledge of how corporations work to political offices. Law makers possessing high level corporate backgrounds know of the need for ever growing quarterly earnings. As might be expected, these people view labor and environmental regulations as being impediments to earning profits, and or they claim taxes are too great, and or the government is too large. So they bring their anti-government attitudes into political offices and demand such things as deregulation and the privatization of government services. With the ideological impetus that only sizable amounts of money can purchase, politicians co-dependent with corporations quickly buy into the erroneous notion that economies dominated by publicly traded companies bring about some sort of prosperity for all of the people of the world to share in, even though the evidence developed over the last thirty years strongly suggests otherwise.

A quick perusal of current top White House officials and other politicians during the two terms of President George W. Bush provides a glimpse as to how many politicians are really co-dependents of corporations. John Snow, for example, replaced Paul O'Neil as Bush's treasury secretary. He had been chairman of CSX Corp., a railroad company and a noted tax dodger.[39] As mentioned in chapter two, Snow's predecessor, Paul O'Neil, had been the CEO of Alcoa, Inc. William Donaldson became head of the Securities and Exchange Commission in the wake of the corporate accounting scandals during the first term of President Bush (2001-05). Among other positions, he had been president and CEO of Aetna, Inc. from 2000 to 2001. He had also established a Wall Street investment firm, and was chairman and CEO of the New York Stock Exchange from 1990-95. We already know that President Bush had mismanaged several corporations into the ground. And we know that Vice President Dick Cheney had been CEO of Halliburton Inc. Defense Secretary Donald Rumsfield had been the corporate hero of G.D. Searle, a pharmaceutical corporation. White House Budget Director Mitch Daniels had once been a senior vice president at Eli Lilly, another pharmaceutical corporation.

Many members of the U.S. Congress are also co-dependents in one way or another with publicly traded companies. Senate Majority leader Bill Frist of Tennessee and other members of his family own millions of dollars of stock in the Hospital Corporation of America, a firm founded by his father and brother. As of the year 2005, Senator John Kerry of Massachusetts was married to a billionaire. His wife had inherited the Heinz Ketchup fortune.

Some politicians may not necessarily have ever been directly involved with corporations, but many of them are rich and co-dependents in one way or another. Because of their lofty financial status, or perhaps because they are wannabes, some people in Congress may feel a solidarity of interest with rich people and corporations. As of 2003, approximately forty U.S. Senators were worth millions of dollars, and there were probably more but for the likelihood that many understated their values. Senator Hilliary Rodham Clinton, for example, was reported to have assets that ranged somewhere between $352,000 and $3.8 million, but she was not listed as one of the forty.[40] As of 2004, 28 percent of the members of the U.S. House of Representatives were known millionaires.[41]

It is difficult to imagine how any member of the White House or of Congress would not possess a fair degree of bias in favor of publicly traded corporations when these people were once exceedingly well paid former employees, or when they own corporate stock, or when their law making favors are being purchased with thousands of dollars in campaign contributions from these businesses every year, or when they come under the influence of millions of dollars of corporate lobbyists every day. This corporate bias can only become stronger when valuable perks are dangled under their noses, such as well paying speaking engagements, vacations disguised as government business, or even corporate jobs after they leave office. The results of all of these corporate influences in government are conspicuous. Many senators and representatives, millionaires or not, as well as the people in the White House, have a vested interest in ensuring that income and wealth is continuously transferred from poor, working, middle class and small business people to the shareholder class.

Given the solidarity of interests between what appears to be the vast majority of state and federal politicians on the one hand, and corporations and the shareholding investor class on the other hand, patriotic citizens should never anticipate that lawmakers will want to do something beneficial for working people anytime soon if by doing so there may exist the potential for lowering the free income that is transferred from the general public to the shareholder class. Our democratic rights as citizens and patriots are being washed away by a flood of corporate money showered on our elected representatives, and increasingly so. So don't expect a majority of those in the White House and Congress to think too seriously about rejecting GATS when it comes time to vote on it; and don't expect these corporate loyalists to authorize any serious re-negotiation with Canada and Mexico to eliminate the chapter eleven provision of the NAFTA accord. Rather, it should be expected that additional treaties will be negotiated giving corporations more legal rights to render our democratic institutions powerless and meaningless, as well as to steal our lives, livelihoods, health, wealth and land. Such legal actions will allow corporate earnings, dividends and stock prices to surge ever upward.

Perhaps it's time for those of us who work for a living to organize ourselves into a sizeable political force bent on reversing corporate rights, and perhaps even eliminate them. However, if history shows us anything, it's that such a social movement will encounter violent and criminal retaliation from its adversaries. This history is worth a quick examination.

Notes

1. Ivins, Molly, "The state of the union goes to the high bidders," *Oregonian*, Jan. 29, 2003, p. B-11.

2. Press, Bill, "Enron case shouts for campaign finance reform, CNN.com, February 13, 2002.

3. Press.

4. Press.

5. Press.

6. Behr, Peter, "Overcharges in Calif. Estimated Energy Firms Faulted, but $1.8 Billion Sum Is Less Than Sought," *Washington Post*, December 13, 2003, p. E3.

7. www.monitor.net/monitor/0202a/enrontimeline.html.

8. www.progress.org/archive/enron.htm.

9. The Internet site www.progress.org/archive/enron.htm provided my figures, which were originally obtained from www.commoncause.org.

10. Opensecrets.org.

11. Kosseff, Jeff, "Lobbying propels bankruptcy reform," *Oregonian*, March 20, 2005, p. E1.

12. Opensecrets.org.

13. Bielke, Rick, www.Publiccampaign.org/, "State of the Union: Big Political Investors Get Paybacks from President Bush," January 29, 2003

14. Hauter, Wenonah, "A nuclear Swindle," TomPaine.com, July 27, 2005.

15. Editorial, "Energy Prices: playing with time," *Oregonian*, July 28, 2005 p. D8.

16. Ivins, "The state....

17. Ivins, "The state....

18. Ivins, Molly, "Wall Street's dream team," *Oregonian*, December 15, 2002, p. B5.

19. Rogoway, Mike, "Oregon corporate taxes on wane," *Oregonian*, May 16, 2005, p. D1.

20. Sandoz, Margorie, "Corporate Tax Breaks" (A letter to the editor), *Oregonian*, March 9, 2003, p. E3.

21. Metcalf, Steven, "Reading Between the Lines," *Education, Inc.*, Heineman: New Hampshire, 2002, pp. 52-53.

22. Metcalf, pp. 51-53.

23. Metcalf, p. 51.

24. Metcalf, p. 51.

25. Feller, Ben, "Suit Targets No Child Left Behind," *Oregonian*, April 21, 2005.

26. Kaplan, Geoffrey, "Consent of the Governed," *Orion*, November/December 2003.

27. Kaplan.

28. Kaplan.

29. Kaplan.

30. Kaplan.

31. Kaplan.

32. Kaplan.

33. McIntosh, Don, "Trade treaties target service, information, public sectors," *Northwest Labor Press*, Volume 104, Number 5, March 7, 2003, p. 1.

34. Gribskov, Margaret, "Why Americans Are Free and Why Foreign Corporations Are Attacking Our Freedoms," Economic Justice Action Group: Portland, OR, June 2002, p. 15.

35. Scott, Alwyn, "Canadians want U.S. to pay for beef ban," *Seattle Times*, February 23, 2005.

36. Iritani, Evelyn, "State Laws Take Back Seat to Trade," *Los Angeles Times*, December 5, 2004.

37. Huffington, Adrianna, "Nafta sells out democracy; America pays," *Oregonian*, Feb 3, 2001.

38. Gribskoy, p7.

39. Ivins, Molly, "Wall Street's dream team," *Oregonian*, December 15, 2002, p. B5.

40. Loughlin, Sean, and Yoon, Robert, "Millionaires populate U.S. Senate," Cnn.com, June 13, 2003.

41. Tompaine.com.

Chapter Ten

HISTORY OF THE CORPORATE ECONOMIC SYSTEM

On December 31, 1600, Queen Elizabeth of England issued a charter giving life to a corporation called the British East India Company. The purpose of this investor union, then known as a joint-stock company, was to obtain profits via international trade. Her royal highness also granted the company many special privileges not given to people of the lower social classes, including monopoly rights to trade with the East Indies, the abilities to negotiate with foreign governments, and the legal rights to develop a standing army. Such special privileges were typically reserved only for wealthy aristocrats, and these people also just happened to be the people who controlled the government of England. So it should not come as any great surprise that this new business entity was created out of legislative thin air in favor of only one very wealthy person—Queen Elizabeth I. She was reported to be the sole shareholder; And so it was for the benefit of England's most powerful politician that a new form of property had been created.

In the Netherlands, another corporation, the Dutch East India Company, was formed in 1602. Several small trading companies merged together to form one new investors union. Only together, armed with legal advantages provided by the Dutch government, could the former competitors obtain larger profits than before incorporation, because their union eliminated any competition between them. The Dutch government gave the company the legal rights to enter into treaties with foreign countries, maintain military forces, and to coin money. Among other ventures, the new business brought spices to Europe from the East Indies. It also hired Henry Hudson to explore the Hudson Bay and the Hudson River in a vain attempt to discover the elusive western route to China and India. By 1669, the company owned more than 150 merchant vessels, forty warships, a private army of over 10,000 troops, and had over 50,000 employees. That year it paid dividends of 40 percent.

Most if not all shareholders of these early corporations were members of the aristocracy, and they had ready access to national politicians. Many of the aristocrats were elected officials. The merchants of these companies often possessed financial and blood ties to the nobles of their home countries. Unlike members of the aristocracy, the citizens of the working classes, such as yeoman farmers, butchers, wheel makers, carpenters, laborers of all kinds, did not possess the political power to obtain exclusive favors from their governments. Incorporation was solely a special privilege of the wealthy and the politically powerful.

In addition to such things as state granted monopolies, typical special privileges that came with incorporation included the fact that shareholders did not have to work, or even know anything of what their corporations produced because management was delegated. The transfer of ownership was made easy through the sale of existing stock, and there came a time when the legal liabilities of the owners evaporated. Typical benefits, usually not cited, included the fact that investors in these joint-stock companies no longer were required to compete against each other. Meanwhile, the butchers, the bakers and those jolly old candlestick makers still had to labor for their livelihoods, and they still had to compete against their rivals. You can rest assured that when put in a state of distress by their competitors, it was unlikely few politicians ever came to their rescue.

You can imagine how difficult it was for aristocrats living in London, England to manage their corporations that were engaged in business activities all over the known world. These people were clueless as to what was going on in their far flung financial empires. How could they possess any such knowledge if contemporary CEOs are still largely clueless as to what goes on in their businesses despite all of the advances in communication technologies that have occurred since then? The inability to manage these companies efficiently is precisely what ensured the need for special legal privileges. And that's why these inefficient organizations were no match for the hardworking, experienced and sagacious common people in competition with them. When the managers of a corporation called the Royal African Company discovered they could not compete against owner-operated businesses, the British Parliament enacted a 10 percent tax on its rivals in 1698.[1] Then there was the time when the East India Company was facing bankruptcy in 1773. Rather than allow it to become insolvent, which would have rendered their stockholdings valueless, the aristocrats of the British Parliament gave the firm a virtual monopoly to export tea tax free to the American colonies. This gave the corporation a sizeable financial advantage over colonialists engaged in the tea trade because the latter had to pay the tax.[2]

Obviously, corporations were not formed in the name of greater efficiency in the production of goods and services, or competitiveness. This wasn't lost on people living in those bygone days. In 1776, the poster boy for modern conservatives, the economist Adam Smith, noted that the result of corporate management was "Negligence and profusion…in the management of the affairs of such a company."[3] In those days, profusion was synonymous with the word "waste." Smith also wrote,

> The trade of a joint-stock company is always managed by a court of directors (board of directors). This court, is frequently subject, in many respects, to the control of a general court of proprietors (shareholders). But the greater part of those proprietors seldom pretend to understand any thing of the business of the company; and when the spirit of faction happens not to prevail among them, give themselves no trouble about it, but receive contentedly such half yearly or yearly dividend, as the directors think proper to make them.[4] (Parenthesis mine.)

Smith clearly recognized that shareholders had little or no idea of what was occurring in the management of their companies, and neither did the members of the boards of directors. Managers called the shots, and like modern CEOs, often for their own benefit. Smith wrote,

> It is merely to enable the company to support the negligence, profusion, and malversation of their own servants, whose disorderly conduct seldom allows the dividend of the company to exceed the ordinary rate of profit in trades which are altogether free, and very frequently makes it fall even a good deal short of that rate.[5]

Smith's assessment of the efficiency of corporations engaged in manufacturing was just as harsh.

> The joint-stock companies (business corporations), which are established for the public-spirited purpose of promoting some particular manufacture, over and above managing their own affairs ill, to the diminution of the general stock of the society, can in other respects scarce ever fail to do more harm than good.[6] (Parenthesis mine.)

It was obviously not lost on Smith and others that corporations were founded solely to be conduits to supply labor-less profits to members of the aristocracy. They were never intended to cost-effectively produce goods and services to the underlying citizens, or to raise the standards of living for the great majority of the people of any country. Any benefits for working people resulting from the existence of corporations were purely coincidental because these business structures, like their modern descendants, relied heavily on transfer's of income and wealth from working people and small businesses to help stimulate profits.

The Twin Pillars Of The Industrial Revolution

Samuel Slater, an Englishman who immigrated to the United States, ushered in the Industrial Revolution in North America when he opened the first textile factory in Pawtucket, Rhode Island in 1789. The first employees in Slater's mill were all children, and they were paid less than what adults normally earned.[7] During the next forty years, the textile mills spread rapidly throughout New England. The industry grew because of the labor of young people. By 1832, two of every five workers in the textile factories were children between the ages of six and seventeen. The rest of the work force was composed of young women under the age of twenty-five.

The conditions under which these people lived and worked were often extremely harsh. Typically, "work began at five o'clock in the morning." Workers received a short break for breakfast a little more than two hours later. Lunch began at noon and lasted half an hour. The workday ended at half past seven in the evening. Woman and children worked six days a week. The labor was performed under low ceilings in buildings that were often several stories high. Windows were shut all through the year, even during the summer. Air conditioning had yet to be invented. These people worked and breathed thick cotton dust that mixed with "smoky fumes from whale-oil lamps," all of which made it difficult to breathe, much less to work.[8]

The terrible working conditions of these young people sometimes led them to be suspicious of the motivations of some of the decisions made by management. In 1828, the first known factory strike in American history occurred. The owners of a textile factory wanted to switch the lunch hour from noon to one o'clock. The children suspected this was simply a ruse to put an end to their lunch all together. They objected to this demand and when the owners persisted, the children went on strike. As is the case with many adults, the proprietors wanted the children to be obedient and to take them seriously, and so they called upon the local militia to break the strike.[9] This was the first time in U.S. history that factory owners used their political influence to bring the armed might of the government against exploited people, and it would not be the last.

The children and the young women who toiled under such harsh conditions during the early years of the nation represented one of the two pillars on top of which the Industrial Revolution first developed and then evolved. In the New England textile mills, these unsung heroes spun out shirts, pants, dresses, drapes, blankets and many other items made of cotton. As the nation tossed the natives off of their lands further west, some mills spread into new states, such as Ohio, Indiana, Illinois, and so forth, but the industry remained based mostly in the Northeastern states along the Atlantic coast. By 1860, on the eve of the civil war, the Industrial Revolution, and its reliance on the cheap labor of women and children, had been under way for several decades.

Prior to 1793, cotton farming was a time consuming and relatively expensive process. In the Southern states where the crop was cultivated, the seeds were separated from the fiber by hand, a slow and mind-numbing procedure most frequently performed by slaves. Eli Whitney revolutionized the entire industry in 1793 when he developed the cotton gin, a machine that separated the fiber from the seeds many times faster than could be accomplished by hand. Later innovations of the gin made cotton growing highly profitable, and expanded its cultivation halfway across the North American continent. The gin made cotton the least expensive and most extensively used textile fabric in the world. It also brought about a huge demand for slaves to work the cotton fields until there lived 4 million of them in the South just prior to the civil war.[10] Slavery was the second pillar on which the Industrial Revolution developed.

Economic And Political Trends After The Civil War

Simply releasing the slaves from their burden was perhaps the cruelest of actions that resulted from the conclusion of the civil war in 1865. Most of these people could not read or write, and as a group they possessed few marketable skills beyond working in the fields. They typically lacked any propertied assets that might alleviate the intense poverty into which they had been thrust. Their dearth of expertise and assets made them extremely vulnerable to the whims of the white ruling class of the South. Immediately after the war, the former slaves had no jobs by which to support themselves while the plantation owners no longer had any workers. Many of the newly freed people were compelled by these circumstances to become sharecroppers, while a smaller number were forced into tenant farming.

Both types of farmers cultivated the land of the plantation owners. Sharecroppers gave the landlord a portion of their crops in exchange for shelter, land to cultivate, food, tools and mules. Tenant farmers rented land from their former masters, but ultimately a large percentage of the crops they cultivated were used to pay the rent, and they received little else in the bargain. The tenants needed to provide their own tools and mules.[11] These arrangements were nothing more than a new form of servitude forced upon the freed people.

Regardless of their race, many farmers throughout the United States battled an enemy they could not win against when crop prices continuously dropped for several decades after the civil war. Farming was then a highly competitive industry without government subsidies and protections. With increasing efficiency, thousands of farmers competed against one another and produced more and more crops of every kind, but ultimately efficient production coupled with rigorous rivalries forced crop prices downward. Many of the independent farmers of the South and West found themselves unable to repay their bank loans as the prices they received for their wheat, cotton, apples, corn, tobacco and other goods drifted lower and lower. The results were higher and higher rates of farm foreclosures.

The Industrial Revolution in the South and the West was insignificant compared to what was occurring in the North and Northeast, and jobs in new urban industries were relatively scarce in these areas. As the foreclosure rate of independent farmers remained high throughout the United States for decades after the civil war, and with relatively few opportunities in industrial employment, hundreds of thousands of the formerly independent farmers were forced into tenant farming and sharecropping, especially in the South. Worst yet for farmers of both races, many regressed to the status of day laborers.[12]

The sizes of tenant farms shrank appreciably from 1865 to 1900 as more and more independent farmers were forced to leave their lands due to bank foreclosures and shifted to tenant farming. Nobody was making any more land, but the numbers of people demanding parcels on which to farm as tenants and sharecroppers rose, and so the plantation owners simply reduced the sizes of their lots to make room for those seeking a place to cultivate their fields. This decreased the potential yield of crops each time the lands were sliced into smaller parcels, and the depth of poverty among farm families correspondingly rose. Some tenant farmers received as little as $38 per year per capita in the lower Mississippi Delta.[13] For millions of farm family's life just got worse and worse between 1865 and 1900.

Throughout the South, tenant farm families lived in shacks with holes in the walls and roofs that leaked whenever it rained. The typical diet of these people consisted mainly of meal, molasses, and occasionally meat. Newly born babies spent much of their time lying in furrows while their mothers worked the fields.[14] Children began working beside their mothers and fathers in the fields when they were six years old.[15] Education for these people was virtually non-existent. They grew up in the cotton fields, married early, had children early, and continued a life cycle that propelled successive generations ever deeper into destitution and helplessness. On the other hand, diminishing farm sizes and falling crop prices were not the only factors that contributed to their growing poverty.

Corporations added to the growing misery of farm families during this period. Farmers had to buy expensive manufactured goods from U.S. corporations, because these businesses had purchased high tariffs from their government and prevented cheaper European products from getting to the farmers. Rather than responding to supply and demand, railroad rates often reflected the corporate need for rising dividends and stock prices, and the farmers and others were made to pay the difference when shipping their crops to far away markets.

In response to their faltering fortunes, white farmers formed into associations, such as the Grange movement and the Farmers Alliance. The latter led to the development of a grave threat to corporate dominance over the political and judicial processes of the United States.

The Farmers Alliance was formed in Texas in 1877 because of the continuous fall in the prices of farm products, and as might be expected these people weren't overly thrilled with the corruption displayed by corporations. And there were plenty of examples of illegal business activities occurring throughout the nation in the farmlands, the cities and the halls of the U.S. congress. For example, some years after the Alliance was founded, eight American business firms fixed the prices of jute bags at an extremely high level compared to previous years. These bags were extremely important for cotton farmers because they held together cotton bales. Alliance members boycotted the jute bag conspiracy, and they obtained better prices through their actions. In the summer of 1886, in Cleburne, Texas, Alliance representatives wrote the "Cleburne Demands." They were written in response to "onerous and shameful abuses" working people had endured for decades because of "powerful corporations." The farmers demanded "regulation of railroad rates, heavy taxation of land held only for speculative purposes, and an increase in the money supply."[16] According to Southern historian C. Vann Woodward, the political and wealthy vested interests of the South were tied to "corporate, industrial and railroad interests." So naturally they were against adopting Alliance ideas "about money, banks, railroads, and agrarian reforms."[17] During this period the Augusta Chronicle of Georgia called railroad baron Jay Gould the richest man in the United States. Gould and several other millionaires…"'controlled over 40,000 miles of railway lines,'" much of them in the South.[18] All of the demands made at Cleburne would have helped to improve the plight of many dirt-poor farmers if they had been legislated into law, but they would also have cut into ever-rising corporate profits and dividends for politically powerful millionaires. Enacting the demands of the farmers into law would have meant that railroads would not have been able to raise their freight rates on a whim, nor would corporations have been able to speculate on land, and a rise in the money supply would have cut interest rates banks and stores charged farmers, which were often as high as 25 percent.

The Alliance faced several daunting obstacles from the beginning. Of those long-gone years in the South and the West, Woodward noted, "Even in the modern court the judge tried railroad cases with free (railroad) passes in his pockets."[19] In other words, corporations had fixed the courts and ensured victory over their opponents in these battlegrounds. Quite often, the local police also favored the rich and their corporations. You might think things couldn't get much more one sided, but of course it was because major newspapers were owned by affluent consumers, and they usually closed ranks with their fellow millionaires by providing unfavorable news coverage of the Alliance and its members. Dirt poor subsistence farmers also lacked the political experience, connections and sophistication compared to their opponents, especially when it came to fixing elections. In this regard, the rich were in a league of their own. Despite all of these obstacles, the strength of the Alliance continued to grow. There were 100,000 white members by 1886. The numbers continued to swell until peaking at approximately three million during the 1890s.

In the South, on December 11, 1886, a "Colored Farmers National Alliance" was formed. Membership possibly exceeded 1 million during the 1890s. Many people of both colors saw the need to unite in order to achieve similar goals, and joint conferences were held between the two organizations. According to historian Howard Zinn, "A leader of the Florida Colored Alliance said: 'We are aware of the fact that the laboring colored man's interests and the laboring white man's interest are one and the same.'"[20]

At a joint conference in 1889, an African-American delegate suggested the two groups begin putting their own people into elected offices. In Kansas that year, the Alliance began doing just that. In 1890, thirty-eight Alliance people were elected to Congress. In the South, the two groups managed to elect sympathetic governors in Georgia and Texas. By 1892, a political revolution had emerged when the alliance of blacks and whites congealed into a third major political force called the Populist Party. And it wasn't just a white mans party either; African-Americans were elected to state executive committees, as well as local, state, and federal offices.[21]

William Garrott Brown, a historian who lived through the movement wrote, "'I call that particular change a revolution, and I would use a stronger term if there were one; for no other political movement—ever altered Southern life so profoundly.'"[22] In those very early days of the party, conflicts erupted over racial issues to be sure, but for the most part, rich folks of the South found themselves in a state of shock at how well the two races got along. Woodward noted, "Populist sheriffs saw to it that Negroes appeared for jury duty; and Populist newspaper editors sought out achievements of Negroes to praise in their columns."[23] During the electoral campaign of 1892, members of the Ku Klux Klan threatened to lynch an African-American Populist. However, they decided not to carry out their threat once two thousand armed white Populists responded to a call for help, and guarded the man "for two nights at his home to avert the threat of violence." Some of the farmers rode all night to respond to the plea for assistance.[24]

As the Populists began electing officials to all sorts of political offices, corporations and their political allies fought back with any means necessary to maintain the political and economic status quo. According to Woodward, they used "fraud," "intimidation," "bribery," "violence," and "terror."[25] Populists were even "turned out of church, driven from their homes, and refused credit because of their beliefs." One Southern Populist complained of being shot at several times. "Grand juries, he complained, will not indict our assailants. Courts give us no protection."[26] Of course, he may not have known the courts were fixed against him and his fellow Populists. In the 1892 Georgia state election, members of the Democratic Party killed an estimated fifteen African-American Populists.[27] Vote fraud was common. The millionaire clubs known as the Democratic and Republican parties used every means necessary to defeat the majority of voters, including "ballot-box stuffing" and "voting of minors."[28] According to Woodward, in Augusta, Georgia during the 1892 campaign,

> Negro plantation hands and laborers were hauled to town in wagon loads, marched to the polls in squads, and voted repeatedly. Negroes were hauled across the Savannah River from South Carolina in four-horse wagon loads and voted in Augusta. Whiskey was dispensed by the barrel in Augusta wagon yards, and cash payment made to voters.[29]

Woodward noted that "Time after time the Populists would discover that after they had carried the white counties, fraudulent returns from the Black Belt counties padded with ballots the Negro did or did not cast were used to overwhelm them." The Populists in 1896 carried four-fifths "of the parishes of Louisiana that had white majorities," but fraudulent votes from black communities ensured their defeat. "The *New Orleans Times-Democrat* cynically remarked that white supremacy had once again been 'saved by negro (sic) votes.'"[30]

Disillusioned, the dirt poor white farmers of the Alliance grew disenchanted with their African-American allies, who they assumed were voting against their own interests. In reality, Alliance members of both races were cheated by massive political corruption engineered by those with political and financial ties to corporations.

The rich people who ruled the South, desperate to stop any reforms that might allow their working class rivals to rise up from their poverty using their own labor, came up with a brilliant series of ideas that could be legislated into action. Lawmakers of the old Southeastern states enacted segregation laws over almost every possible way imaginable to separate the poor whites from the poor blacks. Among hundreds of possible situations, these laws made it illegal for blacks and whites to: sit together in public transportation; intermarry; use the same public water fountains and bathrooms; go to the same public schools; frequent the same restaurants, taverns, and other public places. They even had to enter court houses from different doorways. One court made black witnesses swear to tell the truth, the whole truth, and nothing but the truth using a different bible than white witnesses.

Using their power in state legislatures, affluent whites and their corporate allies also erected barriers to prevent African-Americans and poor whites from voting. One such law required property qualifications in order to vote. Day laborers, sharecroppers and tenant farmers automatically lost their legal rights to cast their ballots simply because they didn't own land. Literacy tests were adopted by many states, and they were often quite complicated. Nobody was allowed to vote if they could not pass the test. Naturally, people with little or no education failed to get the necessary scores to vote. Under the circumstances, and as might be expected, governments weren't too keen to allocate money that would be used for educating poor whites, and this was especially true for black people. According to Woodward, the poll tax was devised to curtail the voting rights of African-Americans and "objectionable whites as well," and this included Populists who objected to the racism being played out.[31] In some states, poll taxes were enacted into law. Citizens needed to pay the tax in order to vote, and poor people were unlikely to vote if they didn't have the money to pay.

Woodward noted that the movements to take away the votes of African-Americans, and to segregate them from whites, "...met with stout resistance and succeeded in some states by narrow margins or the use of fraud." He also pointed out that, "In order to overcome the opposition and divert the suspicions of the poor and illiterate whites that they as well as the Negro were in danger of losing the franchise (the right to vote)—a suspicion that often proved justified"—the leaders of the anti-Populist movement resorted to an intensive propaganda campaign of white supremacy.[32]

In 1870, congress had passed the fourteenth amendment to the Constitution which made it illegal for these actions to occur. The amendment had been approved in order to ensure that the freed slaves would not be deprived of their civil rights. Section one of the amendment reads as follows.

> All persons born or naturalized in the United States, and subject to the jurisdiction thereof, are citizens of the United States and of the State wherein they reside. No state shall make or enforce any law which shall abridge the privileges or immunities of citizens of the United States; nor shall any State deprive any person of life, liberty, or property, without due process of law; nor deny to any person within its jurisdiction the equal protection of the laws.

The actions of the vested interests of the South were obviously in violation of the section one, and yet federal officials, at least some of whom likely had many railroad passes in their pockets, refused to enforce this provision of the constitution. This refusal resulted in the elimination of the constitutionally guaranteed rights of African-Americans for decades.

The lesson to be learned from the Populist people's movement is that when citizens of the lower classes demand genuine democracy in the U.S.A, and especially if they threaten the very existence of the corporate/government alliance, the latter will strike with whatever means is necessary to continue ruling from the top down. This includes being willing to violate the Constitution using any means necessary. In contemporary times, such actions will be justified through the hoax of "national security."

Rise Of The Corporations

Prior to the civil war, corporations were given the legal right to exist by state charters, and they usually came with a provision that they provide a public good, such as build a canal or a railroad. Some charters stipulated corporations could only have limited life spans. Stockowners were often legally liable for damages caused by their companies. These early charters also stated that corporations were "artificial persons." These early corporations were legalized investor unions in the United States, but the scope of the work they could take on was limited by their charters.

After the civil war, in the court systems and in local, state and federal governments, corporations whittled away at the rights of citizens to control them. Some of their gains in state legislatures included limiting the liability of shareholders and managers, and state corporate charters were issued in perpetuity.[33] It is difficult to suggest how much of these corporate gains were due to bribery. However, given the over-abundance of shady political deals at the time, it is likely that bribes played the primary role that allowed corporations to gain constitutional rights.

Intertwined corporate and political corruption was nothing new during the nineteenth century. The people whose financial fortunes were weaved together with corporations were often quick to bribe public officials to enact legislation beneficial to them selves. These enticements often led to "tariff, banking, railroad, labor and public lands legislation."[34] Tariffs were raised to high levels on imported European manufactured goods, making them more expensive than those things produced by U.S. businesses. This forced citizens to pay higher prices for such items than would otherwise have been the case. Railroads received public land and money in order to build new lines.

The administration of President Ulysses Grant, in particular, is often cited for its corruption. Even before he became president, the liquor industry for years had short-changed the federal government of an immense amount of taxes. Distillers bribed low paid revenue agents to ensure that taxes did not have to be paid. Grant authorized an investigation when he was confronted with evidence of the dishonesty. Treasury agents swarmed into distilleries and bottling plants in numerous Midwest cities, including Chicago, St. Louis and Milwaukee. All of the Internal Revenue offices were put under Treasury custody because of the pervasive corruption of its officials and agents. Nearly every Republican in political office had benefited from unlawful distilling. Another scandal involved Grant's attorney general, George Williams. He was forced to resign when it was alleged that his office had abandoned legal action against Pratt & Boyd, a mercantile business, following a suspected $30,000 bribe to Mrs. Williams. The convincing evidence showed the business had made "fraudulent customs house entries" involving large amounts of money.[35] The Grant Administration was tainted by scandals, yet these were hardly a novelty for the era.

The political and economic corruption of our wealthiest consumers, along with their corporations, was exemplified by the battle for the Erie Railroad. In 1868, Commodore Vanderbilt began purchasing Erie stock in order to gain control of the company. Jay Gould, Jim Fisk and Daniel Drew, members of the board of directors of the Erie, also wanted to control the railroad. In order to fend off Vanderbilt, the three began printing Erie stock in the hope that they would be able to financially break the Commodore. They simply flooded the market with these certificates. When he discovered what game was afoot, Vanderbilt used his fortune, lawyers and accommodating judges to halt this affair through the use of court injunctions. Eventually, to avoid arrest in the state of New York, the three directors fled to New Jersey, whereupon the state legislature incorporated the Erie, and amazingly authorized the trio to issue Erie stock at will. There is no telling how much money the three paid the legislators for these two favors. Gould then attempted to get the same authorization from the legislature of New York, "whose members for the most part sold their votes at open bidding in the corridors of the State House." New York state Senator A.C. Matoon sided with Vanderbilt after receiving a $20,000 bribe (which would equal hundreds of thousands of dollars today). He then switched sides when Gould bribed him with $20,000, and this was after the Commodore had given him another $15,000. The Senate approved the Erie bill on April 18th, leaving Vanderbilt so disgusted that he pulled out of the "bribery contest." The members of the Legislature were so outraged at this withdrawal of bribes that they voted to pass the bill 101 to six. When the Commodore's money was still circulating a few weeks before, they had defeated it eighty-three to thirty-two.[36] Afterwards, the Assembly also tried to find ways to hurt Vanderbilt for failing to continue to bribe them.[37]

Five years later, the New York Legislature investigated the corruption of itself during this affair. The Report on the Select Committee of the Assembly concluded that Gould had spent over a million dollars bribing lawmakers during the battle for the Erie Railroad. "What the Erie has done other great corporations are doing from year to year," the report stated, "'Combined as they are, the power of the great moneyed corporations of this country is a standing menace to the liberties of the people. The railroad lobby flaunts its ill-gotten gains in the faces of our legislatures, and in all our politics the debasing influence is felt.'" Gould testified to this same committee that he could not remember how many elections he had purchased.[38] Both he and Vanderbilt were not alone in this political corruption.

Collis P. Huntington was the "operating genius" of the Southern Pacific Railroad and its subsidiary, the Central Pacific. He was "sometimes referred to as the 'Jay Gould of the Pacific Coast.'" He was a politically influential figure, which was made necessary because of Gould's attempts to push his railroad lines to the Pacific Ocean, which might have hurt the profitability of the Southern and the Central. Huntington had written that the U.S. Congress "was a 'wild set of demagogues,' who were easily bribed but hard to pin down on their promises." He once complained that the lobbyists of Gould had pushed the price of a congressman "to $10,000."[39]

Given the abilities of powerful and influential corporate aristocrats such as Vanderbilt, Gould, Drew, and Huntington to bribe public officials, it should not be too surprising to discover that the judicial system was not immune from such incentives, especially given that judges often had free railroad passes in their pockets even as they presided over cases involving railroads.

When President Benjamin Harrison was in office, he appointed George Shiras to the Supreme Court on the recommendation of Andrew Carnegie, a corporate aristocrat who had contributed heavily to Harrison's campaign. Shiras was Carnegie's attorney, fishing buddy, and close friend. As a Supreme Court Justice, his pro-corporate bias was made conspicuous in January 1895 when he decided that the American Sugar Refining Company was not a monopoly in violation of the Sherman Anti-Trust Act, although it controlled 90 to 98 percent of the sugar refining industry.[40] In May of that year, "he voted to sustain an injunction the federal government used to smash a strike at the Pullman Company.[41] Whether purchased by corporations or not, other justices had pro-corporate biases and backgrounds. Chief Justice Morrison Remick Waite had been an attorney for the railroads prior to being appointed Supreme Court Justice by President Grant. Supreme Court Justice Stephen Field was closely associated with the Southern Pacific Railroad, and continuously demonstrated favorable bias toward the railroads as a justice of the Supreme Court.[42] It is conceivable that most courts, if not all, at all levels throughout the nation, including the Supreme Court of the United States, were loaded with cronies of wealthy corporate interests.

Therefore, in 1886 nobody should have been too shocked when the United States Supreme Court, in Santa Clara County vs. the Southern Pacific Railroad Company, ruled that Collis P. Huntington's corporation was entitled to all of the constitutional rights of human citizens guaranteed by the Fourteenth Amendment. The case was a simple tax assessment issue, and had nothing to do with whether a corporation was or was not a person under the Constitution of the United States. Just prior to the opening arguments in the case, the former railroad employee, Chief Justice Morrison Remick Waite said, "The court does not wish to hear arguments on the question whether the provision in the Fourteenth Amendment to the Constitution, which forbids a State to deny to any person within its jurisdiction the equal protection of the laws, applies to these corporations. We are all of opinion that it does." Waite's reasoning reversed earlier rulings. Corporations had argued before the Supreme Court in cases prior to 1886 that since they were chartered as "artificial persons," they were persons with all of the protections of the Fourteenth Amendment, but they had lost each time.

Waite and the rest of the members of the Supreme Court knew that in the Constitution of the United States no mention was made of corporations. They also knew the Fourteenth Amendment had been written to ensure the legal rights of the recently freed slaves. According to the amendment, in order to be a citizen a "person" must be "naturalized" or "born" in the United States. Waite and his fellow justices knew corporations, given life by legislative fiat, could not be given the legal rights of citizens because they were not "naturalized" or "born." This decision by the Supreme Court also brought about a legal contradiction. Under the reasoning of the justices, corporations were persons with all the protections of the Constitution of the United States. However, these persons are owned by shareholders, which is a condition of slavery. Under the Thirteenth Amendment, slavery is forbidden. The whole idea that corporations were somehow people defied both logic and law.

What compelled the Supreme Court to decide that corporations were somehow legally entitled to the same rights as citizens, especially given all of the legal contradictions within its decision? Since this decision defied both logic and the law, and given the immense corruption of the times, a person might rightly come to the conclusion that political and judicial corruption played the central role in the decision made by the Supreme Court.

Strange as it may seem, the time period from 1886 to roughly 1910 witnessed the destruction of constitutional rights for poor whites and African-Americans that were supposed to be guaranteed by the Fourteenth Amendment. When these citizens were dispossessed of those rights, it ensured that wealthy corporate interests and their political allies benefited handsomely. Meanwhile, in 1886, using the Fourteenth Amendment, corporations were elevated to the status of citizens although they could not vote, eat, drink, procreate, be drafted into the military, etc. However, through their new legal status, they were able to steal more money from farmers and other people who worked for a living, all for the benefit of a few wealthy consumers who largely controlled the political, police, military and judicial apparatus of the United States.

The Anti-Labor Movement

The power brandished by the U.S. federal government, as well as governments at the state and local levels, has long been used to stifle the voices of dissent whenever protests grew too loudly against habitually rising corporate profits and corrupt political power, as well as the mal-distribution of the fruits of labor. The labor union movement has been a seemingly constant target. Yet the only thing labor union members have typically desired are the rising standards of living falsely guaranteed by the prophets and defenders of the system. Typical government tactics used against the labor movement include committing acts of terrorism against citizens. The history of the textile industry after the Civil War is one of many excellent examples of the bias elected officials have usually possessed toward corporations, rich shareholders and CEOs, while also showing their disdain for working people.

In the decades following the civil war, the corporate form of business gradually displaced sole proprietorships and partnerships in the textile industry. By
1900, corporations were the form of ownership of 84.1 percent of all cotton
goods businesses. This included the mills where cotton was spun, the weaving of
piece goods, and the manufacture of such items as lamp wicks, corset lacings,
and tape. Moreover, corporations had become the dominate form of ownership
in 50.2 percent of all dyeing and finishing textile firms, and in 26.9 percent of
the businesses that manufactured men's furnishings.[43] Because of the transformation to the corporate form of doing business, there also arose the need to continuously enhance earnings one quarter after the next, which was an outcome
that had been unnecessary under the older forms of doing business. Sometimes,
corporations were ineffective at using their political strengths to augment or
keep earnings rolling upwards, and when that was the case, they simply moved
their production facilities to where they did wield such power.

In 1898 the legislators of Massachusetts passed a law prohibiting people
under the age of fourteen from working, and the state strictly enforced it. In
1907, the same state prohibited the work of women and children in textile mills
after 6 p.m. Four years later in 1911, Massachusetts legislators passed a law
mandating a fifty-four hour work week.[44] As restrictions on child labor occurred in the Northeast, from 1890 onward, restrictions on the use of such labor
in the Southeastern United States were relaxed, and this helped to lead a movement of textile factories from New England to the South. Alabama had enacted a
law in 1887 that prohibited child labor under the age of fourteen. This law also
fixed an eight-hour workday for those who were under sixteen years old. However, in what would become repeated throughout modern economic history, a
northern mill "that had moved into Alabama" successfully fought to abolish
this law.[45] According to historian Gary M. Fink, in Georgia around this same
time, the law prohibiting children less than ten years old from working in the
mills was a sad joke due to lax enforcement and numerous loopholes.[46]

More than 100 years ago, author A.J. Mckelway argued, "In any child-
employing industry the wages of the adult are measured by the wages of the
child." He showed that adults earned what children were paid in the cotton mills,
and both adults and children often worked over sixty hours per week.
McKelway cited a study by The Federal Labor Bureau that found in some mills in
South Carolina adults actually received wages that were less than those earned
by children for the same work.[47] In such situations, adults competed against

their own children in the labor markets. With meager wages, additional family members were forced into the job market which lowered wages even further. This accounts for why children as young as seven years worked in the mills.

Some cotton mills actually owned complete towns in which their employees lived, and as might be expected the local police owed their positions and loyalty to management. Employees purchased their groceries in company stores and were forced to pay the prices offered by mill managers. Sometimes the workers went to schools and churches owned by the companies. Taking part in labor union activities meant being expelled from those institutions, including their homes. During times of turmoil, the police often interfered violently on the only side with political and economic powers. Consequently, the deck was stacked against the workers of company towns whenever conflicts erupted between them and management.

In cities and towns not owned by any mills, local vested interests of the South went out of their way to attract investments from the North. This was not done in order to increase the standards of living for the vast majority of working citizens, who were expected to be cannon fodder in the cotton mills. In 1929, the Marion, North Carolina Chamber of Commerce issued the following announcement, and it is indicative of the attitude of many Southern and Northern business and political leaders.

> There are tax assessments to be adjusted, and Marion's attitude is fair
> and constructive. There are water, sewage, and utilities to be supplied,
> and Marion's spirit is liberal. *There are police and legal protection to be*
> *provided, and Marion's response is certain.*[48] (Italics theirs.)

And they weren't kidding. The leaders of the city of Marion were attempting to attract businesses from outside the area, and they were willing to provide a fair number of publicly promised favors in order to achieve this result. That very year of 1929 the police and the legal system of the city were used in very brutal ways to achieve the desired outcomes.

It was in Marion that the United Textile Workers (UTW), an affiliate of the American Federation of Labor (AFL), attempted to organize the labor forces of the Marion Manufacturing Company and the Clinchfield Mill. The workers demanded a fifty-five hour work week with no reduction in pay. The management of both companies refused so the employees decided to go on strike. A judge issued an injunction on behalf of the companies that prevented strikers from assembling inside the mill village. The injunction also restrained the repre-

sentatives of the UTW from encouraging strikers to picket, a clear violation of
the Second Amendment of the Constitution of the United States. A settlement
was eventually reached, but it was violated by the owner of the Marion mill. As
a second strike loomed, the local sheriff and several heavily armed deputies ar-
rived at the Marion plant. Along with several foremen, the law officers antago-
nized the labor force as they worked. After approximately five hours about 250
workers decided they had had enough of the harassment, and they decided to go
on strike. The sheriff demanded that they disperse. When the strikers refused to
do so, the officers fired tear gas into the crowd. A striker then attacked the sheriff
with a cane, whereupon the deputies fired their guns into the assembled employees, killing sixteen and wounding eighteen more. The officers of the law were
charged with murder, but they were released on bail. The sheriff then issued
warrants against thirty-two strikers on charges of insurrection and riot. Families were evicted from the mill town within a month. More than 100 strikers
were dropped from the rolls of the East Marion Missionary Baptist Church. On
November 30, four of the strikers were found guilty of inciting a riot. On December 22, the sheriff and his deputies were found not guilty of murder. In order
to protect corporate profits, the mill owners, the police system, the court system
and the church used terrorism, harassment, murder and religious ostracism
against their fellow citizens.[49] And believe it or not, these were common tactics
the corporate/government alliance used against people who worked for a living
in the United States.

During this same period, several mills in the Appalachian highlands of
South Carolina went on strike. In March 1929, in the town of Gastonia, North
Carolina, the National Textile Workers' Union (NTWU) organized a strike
against the Loray Mill, which was owned by a company located in Rhode Island.
On the eighteenth of April, despite the presence of the National Guard, approximately one hundred masked men demolished the union store and destroyed its
relief groceries. Strikers then established a tent city with armed guards. The
managers of the mill convinced a fair number of their workers to break from the
strike, and these people went back to work. Despite this, those still on strike kept
the mill from operating at its full capacity. On June 7th, sheriff deputies and the
police attacked about 150 strikers. Later that night, the Chief of Police, Orville
Aderholt, and four other policemen attempted to enter the tent city without a
search warrant. The strikers were naturally nervous due to the previous destruction of the union store, and the attack earlier that day, and they weren't

going to allow these assaults to happen again. They were on guard. No one really knows who fired the first shot, but plenty of guns were ablaze and Aderholt was killed. A grand jury indicted sixteen union members for murder and seven others for assault with deadly weapons. A mistrial was declared. Afterwards, a group of about five hundred men raided the strikers' headquarters at Gastonia and Bessemer City. Union men were kidnapped and beaten. The leaders of the NTWU then called for a mass meeting on September 14, but this was stopped by an anti-union mob. Ella May Wiggins was killed when shots were fired into a group of unarmed strikers. Although Horace Wheeler, an employee of Loray Mills, was identified as the killer of Mrs. Wiggins, and despite many witnesses' that testified to this, the jury in his trial determined that he was innocent of the crime. Despite many instances of union organizers being shot, kidnapped and flogged, no one was ever convicted of any of these crimes. However, in the retrial of the killing of the Chief Aderholt, seven men were convicted of second degree murder.[50]

This kind of state sponsored terrorism was used against working people throughout the history of the United States, and in every region of the country. The New Deal programs of President Franklin Roosevelt provided citizens and their labor unions greater rights to organize in order to achieve higher standards of living. However, these rights were never as great as the privileges enjoyed by wealthy investors, inasmuch as average union members simply did not have the financial clout necessary to make purchases in the supermarkets of politics to the same degree as wealthy investors. In addition, much of the advantages obtained by the wealthy had already been established by such bizarre things as the Supreme Court decision of 1886 giving corporations the legal rights of personhood.

Conclusion

As the corporate economic system continues its slow erosion and eventual collapse, citizens will organize and begin political and economic actions to ameliorate their worsening conditions. The fight to end corporate control over our economic and political lives will then begin in earnest. Our corporate heroes and wealthy shareholders will use their overwhelming financial power in the political markets and over the court systems to fight back. They will want to continue to transfer income and wealth from working people to themselves in order to sustain the system for as long as is possible. The same forces that brought about the end of the Populist Party and bludgeoned, terrorized and murdered members of labor unions will be brought to bear against any sizeable anti-corporate movement, although the tactics used against them will be more subtle. Typically, the FBI will plant operatives into any organization in order to sow the seeds of dissension. Nowadays, it likely will go farther than that with the new homeland security apparatus. And when it comes to the legalities of the tactics that might be used against human rights organizations, you can reasonably guess where the sympathies of any court justice might lay. At least one justice of the Supreme Court has gone duck hunting with his favorite corporate welfare queen during the last few years. Studies of history has shown us that we can expect a difficult and prolonged struggle to bring about the end of corporate power, to re-establish an economic system in which the abilities of people to produce goods and services determine their fortunes, and to re-establish a government of the people; and not just for the wealthy few who reap the benefits of the economic and political systems at the expense of everyone else.

Notes

1. Smith, Adam, *An Inquiry into the Nature and Causes of the Wealth of Nations*, The Modern Library: New York, 1937, p. 702.

2. Commager, Henry S., Morris, Richard B., *The Spirit of Seventy-Six*, Castle Books: New Jersey 2002, p. 1.

3. Smith, p. 700.

4. Smith, p. 699.

5. Smith, p. 712.

6. Smith, p. 715-716.

7. Winthrop, Jordan; Greenblatt, Miriam; Bowes, John, *The Americans: A History*, McDougal, Littell & Company: Illinois, 1992. Pg. 251.

8. The Americans, 251.

9. The Americans, 251.

10. Todd, Paul; Curti, Merle, *Rise of the American Nation*, Harcourt Brace Jovanovich Publishers: San Diego, 1982, p. 298.

11. Kester, Howard, *Revolt Among the Sharecroppers*, Arno Press: New York, 1969, pp. 8-21.

12. Kester, p. 22.

13. United States, Federal Emergency Relief administration, Division of Research, Statistics, and Finance, "Farm Tenancy: Report of the President's Committee," Washington: 1935, pp. 55-56.

14. Kester, pp. 46-48.

15. Kester, pp. 46-48.

16. Zinn, Howard, *A People's History of the United States*, Harper Perennial: New York: 1995, p. 280.

17. Woodward, C. Vann, *The Strange Career of Jim Crow*, Oxford University Press: New York, 2001, p. 77.

18. Woodward, C. Vann, *Tom Watson: Agrarian Rebel*, Oxford University Press: New York, 1963, p. 179.

19. Woodward, *Tom Watson*, p. 172.

20. Zinn, pp. 283-284.

21. Zinn, pp. 276-282.

22. Woodward, *Jim Crow*, p. 78.

23. Woodward, *Jim Crow*, pp. 63-64.

24. Woodward, *Jim Crow*, pp. 62-63.

25. Woodward, *Jim Crow*, pp. 76-77.

26. Woodward, *Tom Watson*, p. 223.

27. Woodward, *Tom Watson*, p. 237.

28. Woodward, *Tom Watson*, p. 241.

29. Woodward, *Tom Watson*, p. 241.

30. Woodward, *Jim Crow*, p. 80.

31. Woodward, *Jim Crow*, p. 84.

32. Woodward, *Jim Crow*, p. 85.

33. Korten, David C., *When Corporations Rule the World*, Kummarian and Berrett-Koehler: West Hartford and San Francisco, p. 58-59.

34. Korten, p. 58.

35. Smith, Jean Edward, *Grant*, Simon and Schuster: New York, 2001, pp. 583-84.

36. O'Connor, Richard, *Gould's Millions*, Doubleday & Company, Inc: New York, 1962, pp. 64-83.

37. Klein, Maury, *The Life and Legend of Jay Gould*, The Johns Hopkins University Press: Baltimore and London, 1986, p. 85.

38. O'Connor, p. 76.

39. O'Connor, pp. 223-227.

40. Some sources suggest that the corporation controlled 98 percent of the industry. See Todd, Curti, *Rise of the American Nation*, pp 451-52. The Sherman Anti-Trust was an alleged anti-monopoly law.

41. Krause, Peter, *Carnegie*, John Wiley & Sons: Hoboken, New Jersey, 2002, pp. 252-53.

42. Hartmann, Thom, *Unequal Protection: The Rise of Corporate Dominance and the Thief of Human Rights*, Rodale:city unknown, 2002, Chapter 6.

43. United States, Census Bureau, *Character of Ownership: Summary for the United States, for all Industries Combined, Washington*: Volume 8, 1910, pp. 137-138.

44. Conant, Richard, "The Textile Industry and Child Labor," The Child Labor Bulletin: May 1913, p. 92.

45. Lovejoy, Owen, "Edgar Gardner Murphy," *The New York Evening Post*, Rpt. in "The Child Labor Bulletin," National Child Labor Committee: New York, Nov. 1913, pp. 50-51.

46. Fink, Gary, *The Fulton Bag and Cotton Mills Strike of 1914-1915*, ILR Press: Ithaca, New York: 1993, p. 51.

47. McKelway, A.J., *Child Wages in the Cotton Mills: Our Modern Feudalism*, The Child Labor Bulletin: New York, May 1913, p. 10.

48. Meiklejohn, Kenneth, and Peter Nehemkis, *Southern Labor in Revolt*, The Intercollegiate Student Council for the League of Industrial Democracy, New York: 1930, p. 6.

49. Yellen, Samuel, *American Labor Struggles: 1877-1934*, Anchor Foundation: New York, 1988.

50. Yellen, pp. 308-316.

Chapter Eleven

THE NEW AMERICAN REVOLUTION

During the bleak months of 1932, as the unemployment rate raced upward to 19 percent and beyond, and eliminated any notions of an immediate reversal of fortunes, save for a few obtuse defenders of the old system, a voice of reason offered a simple question. The economist Stuart Chase had asked in his latest book *A New Deal*, "What is an economy for?" Chase had been an accountant most of his early adult life, but then he switched to studying economics while in his forties. In the early 1920s, he enrolled in classes at the New School for Social Research where he studied under Thorstein Veblen. Chase became a prolific economics writer for more than a decade afterwards. Perhaps his most influential book was *A New Deal*. It has been credited with providing the name of Roosevelt's series of programs that were collectively named after the title, and it offered several remedies to the dismal economic situation. Chase also worked as a minor official within Roosevelt's administration, and then he faded into history.

Chase had come up with an intriguing question pertinent to contemporary times. So what is an economy for? As citizens of the United States, should we have an economic system that has been constructed to bring about always increasing income and wealth transfers from those who work for a living to the politically and financially powerful? Is that what we should work for? Should the wealthy be allowed to acquire ever rising unearned income without ever lifting a finger to produce anything? Should we continue to allow the raping and pillaging of public institutions by corporations under the transfer of income scheme known as "privatization," just so their earnings can be made easier? In the name of efficiency, should we allow businesses to be so large that CEOs have few ideas of what is actually occurring throughout their vast financial empires? Should corporations be allowed to injure people and pollute the environment without the owners or chief officers of the firm possessing any responsibilities for their decisions? Should we have a system that requires most people to increase their productivity and work more and more hours, while earning less and less in salaries, wages, health and retirement benefits, as well as vacation time? Unless you have significant financial ties with one or more publicly traded corporations, to answer yes to any of these questions is completely crazy if not down right insane. Are these the things for which an economy is for? I don't think so, so why is the current system structured to achieve these objectives?

An important parallel question needs to be asked, "What is a government for?" More and more, corporations are gutting the democratic rights of people throughout the world, including the United States. Sure, these governments are still called democracies, but in reality they serve corporate interests for the most part, and increasingly so. Corporate democracies are not democracies for people because we know the needs of corporations quite often diverge from the interests of the great majority of the world's people. This is proven every day in any number of ways, but the most obvious one is the constant stream of income and wealth trickling upward from the bottom so that those at the top can receive their ever growing unearned revenue. It's true the vast majority of politicians will gladly broadcast all of the ways in which they have served the people, but such rhetoric is only a game to deny what has largely become reality. And to be sure, there are still a few old fashioned legislators in the halls of congress and in state and local governments who actually represent the people, but they are a small and nearly extinct minority, or so it seems. To be fair, a number of elected officials have a foot in each camp, but stubbornly and slowly they too appear to be fading into the history books. Of course, that leaves us with the pressing question. Should corporations and rich shareholders exercise control over the governments of the world to the detriment of the vast majority of the people? I don't think so, especially since these persons rely on the current economic system for their income, and it is highly unlikely they would want to reform or replace such personal goldmines of free income, except perhaps under grave economic circumstances. The promise and justification of capitalism was that living standards would rise for everybody, but this promise was always a lie. If it ever existed, this potential was reversed by the cancerous rise and dominance of publicly traded limited liability companies. Corporate control over the economies and governments of the world have largely been increasingly unpleasant and even disastrous for working people, but such domination has been very lucrative for small numbers of rich folks.[1] Just look at Mexico, a nation where wages have plunged precipitously in only twelve years since the enactment of the corporate negotiated NAFTA treaty.

Reform is thought to be possible for publicly traded businesses. Seventy years ago, during the early years of the Great Depression, Chase argued that a standard "conventional dividend" could be paid to stockholders at a set rate, eliminating much of the speculation that drives the stock markets. He claimed that a dividend amounted to a tax, and the economy of that time could easily have supported such a thing.[2] Unfortunately, a "conventional dividend" would not have eliminated the speculation from which investors receive their income. Just like today, dividends, earnings and share prices always needed to rise higher than previously in order to keep the system afloat. A fixed "conventional dividend" most likely would have been unable to attract all that many investors, who for the most part prefer always rising earnings and stock prices. Therefore, the enactment of Chase's proposal most likely would have brought about a general retreat of investors from the stock markets, sent share prices skidding, and led directly to the collapse of the markets. Consequently, failure to eliminate the speculation from the financial markets means the idea of a "conventional dividend" should have been laid to rest 70 years ago, and so it was. It's a thought that might have worked to some degree, but other changes needed to accompany a legislated "conventional dividend" for it to have achieved the desired effect. Even if such a thing were made into law by the federal government under pressure of some grave economic crisis in the future, it would surely be reversed when such a threat passed. Besides, no government, controlled or heavily influenced by corporations, would think it a good idea to reform the system too much, although democratic representatives might fiddle with it, provided such tinkering redounds to aid the increasing of profits. Any benefits that might come to the citizenry due to legalistic fiddling with the system would most likely be entirely coincidental.

This suggests reforming the system would be wishful thinking, and leads us to ponder the benefits and negatives of actually getting government to legislate publicly traded corporations out of existence. This should also include corporations that are privately held, but whose political and economic powers are so great that they are at risk, or they are in the act, of perverting the democratic processes. What can we replace the current system with? A communist structure is out of the question since it is a proven failure. Socialist economies such as those in Europe seem to work okay, but they are weighted down by the needs of their publicly traded corporations, and this has ensured that high unemployment has become a permanent condition in many of these countries. On the other hand, throughout the world there are millions of owner-operated businesses that are very successful and are creating the vast majority of the world's jobs.

The centerpiece of the new economy, therefore, ought to be locally based and ecologically sustainable small businesses. There are plenty of examples of such organizations just about anywhere in the world. These include cooperative stores, organic food stores, credit unions, local restaurants, retail stores, farms, ranches, music stores, laundries, taverns, homebuilders, auto repair shops, flea markets, local construction firms, local plumbing businesses, and manufacturing companies. Many of these types of businesses are S-corporations, which are small non-publicly traded businesses in which many of the employees are part owners. They should be carried over into the new economy.

An economic system comprised solely of non-publicly traded businesses would enhance the abilities of local people everywhere to take care of themselves and their families. Producing food for local consumption, for example, is an economic development plan that provides fresher and more readily available food supplies for the people of every community in which such plans are undertaken. Compare this to the scenes outlined earlier of Central Americans starving by the roadsides because they could not eat the coffee they had successfully cultivated, nor could they sell it because the prices offered to them were less than what it had cost to grow their crops. These people were following the alleged economic development plans of the IMF. As shown earlier, growing coffee and other non-consumable goods in order to generate export earnings was an anti-development plan that only benefited multi-national corporations. Developing small-scale economies to meet local needs would eliminate many of the scenes of people starving to death because they have been compelled to produce non-edible goods due to political circumstances beyond their control. In a small business world, as individual and collective work productivity increases, so too should the standards of living correspondingly rise for the majority of the world's working citizens because increases in work productivity would not be diverted toward always rising dividend payments.

The owners of small businesses typically supervise their company's operations, making them far more efficient than corporations spread across small and wide geographic areas'. As demonstrated earlier, skills in managing operations are not necessarily a requirement of the job of CEO because most publicly traded corporations are simply too large for one or even a small group of people to manage efficiently anyway. Imagine having a CEO who is a master lathe operator, drill press operator, seamstress, accountant, advertising professional, computer programmer, product designer, electronic engineer, wall framer, scientist, as well as a top-notch salesman who understands and can direct how corporate operations occur throughout the world among hundreds or thousands of employees, while being able to inspect the quality of the goods and services produced by his or her company, as well as those it receives from many contractors and sub-contractors from around the world. It's just not possible for one person to do all of these things, or even for a small group of people. This is why corporations so often pick inefficient life-long government bureaucrats (like Dick Cheney) who have little or no experience working in private business to be their CEOs. These people provide political connections so that their firms can more easily acquire government handouts than would otherwise be the case. Since large publicly traded corporations cannot be managed efficiently, but need constantly growing earnings, they require increasing amounts of taxpayer charity. Locally owned businesses, on the other hand, provide goods and services on a competitive basis, typically under the direction of owners who have experience in their fields. For this reason, their operations are managed far more efficiently than most—if not all—publicly traded corporations. Obviously, an economic system without publicly traded companies would provide citizens with many benefits indeed!

An economy comprised solely of small businesses would bring people closer together because each person within the range of operations might potentially be a customer, or a neighbor. Being nice might prove to be more profitable, especially if an owner has to directly confront their neighbors as irate customers. No longer would people need to talk to machines or people living thousands of miles away when they have a complaint or a compliment.

Another benefit is that local business owners may be more likely to ensure that the environments of their communities are maintained or improved, which is often a radically different sentiment expressed from far away corporate headquarters. Consequently, local businesses rather than distant corporations would also be less likely to pollute the air, land and water upon which they and their neighbors rely. Besides, local polluters might need to confront their victims now and then, people who might be their neighbors, customers and business associates. Their livelihoods would depend on being a good neighbor. This is a problem far away CEOs do not normally deal with.

Although largely in its infancy, ecologically sound and self-sustaining economic development has been occurring all over the United States from the splendor of the Shenandoah Valley of West Virginia and Virginia to the natural beauty of the Pacific Northwest, and from the stormy coast of Maine to the sun drenched beaches of Southern California. There are plenty of examples of businesses leading the way toward the development of more healthy economic systems than the corporate system can currently produce.

For many decades, the Appalachian region of Tennessee and Virginia has suffered from economic decay due to the consequences of out-of-state corporate ownership. In 1995, local citizens formed an organization called Appalachian Sustainable Development (ASD) with the intention of bringing neighboring communities together to regenerate the local economy and culture from within. The goal of these people was to develop an ecologically sustainable economy encompassing a ten county area that overlaps the two states. These counties were suffering from high unemployment, which was nearly 20 percent in some of them. The people at ASD wanted a sustainable alternative to the corporate economic system, one that would be reliant on local sources of food, timber and sales outlets. Therefore, the organization focused on two of the strengths of the area in which to begin real economic development: agriculture and timber.

ASD developed a network of twenty-seven local farmers and began marketing their produce to local and regional food stores. These farmers work as a cooperative. They meet every month from October through March and decide what each will cultivate. Some of them grow up to ten different crops. Collectively, they also determine the amount of each food to be grown and when each will be planted. This cooperation ensures that there flows a steady stream of locally cultivated food to markets throughout the area.[3]

ASD also developed a locally based, sustainable and ecologically sound forestry and wood products industry. The organization purchases timber if it is harvested by their standards, made into boards and dried in their kiln (a furnace or oven). Other local companies transform the wood into cabinets, floor materials, and other useful products. Since the trees are near their markets, and because every step of the process from raw timber to finished product adds value, loggers and landowners receive relatively high amounts of compensation for their labor, time and trouble. This economic process has been developed so as to ensure its ecological sustainability. Landowners formulate plans with ASD personnel to preserve water areas, such as streams, and provide a place for wildlife to live. There is no reliance on clear cutting large areas, which is something the Louisiana Pacific wafer board factory relied upon until it closed without notice to its 100 employees in 1996.[4]

Real economic development is also happening in Portland, Oregon. New Seasons Market is a locally owned and operated food store chain. It sells both organic and non-organically produced goods. In the produce section, signs by every display of fruits and vegetables tell exactly where each is grown, and whether or not they are organically produced. Citizens then have the option to buy locally and organically, and they are also free to choose to purchase contaminated imports for themselves, friends and family members. This is important information since citizens should have the right to know what they are being sold, and from whence and under what circumstances the food they buy is produced.

Of the food imported into the United States, 98 percent is never inspected, which is in harmony with recent trade agreements. Foreign nations are able to export low cost food because most farms in these countries pay farm workers poverty level wages, and they often use pesticides that have been banned in the United States for decades. Some of these farms are owned or influenced by U.S. corporations.[5] Supposedly, pesticides are used to kill and control pests that might eat whole crops. However, some of the pests killed every year by these toxic chemicals include roughly 20,000 farm workers from around the world. Pesticides also cause cancer, reproductive and hormonal problems, and create additional sensitivity to chemicals in humans.[6] By the time these fruits and vegetables get to kitchen tables throughout the U.S., pesticide residues still remain, and we eat them.

Genetically modified foods (GM) have also proven to be a danger to human and other animal health. Not so long ago, the Ecologist magazine reported that "one genetically engineered bacteria used in the production of the food supplement tryptophan produced dioxins that killed 37 people and permanently disabled 1500 others." In one experiment, according to the publication, rats were fed GM potatoes and "suffered stomach and intestine damage." The magazine also cited other examples providing even more evidence that these foods are dangerous to human health.[7]

The sale of local and organic produce by New Seasons is healthier, fresher and a better way of doing business than what many corporations are willing to provide. There are obviously important reasons why consumers have a right to know what it is they are buying and eating, as well as the country of origin, the use of pesticides, and whether or not foods are genetically modified, or are used as ingredients in other products. By selling locally produced organic foods, New Seasons provides this valuable service to its customers.

People living in economically and politically disadvantaged neighborhoods also can benefit from real economic development. The Rebuilding Center in Portland, Oregon is proving this by earning nearly $2 million in revenue each year as a non-profit corporation. The company dismantles houses and apartment buildings by hand and sells whatever is possible.

Shane Endicott, one of the founders, coveted work that would benefit his neighborhood. He also wanted an organization where everyone would have equality in determining how the business was managed, and he desired to work with people who possessed similar values. Endicott also did not want to use natural resources or create hazardous wastes. Therefore, it was more appealing for him to recycle materials than use up more natural resources and electricity to produce new things.

Roughly 80 percent of the Rebuilding Center's employees come from the local neighborhood, which has been economically challenged for decades. As of the year 2002, employees start at ten dollars per hour for unskilled labor, but they receive work reviews and pay raises as a matter of routine. They also have full medical and dental coverage. Endicott also reduced the huge disparities in pay between management and labor at his firm.

The Rebuilding Center was praised by a neighborhood newspaper as a keystone to the revitalization of the neighborhood. Says Endicott, "'We used to think we could attain quality of life individually, by making more money...but with our water and air increasingly polluted and so many people isolated and unhappy, the only way we'll get that quality of life is to evolve new ways to do business and to live together in communities that are value-based, not money based.'"[8]

There are plenty of examples of how a thriving values oriented economy can function without being part of the corporate economic system. There are even networks of such businesses. For example, the purpose of the "Business Alliance for Local Living Economies" is to create an interconnected nationwide movement.

Such alliances indicate that there are many people coming to the conclusion that publicly traded corporations have no place in any economic system, except to serve a small, but politically and economically potent, non-productive leisure class.

Of course, there are some who might argue that large corporations are necessary because some products require huge investments in research and development beyond what a small locally owned and operated business possibly could acquire. Besides, who would fund the retirements of working people in the absence of publicly traded corporations and the financial markets? Of course, I can't pretend to have the answers for everything, but some of the concerns of both issues are examined below starting with capital formation.

Currently, many corporations hire contractors and subcontractors to produce their goods and services. For example, athletic shoes and accessories are made primarily by relatively small contractors and subcontractors in Asia and elsewhere. The final products are shipped to the United States and Europe where they are distributed by major athletic corporations. Thousands of goods are produced and distributed in this way. There may not be a single reason why networks of small businesses, like ASD above, could not operate along similar lines in developing new goods and services, or in distributing products that require large amounts of investment in order to bring them to market. In manufacturing, for example, each member of a network could develop some portion of a new product, while another company acts as a hub to put the finished good together, and then others can market and distribute it. The differences between the networks that currently exist in the athletic shoe industry, and those that can exist, is that publicly traded corporations can be eliminated, along with the need for constantly rising profits, dividends and share prices.

When some businesses are so large no one can manage them sensibly, many of them should be broken up into multiple parts, like American Telephone and Telegraph (ATT) agreed to do back in 1982. Once broken apart, each new business unit can contract with its former fellow units to supply it with the necessary parts and expertise to produce its end products. New or established small businesses might arise to help fill voids left by the breakup of major corporations. Under the above scenario, a product designing business can hire via contract an engineering firm to develop a consumer item, and then take the final plans to a manufacturing enterprise. Along the way marketing and distribution firms can be employed to help ensure the product's arrival on store shelves. Although many pro-corporate people may mock such suggestions, many corporations already take these steps now. They design and engineer items in the United States, and then they contract with overseas manufacturers to make their products. They also hire via contract package designers, shippers, marketing and public relations firms, as well as local distributors to put their goods on market shelves. Marketing contractors, for example, then subcontract with graphic designers and other businesses to fill voids in needed areas. Corporations also engage business firms in India and elsewhere to provide product support and or customer services. And this reality demonstrates that there really are few reasons not to break apart publicly traded, limited liability corporations, and ensure that most businesses are established on local levels wherever plausible.

The replacement of large, politically powerful, monopolizing pharmaceutical drug corporations by small local businesses, or networks of them, might concern some people. Would these new business forms be able to obtain the large chunks of cash necessary to develop new drugs that the industry currently attracts from investors? It might shock some people to discover that the corporations of this industry spend more money marketing products than they spend on research in developing them. Further, if "copycat" drugs are excluded, most drug research is publicly funded.[9] Universities are the primary conduits through which pharmaceutical drug research takes place. Therefore, the elimination of corporations in this field would not necessarily create such a big research void since public funding of university research would still continue. However, the primary engine constantly driving up the price of pharmaceutical drugs for citizens, the need for ever rising earnings and dividends, would be eliminated by legislating publicly traded, limited liability corporations out of existence.

Monopoly patent rights are currently given to pharmaceutical corporations even if their drugs are developed with public money, which is another corporate welfare scheme benefiting affluent shareholders. It would be more competitive and cost effective for citizens if legislators were to limit or make non-existent any monopoly rights for any business in the pharmaceutical industry that receives any public help in the development of new drugs, whether the current structure of corporations is retained or reformed, or a new business structure replaces them. The public should not be required to subsidized business earnings in the pharmaceutical industry, and then be forced to experience the continuous inflationary spiral of the prices of these products, as is now the case. Since small localized businesses in this industry would not be publicly traded corporations, there wouldn't be a need for constantly expanding earnings, and this would extinguish the necessity for monopoly patent rights on publicly funded pharmaceutical drug research.

In the absence of publicly traded corporations, funding retirements should not be a problem. Already, even with the corporate system, in the United States tens of millions of people retire with only social security benefits, and this suggests that the corporate economy is not all that great for helping to plan retirements anyway. So why not replace this grossly inefficient system? In the new economy, the social security program should remain intact to provide a bare minimum necessary to fund retirements, and it should not be privatized in any way. Legislating publicly traded corporations out of existence will allow citizens to enhance the amount of monthly disbursements they will receive from this program, because their income will rise once the income and wealth transfer mechanisms of the corporate system are dismantled. This will permit working citizens to contribute more to the program with each paycheck, and without raising the current rate at which they pay into the system, they will be able to enhance their monthly benefit payments when they become retirees.

To augment the social security program, people will be able to sell their businesses and retire on the proceeds. And small S-corporations should continue to exist. They issue shares to individual owners. Along with wages, salaries and benefits, dividends are paid to the proprietors from the earnings of the business. Nowadays, many people either sell their shares in S-corporations when they retire, or they retain ownership and live off the dividends. People could also invest in government bonds to boost their retirement earnings. In its history, the United States government has never failed to pay back money it has borrowed. To be a member of a credit union, you need to purchase one or more shares of these businesses. Each share receives interest payments every year, which can be used to augment retirement income. Private land could be purchased as a means to fund retirements. Typically, the price of this commodity is always rising making it a pretty safe investment. Besides, no one is making anymore of it.

It might also be possible for some publicly traded corporations to continue to exist if they provide public services reasonably efficiently and cheaply to citizens, as well as provide decent or better standards of living to their employees. Some industries are currently heavily regulated, such as some electric utilities, and some of these are owned and operated by publicly traded corporations. It is possible some of these firms are managed fairly well, and perhaps they should be allowed to continue operating under the current scheme of things. Stocks and bonds can be purchased from these businesses just as is the case nowadays. This is the situation in which a quarterly or yearly "conventional dividend" can be paid. This would eliminate the pressure on CEOs to always keep pushing stock prices upward via ever rising dividend payments, and make it more likely they would be beholden to those with stakes in the system—their captive customers.

The oil industry, because of its size and its heavy influence on the economy, might be a prime candidate for either heavy regulation or government ownership. Of course, it might just be easier to tear each oil company into its constituent parts, and let them function on their own as smaller businesses, but with strict price controls and heavy regulation. In any case, eliminating their ties to the financial markets means it might be possible for these businesses to offer "conventional dividends," and this could help to enhance the retirements of individuals, as well as put downward pressure on gasoline prices.

My intention above was to provide only a brief overview of potential sources in which to invest for retirement in a new small business economy. By the outline above, it should be obvious there are already numerous methods by which to do so, and more that can be put in place.

A Sustained People's Movement To Liberate Society

It is highly unlikely an economy comprised of small businesses will displace financially and politically more potent publicly traded corporations. Any assumption that an emerging small business economy will someday displace the corporate economic system by itself may be very foolish indeed because this thought ignores the fact that big corporations often purchase successful local businesses, and many small businesses have eventually evolved to become multi-national corporations. Consequently, we need something more than some hoped for evolution of the economy in which small businesses play the role of mammals and corporations are the soon to be extinct dinosaurs. That just isn't going to happen. We need a better vision of how to get where we need to go. A good place to begin is in the development of a sustained people's movement to roll back the increasing political and economic clout of corporations. Taking back our governments at all levels is probably the first step, and that means rolling back the illegitimately gained legal rights of corporations.

In the USA, corporations have stolen human rights through a corrupt process, resulting in unequal protection under the law. For example, they never go to prison, nor are they sentenced to death if they commit crimes such as treason, fraud, manslaughter or murder. Of course, how can an idea given existence ("life" really is too strong of a word to use) by legislative fiat be locked away in a prison? Or sentenced to death? Humans are also unequally taxed. You would have a hard time finding a local automobile mechanic who has received a $100 million rebate on taxes he or she never paid, but there are plenty of corporations that have received such refunds, year after year after year. In life, there is not, nor has there ever been, economic and political equality between human beings and corporations. It's simply not possible. So how can anybody suggest that corporations should have equality with human citizens by right of the Fourteenth Amendment of the Constitution of the United States? That's just plain nonsense. The Constitution was written for people, not for corporate conduits created to transfer income and wealth from working people to rich stockholders. Since this is a nation of people, perhaps most, if not all, publicly traded corporations need to be legislated out of existence in order to re-establish a government and an economic system for people only, just like the founding fathers intended. Perhaps that should be the ultimate goal, but along the way other measures can be taken to roll back corporate rights that really should never have existed in the first place.

The place to begin is to establish an organization that will conduct a campaign to put an end to the legal concept that corporations are somehow "persons," with all of the rights and few of the responsibilities of real citizens. This is an issue that should be decided by the Supreme Court of the United States. Someone, in some way, will need to legally challenge that concept at a local or state level, and then take it all the way to the highest court.

The civil rights movement gave birth to several organizations that can serve as models for the anti-corporate movement to copy and develop and use as vehicles in which to engage the enemies in the legal battlefields to come. As we have seen, in the South, the rights of African-Americans were legally taken away beginning in the 1890s. In 1896, in Plessey vs. Ferguson, the Supreme Court ruled that segregation laws were legal (yes everybody should be suspicious of the motivations that guided the justices to their decision). Even as African-Americans in the South were suffering from stolen voting rights, lynching and segregation, their supporters in the North founded an organization in 1909 called the National Association for the Advancement of Colored People (NAACP). The NAACP still exists and provides us with a working model of an organization that just might be able to achieve the desired goal. This institution successfully challenged the Jim Crow laws of the South in 1954 when its lawyers took the case of Brown vs. Board of Education all the way to the Supreme Court and reversed Plessey vs. Ferguson. There is absolutely no legal reason why the Supreme Court decision of 1886, which granted personhood rights to corporations, should not be overturned, just like Plessey vs. Ferguson.

This new institution can be sustained through the founding of local chapters and the solicitations of contributions from non-corporate sources, which is similar to the ways in which the NAACP funds itself.

Legal battles can be undertaken at local levels in order to chip away at corporate rights. As many municipalities as is possible throughout the United States should be encouraged to pass laws declaring that corporations are not to be considered "persons" in their dealings within the jurisdictions of each of these governments. Recollect that two townships in Pennsylvania have already done this. Hopefully, such legislation should lead to legal confrontations with corporations when these "artificial persons" threaten lawsuits against elected officials and governments in order to force them to back down. In the past, under these circumstances, politicians knew they faced overwhelming financial resources and so they retreated from their positions. But what if, when threatened, these lawmakers could appeal for help from a fully functioning, financially strong, organization bent on re-establishing democracy in the United States by rolling back corporate legal rights? With the help of this new organization, the financial and legal odds facing lawmakers would be considerably more even and may make them itch for the eventual fight just a little bit more than now is the case. Once such an organization is fully operational, the battle over the economic and political destinies of the vast majority of the people on this planet should begin in earnest.

Anytime any corporation tries to exercise their "civil rights," this fully financed and functioning national organization for human rights (NOHR) can challenge them and their "personhood rights" all the way to the Supreme Court. Once a case reaches this point, it is possible the majority of justices, especially the more conservative of them, when considering such a case, will mull over the impact of their potential decision on their stock portfolios, or their relationships with our captains of corporate and political power, or their buddies among the wealthy elite, or their corporate duck hunting friends, and make their decisions accordingly. However, it is also possible they will actually look at the constitutional issues involved. Even the most ideologically obtuse of them should be able to recognize the constitution does not even mention corporations, and then logically deduce that a human citizen is a natural person, but a corporation is not. They should also recognize that the Fourteenth Amendment requires that a "person" needs to be "born" or "naturalized," and that an idea legalized into law is not. They should also already know that the congressmen who voted to enact the Fourteenth Amendment did not intend to give any civil or legal rights to corporations, and decide accordingly. They should be able to see that the idea called a corporation has no constitutional protections whatsoever, nor even a right to exist.

The civil rights era spawned other organizations that helped during the struggles against segregation and the theft of the voting rights of citizens. The Congress of Racial Equality (CORE), the Southern Christian Leadership Conference (SCLC), and the Student Non-violent Coordinating Committee (SNCC, but pronounced as "Snick") all followed the NAACP, and all helped in the struggle to end American apartheid. The Congress of Racial Equality (CORE) was founded in 1942. During the civil rights era, it was a sponsor or co-sponsor of numerous anti–Jim Crow activities including freedom summer of 1964 and the freedom rides of 1961. The Southern Christian Leadership Conference organized protests against all aspects of Jim Crow laws in the South beginning in the late 1950s. It was a powerful organization that helped to force local governments to abide by the Supreme Court ruling desegregating schools. The Student Non-Violent Coordinating Committee (SNCC) was formed in 1960 as a means of coordinating the rising number of student sit-ins that were taking place in restaurants and other public businesses that refused to serve African-Americans. Among its many activities, it co-sponsored freedom summer of 1964. For over a decade, this under-funded group organized voter registration drives and other protests in the battle to overthrow Jim Crow laws.

The Federal Bureau of Investigation (FBI) is alleged to have infiltrated these organizations, and agents were thought to have sowed the seeds of destruction, at least in the case of SNCC. Consequently, any anti-corporate groups will likely become the targets of Homeland Security and the FBI. Investigations of members and infiltrations of organizations will occur allegedly on behalf of national security, but in reality it will be on behalf of the right of corporations to achieve constantly rising earnings. Anticipate that underhanded methods will be used to tear apart any anti-corporate groups, most likely but not necessarily from the inside. Decades ago, such interference did not stop the members of the major civil rights organizations from achieving their goals, and neither should it frighten the leaders of the new civil rights groups.

Just as during the civil rights era, there should be several anti-corporate organizations. While the NOHR can chip away at the legal rights of corporations until they are extinct, other organizations can help win the fight against corporate financial and political power in other ways. For example, one group could push for a three strikes and you're out law against corporations that are convicted of crimes. Under such a scenario, when corporations commit three crimes the result will be that their charter's will be revoked and they will die. This should appeal to President George W. Bush since he supports the death penalty, at least for poor and working class citizens convicted of non-white collar crimes. Among other things, anti-corporate groups could agitate for limitations on the life of corporations, incorporation for particular purposes only, an end to corporate welfare (the granting of which appears to be the primary purpose of the federal government), a tax on currency and stock transactions, and keeping corporate hands off of public assets. In addition, at least one organization should agitate for a law to make CEOs (and perhaps major shareholders) legally responsible for any harm done by their corporations to anyone anywhere in the world. The more severe the crime, the stiffer should be the penalty for these people, and this should include prison time, and depending on the severity of the crime, the death penalty. Under such a law, corporations will likely be far more responsible to the environment and humans. If strictly enforced, it is possible that such a law will bring about the collapse of major corporations by itself simply because few people would want to manage them if they are going to be held legally responsible for their actions and decisions. Not too many rich people want that to happen, especially the more conservative of them.

Another group might act to spread the word about the existence of the movement by concentrating on the development of local anti-corporate chapters throughout the country. Such an organization might be able to stir public support through the development of a free press, which is radically different from the conservative corporate news media.

There is a plausible example of this type of organization successfully operating in Brazil, where inequality of income and political power is sharper than in any other country, with the exception of Sierra Leone. Half of the farmland is owned by 1 percent of the landowners. Thousands of their acres lay idle while millions of poor people have no land at all. In 1986, when the military govern-ment was replaced by a democracy, the new Constitution included a clause pro-viding for land reform. In its wake, a social movement sprang forth called the Landless Workers Movement (MST). Since its founding, the group has settled about 250 thousand families on roughly 15 million acres of land in thousands of villages in nearly every state in the country. More MST members have been killed in the struggle for land reform than the total number of citizens who were made to disappear at the hands of the U.S. backed military dictatorship. It's been quite a struggle for these people, but they have successfully persevered. Al-though it is helping people climb out of landless poverty through land owner-ship, Brazil's media have branded MST as being communistic. The organization attempts to counter such messages by operating more than 30 radio stations. While obviously outgunned, the stations help spread the word about what the organization really does and what it is. This helps to deflect some of the lies and other misinformation provided by the corporate media. MST provides us with a reasonably successful grass roots movement that has been developing its own nationwide independent news media.[10]

Just like the old civil rights groups, some of these new organizations should combine their efforts and resources whenever possible, especially if such alli-ances create opportunities to bring about change, however minor, or simply en-hance public awareness.

One change in which anti-corporate coalitions would seem to be important would be the establishment of a new political party, possibly in alliance with the Green Party and labor unions. Currently, at the federal level, the Democrats are losing their battles to protect the environment and to defend and augment labor rights. More and more, the sympathies of the politicians of the Democratic Party lay with corporate businesses and trial attorneys. The Republican Party, mean-while, is completely awash in corporate money, and these politicians use the abortion, gays, God and guns issues to attract and then disappoint conservative Christians everywhere. On the other hand, the Republicans have alienated many of their moderate members, people who care about the environment, for exam-ple. And the Party has favored more and more federal intrusion into the lives of citizens everywhere, thereby distancing themselves from Barry Goldwater con-servatives. Enough people might be attracted to this new political party to make it a big time player on the national scene if it were pro-environment, pro-free en-terprise, anti-corporate, and anti-federal intrusion into local and state matters;

with strong federal involvement in regulating certain industries, maintaining Social Security, Medicaid and Medicare, as well as enforcing certain laws like the minimum wage and civil rights legislation; and possibly establishing and maintaining a universal health care system (or making the industry more competitive). Such a party might especially be strong if it is linked together with the other anti-corporate organizations. By gaining and exercising influence in government, it is possible change can come with the passage of laws.

The Party should only be built one brick at a time, starting at the local levels. People could campaign for school boards, for example, as well as other local offices. Slowly, as membership rises, candidates should be found to run for state, and then, federal offices. It could take twenty years or more for the development of a powerful people's party, but it should be done.

Conclusion

Why work increasingly more to earn less and less as the months and years pass by? Is that what an economy is for? That's just plain stupid. By eliminating the income and wealth transfer mechanism from the corporate economy, we can change that to "work more and earn more" because people will be rewarded based on their ingenuity and work ethic more so than is now the case. Perhaps that's the kind of economy we should want, rather than one that forces people to work more and earn less because a "kept class" needs everyone else to contribute more and more to keep their wallets fat and their income transferring system afloat. Many good things will happen once publicly traded corporations are more heavily regulated, or hopefully eliminated, from the United States, as well as from the rest of the world. The coolest thing that will occur by sailing into this battle is that the income and wealth transfer mechanisms that come with corporations can be dismantled.

There exists a myriad of other reasons the people of the world will live better without corporations. In the United States, an economy that has to constantly grow to keep those profits forever rolling upward will not be needed, except perhaps with the growth of population. The need for a rising tide of immigrants to sustain the mounting tidal wave of corporate profits, dividends and share prices will end with the demise of publicly traded corporations. Who really wants to experience the doubling of the population of the United States in fifty years or less? Almost all of this increase will be due to immigration. Meanwhile, a world without public traded corporations will reduce the miseries of poverty, hunger, famine, despair and unemployment throughout the lesser developed world. This will diminish the political and economic pressures that force people to emigrate from their home countries. Throughout the world, wages and salaries should go up in real terms making it more likely people will be able to raise themselves out of poverty. Inflation will decrease or desist, and this will bring about a period of stable or declining prices. We will become healthier because corporations are quick to pollute the environment, and they import contaminated food for our consumption. We will be able to end welfare for the rich as we know it, because the end of corporations will put an end to their public assistance programs, and this will significantly reduce the size of government at all levels. This means we will be able to divert tens of billions of dollars every year to take better care of our children, the elderly, the mentally ill, the disabled and veteran's of foreign wars far better than we do now, and we still might be able to more fully fund public schools, and receive tax cuts. The end of corporations may force many members of the over-consuming class to find productive employment. Rather than act as parasites on society, they will be able to add to the joint stock of goods and services. The end of pharmaceutical corporations means prescription drugs will be cheaper. The health care industry in the United States is a financial monster of ever increasing costs to citizens. Corporations of this industry drive their prices upward for the same reasons as everyone else, and once publicly traded companies are extinct or more heavily regulated, either a publicly financed or a truly competitive system can be established in their places, and health care for most people will be far cheaper and more readily available than is now the case.

We cannot forget that the face of democracy will be changed forever with the downfall of publicly traded companies. No longer will massive amounts of corporate dollars flood the political markets in the form of contributions, perks, jobs and lobbyists. This will provide significantly more freedom for our political office holders to use the powers of government at all levels to do the right things for the people they are supposed to represent, rather than provide legislation to ensure ever rising corporate profits. Local people will be able to exercise greater control over their communities since corporations and the rich will be less able to purchase legislative favors in the state capitals, in the halls of congress or the White House. And this means it will be less likely that the federal government will coerce the states into providing de facto public assistance programs for corporations.

When corporations are weakened politically and financially, or simply outlawed, along with other corporate welfare programs, the "No Child Left Behind Act" can and should be repealed as soon as possible. Once that's done, community members everywhere will have the democratic responsibility of determining what it is they really want their children to learn, rather than have distant corporate executives arrogantly decide what other people's children should study in order to maximize their profits. Many of these captains of industry and their children have never even attended public schools, have no idea how children learn, and are ignorant to one degree or another about the learning process. So why should they have any input into what students should study in your public schools, especially if these people live out of your state? Giving ignorant people a voice in these important matters makes absolutely no sense. The great educator Myles Horton once observed that poor people were the experts on poverty, while students who studied the destitute in distant universities were not authorities on the subject at all. Seventy years ago, Horton had a group of poor people come together. He discovered that collectively that could ascertain just what was necessary to alleviate their indigence. Likewise, forty years ago he insisted black people were the authorities on their problems, and Chicanos were the experts on their troubles. People involved in educating children, likewise, are the experts on the problems and successes of public education. Parents, teachers, administrators, board members and other members of the community should all have input on the development of school curriculum and social activities. These people know what kind of skills schools can provide their children to help them survive and prosper in the modern world. On the other hand, distant corporate executives and politicians living plush and carefree life styles are largely clueless about what occurs in public schools, and they are also completely out of touch with the needs and desires of the vast majority of citizens who rely on public education to provide their children with life skills.

On the international front, trade agreements such as NAFTA can be renegotiated once corporations are sufficiently weakened or eliminated. Free trade does not exist when U.S. citizens are not allowed to enter Canada to purchase prescription drugs and then freely return home with them. That's just one of the reasons why this treaty is an illusionary joke. Citizens have been forced to pay taxpayer money to foreign corporations not to poison them, and state and federal officials have decided not to enact legislation to protect their citizens because of the threat of lawsuits allowed by NAFTA. The treaty undermines state and local regulation of food, water and the environment. In addition, due to the agreement, jobs have been lost in all three countries. In Mexico wages have plummeted and poverty has grown, while in Canada wages have stagnated in real terms according to some reports. Nearly a million jobs have been lost in the United States due to the agreement. Obviously, the well being of citizens and democracy are in direct conflict with the corporate interests that negotiated the treaty.

During the renegotiations, the welfare of people can be given more weight than the mere quest for ever rising profits via the exchange of goods and services and through the transfer of income and wealth from productive individuals. The environment, jobs, democratic institutions, health, as well as minimum wages, salaries and benefits indexed to inflation should all be renegotiated so as to ensure rising standards of living for the people of the nations that sign the treaty. Isn't that what an economy is for?

I've barely scratched the surface of the many positive things that can be made to happen once publicly traded corporations are swept out of the way. Obviously, there will be plenty of things that can be done, and should be done. Myles Horton once said the best way to begin anything is simply to begin. He was right on target. The time to begin is now.

Notes

1. Although this book is confined to U.S. corporations and financial markets, the momentum for earnings that pushes the cost of labor downward forces many of the corporations of other nations to follow this lead in order to stay competitive vis-à-vis their U.S. rivals. In addition, although beyond the scope of this study, it can be suggested with a fair degree of certainty that the financial markets of other nations wield similar influences on the decisions made by corporate managements, more or less, as U.S. markets have on the decisions made by the American captains of industry and finance.
2. Chase, Stuart, A New Deal, The McMillan Company: New York, 1932, p. 184.
3. Flaccavento, Anthony, "from the earth up," Yes!, Fall 2002, pp. 25-27.
4. Flaccavento.
5. Gribskov, Margaret, "Why Americans Are Free: And Why Foreign Corporations Are Attacking Our Freedoms," Economic Justice Action Group: Portland, OR, June 2002, p. 14.
6. "Keeping up with Pesticides," Ecologist, March 2003, p. 59.
7. No author, Ecologist, "U.S. on warpath over GM food, " March 2003, p. 46.
8. Dressel, Holly, "breaking down buildings, building up a neighborhood," Yes! Fall 2002, pp. 30-31.
9. A Report of The International Forum On Globalization, Alternatives to Economic Globalization: A Better World is Possible, Berrett-Koehler Publishers, Inc., San Francisco, 2002, p. 149.
10. Lappe', Frances Moore, and Lappe', Anna, "of land and hope," Yes!, Fall 2002, pp. 40-42.

Appendix A:

INCOME AND WEALTH DISTRIBUTION 2003

Census Bureau data reveals that income distribution has become increasingly lop-sided since 1979. That year, the bottom 80 percent of U.S. citizens earned 68.1 percent of the total income in the United States. By 2001, their share had dropped to 53.8 percent. The next highest 15 percent of the population, those in the 80 to 95 percentile income bracket, garnered 27.6 percent of total income in 1979. Their share moved slightly upward to 27.7 percent by 2001. Meanwhile, the top 5 percent of U.S. consumers received 16.4 percent of total income in 1979, but this rose to 22.4 percent by 2001.[1] This trend in favor of the wealthiest consumers hasn't always been the case.

Income for most Americans rose significantly from 1947 to 1973, even when inflation is factored in. During this period, the change in real family income climbed over 100 percent on average for the bottom 80 percent of the population. However, income for the top 5 percent still increased 86 percent. The rich became richer, but so too did working people. Unfortunately, from 1979 to 1998, the bottom 20 percent of the population experienced a reduction of -5 percent in their income. Meanwhile, the top 5 percent enjoyed a raise of 64 percent.[2] More recent statistics from the Census Bureau show the trend continuing. The share of income earned by the bottom 60 percent of all households dropped from 2000 to 2003 while the portion acquired by the wealthiest 20 percent rose during the same period.[3]

These statistics do not even come close to telling the whole truth of the massive lop-sidedness of the distribution of income during the last 30 years because it does not count those who have seen their lives, labor and health expropriated by U.S. corporations in less developed countries which has then been transferred to rich shareholders and CEOs.

There is a difference between income and wealth. Money flowing into your wallets is considered income, while things you already have are considered to be your wealth. When your income increases, you are more likely to purchase things that become part of your total net wealth, such as cars, houses, stereos, savings accounts, art, and stocks and bonds.

The shift in income in the United States and elsewhere is reflected in the fact that most corporate stocks, mutual funds and retirement accounts are owned by the people at the top who receive dividend payments and rising values of their stocks. The top 1 percent own 42.1 percent of all of these assets, the next 9 percent own 36.6 percent, and the bottom 90 percent hold only 21.3 percent.[4] Very few people among the bottom 60 percent of the population hold any of these assets. The vast majority of people in less developed countries, even those who work for U.S. corporations, their contractors and subcontractors, most likely own virtually none of these assets.

From 1983 to 1998, the stock markets shot skyward "1,336 percent" because, in large part, of the transfer of income taking place between working people and mostly wealthy shareholders. This allowed the share of net wealth to rapidly increase for the top group, while the bottom groups saw their wealth directly or indirectly transferred to the rich, and so they lost total net worth. For example, from 1983 to 1995, the top 1 percent of U.S. households saw their total wealth rise 17 percent when adjusted for inflation, while the bottom 40 percent lost 80 percent of their inflation adjusted net worth during this same period. Other groups of U.S. citizen's also experienced total reductions of inflation adjusted wealth.[5] Although there may be slight differences among the sources of information used here, the trends are the same; income and wealth inequality is growing between the most affluent 1 percent of consumers and the rest of the world's citizens.

The re-distribution of wealth and income from working people to rich consumers isn't solely a phenomenon of the U.S. Much of the re-distribution is taking place between working citizens and affluent over-consumers throughout the world, creating a rising tidal wave of people working more and earning less, and in worsening working conditions, while spreading poverty and misery throughout the world. That is precisely the only way income and wealth can be distributed as long as the corporate economic system is the dominant economic model around the globe. The existence of this system, along with growing corporate political power, ensures that economic inequality for the lower 90 to 99 percent of world's population will only grow.

Notes

1. DeNavas, Carmen-Walt, Cleveland, Robert W., "Money and Income in the United States: 2001," U.S. Census Bureau, September 2002, p. 19.
2. Sharpe, M.E., "The State of Working America," Analysis of U.S. Census Bureau data in Economic Policy Institute, p. 37, and U.S. Census Bureau, Historical Income Tables, Table F-3, http://www.ufenet.org/research/income_charts.html.
3. DeNavas, Carment-Walt, Proctor, Bernadette, Mills, Robert, "Income, Poverty, and Health Insurance Coverage in the United States," U.S. Census Bureau, 2003.
4. Wolff, Edward N., "Recent Trends in Wealth Ownership, 1983-1998," Levy Institute Working Paper No. 300, Table 6. Levy Economics Institute: April 2000.
5. Sklar, Holly and United for a Fair Economy, "Shifting Fortunes: The Perils of the Growing American Wealth Gap," www.ufenet.org/press/archive/1999/shifting_fortunes_report.html.

INDEX

THE ESSENCE OF CAPITALISM: The Origins of Our Future

Humphrey McQueen

A timely account of globalization, the consumer culture, and the historical roots of our contemporary dilemmas. By tracking the 130-year history of Coca-Cola (and a number of other large American or transnational corporations), this book details all that is best, worst and most powerful about global capitalism. It is a unique view of the awesome power and single-mindedness of large corporations in pursuit of their own interests.

Highly recommended. All libraries. *—Choice Magazine*

An accessible, yet agreeably densely packed 130 year exploration of capitalism…a seriously entertaining book. *—The Weekend Australian*

Takes the reader not only down the main streets of capitalism but also through less familiar back lanes and sewers of its development. A compelling read…both fascinating and empowering. *—Australian Bookseller*

HUMPHREY McQUEEN features regularly as a commentator on Australian radio and as a contributor to various newspapers, and magazines. He is the author of more than a dozen books ranging through history, politics, and the visual arts.

399 pages, 6x9, bibliography, index
Paperback ISBN: 1-55164-220-4 $28.99
Hardcover ISBN: 1-55164-221-2 $57.99

THORSTEIN VEBLEN AND THE AMERICAN WAY OF LIFE

Louis Patsouras

Thorstein Veblen (1857-1929), best-known for his *The Theory of the Leisure Class*, was an unrelenting critic of the American way of life. A baffling figure in American intellectual history, this important work, undertaken by Louis Patsouras, attempts both to unravel the riddles that surround his reputation and to assess his varied and important contributions to modern social theory. By setting Veblen's work in its social and intellectual context, and by considering Veblen not just as an economist or a sociologist—as has been the case up to now—Patsouras also examines Veblen's politics, then compares and contrasts his ideas with other well-known historical and contemporary thinkers.

LOUIS PATSOURAS is Professor of History at Kent State University. His other published works include *Simone Weil and the Socialist Tradition*, *The Crucible of Socialism*, *Debating Marx*, *Essays on Socialism*, *Continuity and Change in Marxism* and *The Anarchism of Jean Grave* (Black Rose Books).

296 pages, 6x9, bibliography, index
Paperback ISBN: 1-55164-228-X $26.99
Hardcover ISBN: 1-55164-229-8 $55.99